PETER CUSHING

THE COMPLETE MEMOIRS

PETER CUSHING

THE COMPLETE MEMOIRS

Foreword by Joyce Broughton

Introduction by Jonathan Rigby

SIGNUM BOOKS

First published in Great Britain in 2013 by Signum Books,
an imprint of
Flashpoint Media Ltd
173 Mill Road
Cambridge
CB1 3AN

Foreword © Joyce Broughton 2013, 2014
Introduction © Jonathan Rigby 2013, 2014
An Autobiography © the estate of Peter Cushing 1986, 2013, 2014
'Past Forgetting' © the estate of Peter Cushing 1988, 2013, 2014
The Peter Cushing Story © the estate of Peter Cushing 1954, 1955, 2013, 2014

An Autobiography and *'Past Forgetting'* were originally published
by George Weidenfeld & Nicolson Ltd.

A CIP catalogue record for this book is available from the British Library.

ISBN 978 0 9576481 4 2

Edited by Marcus Hearn
Designed by Peri Godbold

Printed and bound in China by 1010 Printing International Ltd.

CONTENTS

FOREWORD

I STARTED WORKING for Peter and Helen Cushing as their secretary in 1959. In those days it didn't seem right to address one's employers by their Christian names, so they agreed to let me call them 'Sir' and 'Ladyboss'. This was a tradition that continued until the end of their lives, and I still can't think of them in any other way.

The time I spent working for my beloved Sir still astounds me. He was a gifted actor, and was similarly accomplished with his art and model-making. He was a real gentleman in every sense of the word.

Sir and Ladyboss lived in Kensington when I first met them, but moved to Whitstable in the early 1960s. This gave Sir the opportunity to swim every day. Ladyboss would be waiting for him when he returned to their seafront house and we would all have tea and toast by the fire. Sir would cover his toast with sticky marmalade and then pretend to rub it on our sleeves, amid great laughter. When the weather was fine he would send me and Ladyboss onto the beach and bring us tea and cakes.

His child-like nature was one of his most endearing traits. In his art studio he would create exquisite model theatres and invite visitors to play board games which he'd designed himself.

When Ladyboss brought him his porridge he would stand on the banquette and drop syrup into the bowl, trying to get higher and higher each time. Sometimes he would entertain us with impromptu shows in his study. He would emerge from behind the curtains to perform tricks, such as placing his feet firmly in front while he leaned his whole body first to one side, and then the other.

Things were never the same after Ladyboss died in 1971, and much has been written about the devastating effect this had on Sir. He entered what he called his Blue Study, and wouldn't see or speak to anyone. I would make the 50-mile trip to his house, only to be dismissed shortly after I arrived.

When he was diagnosed with cancer some years later he came to live with me, my husband Bernard and two teenage children. To my relief he really settled in, started to paint again and found some joy in life. The doctors gave him a year to 18 months, but he lived for another 12 years.

It was during this period that he was asked to write *An Autobiography*. I was glad he had a project that would occupy him. Much of the work was done in longhand, and I would type these pages out for him, returning them for corrections and further dictation if necessary. He was just as meticulous with the follow-up, *'Past Forgetting'*. I am delighted that now, thanks to publisher Marcus Hearn, both books are once more available in this volume celebrating his centenary.

I knew Sir longer than I knew my own father. I cared for him greatly, and my children and grandchildren adored him. For those who weren't lucky enough to know or meet him, these memoirs are an insight into the amusing, generous and talented man I still miss every day.

Joyce Broughton
Kent
April 2013

INTRODUCTION

THEATRICAL COUPLE SIMON and Laura Foster are at almost constant loggerheads but have reached a state of uneasy truce in order to play 'themselves' in a career-rescuing BBC soap. The strain begins to show in spectacular style on the occasion of their 200th programme, after which it's revealed that the young producer, David, has considered writing Simon out of the show via a timely car accident.

'Then,' says Laura primly, 'I was to meet Peter Cushing.'

'Well, I'm damned!' replies Simon.

'We'd been in touch with Cushing's agent,' David admits, before acknowledging shamefacedly that 'Splitting you up would be like splitting up Nervo and Knox.'

How strange, and gratifying, it must have been for Peter Cushing to sit among the audience at the Strand Theatre and hear this exchange performed by his fellow actors Roland Culver (Simon), Coral Browne (Laura) and Ian Carmichael (David). The play was *Simon and Laura*, the author was the lyricist and TV personality Alan Melville, and opening night was 25 November 1954.

If nothing else, it was a startling indication of the meteoric rise Cushing had experienced in just three years. After all, he'd made his TV debut (in JB Priestley's *Eden End*) as recently as December 1951, and already his small-screen stardom was such that Melville, waspishly satirising the burgeoning television industry, considered a Cushing name-check indispensable.

When Melville's play opened, Cushing was in rehearsal for a new TV project that would lead, inadvertently, to the next stage in his career. It was an ambitious adaptation, budgeted at a staggering £3000, of George Orwell's dystopian novel *Nineteen Eighty-Four*.

Finally screened on 12 December 1954, it triggered a massive wave of top-level controversy (with five MPs tabling a motion deploring 'the tendency evident in recent BBC television programmes, notably on Sunday evenings, to pander to sexual and sadistic tastes') and earned Cushing an entirely unexpected sobriquet – 'the Horror Man'.

'Winston Smith, of course, was a hero in what was almost the ultimate in horror plots,' Cushing recalled in a 1970 interview for the *Kent Messenger*. 'Yet it was the horror rather than the heroics of the play that people associated with me. The horror stuck.'

Indeed it did. Hammer Film Productions came calling in November 1956, and by the end of the decade Cushing's physical dynamism, classically precise diction and bird-like nervous tension had not only lent a uniquely dangerous edge to Baron Frankenstein, Dr Van Helsing and Sherlock Holmes; they had also brought him international stardom.

* * *

In 1988, *Simon and Laura* was itself name-checked in Cushing's second volume of autobiography, *'Past Forgetting'*. He got the play's plot slightly wrong (see page 257), but it's clear that he was well aware of the compliment paid him by Melville all those years ago. By the late 1980s, it was a poignant reminder of the celebrity he had enjoyed in the '50s, a celebrity pre-dating the worldwide cult that was to grow up around his horror roles.

Cushing wrote *'Past Forgetting'* in response to the enthusiastic reception enjoyed by his first book, *An Autobiography*. Originally published by Weidenfeld & Nicolson, these two charming memoirs are here made available in one volume from Signum Books, marking Cushing's centenary in May 2013. Marking, also, the fact that Cushing continues to gather new fans who weren't around when the books first came out.

I was myself a fan of long standing by that time, having been fascinated by Cushing's fastidious and febrile performances for over a decade. I can still turn up strange little notes to my 12-year-old self such as this, preserved in my diary for 1975...

> *Sat 8 March – For God's sake remember: HM Show*
> *with P Cushing on Capital Radio*

...and I still have a copy of the letter I wrote to Miss Gladys Fletcher of Ipswich on 24 June the same year:

> *Please find enclosed the form stating my address and,*
> *of course, a £1 note (more suitable than a Postal Order).*
> *I hope my membership of the British Peter Cushing*
> *Fan Club can be arranged.*

Even at this early stage, I was well aware of the painstaking artistry that went into Cushing's performances, and was also beginning to spot some of the recurring mannerisms that so enriched them. There was the 'Cushing finger' – raised in solemn warning or grim admonition, perhaps most memorably when directed at Melissa Stribling in *Dracula* and Christopher Lee in *The Hound of the Baskervilles*. There was the hand passed wearily through the hair, or across the back of the neck, to indicate exhaustion. There was also a peculiarly effective arched-back recoil from pain, whether flung against a pillar in *The Curse of Frankenstein* or (spectacularly) impaled on a hatchet in *Twins of Evil*.

Cleverest of all was his habit of giving dramatic punch to something by contriving a reason to turn away from the person speaking to him – and then turning back on a particularly significant word. The best example of this one is when the guileless Melissa Stribling mentions the word 'anaemia' in *Dracula* and the omniscient Cushing suddenly turns into gimlet-eyed close-up.

Long after discovering all this, I became a student at the University of Kent at Canterbury and lived in nearby Whitstable, whose most famous resident was, of course, Peter Cushing. Seeing him out and about on his bicycle or having his lunch in the Tudor Tea Rooms was by no means uncommon, but I only got to meet him after I'd graduated, in 1986.

An Autobiography came out in March of that year. Like many fans, I rushed to the nearest bookshop and snapped it up at once. Four months later I had a chance to get it signed when Cushing responded to local demand and restaged his recent National Film Theatre appearance at a public school in Canterbury.

In aid of
The League of Friends of the Canterbury Hospitals

An Evening with
Peter Cushing

St. Edmunds School Hall, Canterbury
Sunday, 13th July 1986 at 8.00 p.m.

Admission by Ticket only £2:50
(including light refreshments)

The promise of not merely Peter Cushing but also 'light refreshments' – both of them so typically, invincibly British – was too good to resist. Along with a friend I returned to my former stamping grounds and made a record of the evening's events in my diary.

Having booked ourselves in at the Alicante guest house,
we toiled up the hill to St Edmund's School, where

*An Evening with Peter Cushing began at eight o'clock.
It proved an extraordinary affair. For a long time it consisted
of some obviously rehearsed horse-play between PC (aged
73) and the interviewer (in fact, his devoted secretary's
devoted husband). Suddenly, though, it became clear that this
international film star was nervous, and we warmed to him at
once. And once he'd warmed up too – which he soon did – the
evening was a great success.*

The interview was followed by a signing session in which I
proffered my copy of the book and addressed a few words to the
great man. What to say? I suspect I muttered a word or two about
him being 'an inspiration' – the usual stuff. But then, feeling this
was too generalised, I found myself telling him that I was soon to
enrol at the Central School of Speech and Drama, where I would
be joining a friend of mine called Jason Morell. His ears pricked
up at the name Morell, and I explained that Jason was the son of
Joan Greenwood and Cushing's regular co-star André Morell.

'Ah, dear André,' he smiled, going on to say what a very good
Watson Morell had been when Cushing first played Sherlock
Holmes, a point with which I readily concurred. Then, after a few
more pleasantries, I moved away. Cushing's parting shot: 'Do give
my love to dear Joanie.'

It was a brief encounter, but I was struck by the degree to which
this actor, who just missed out on the Edwardian era, somehow
became more and more Edwardian in person the older he got. It
was all there – the watch chain, the bow tie tucked Holmes-style
under the collar, and the old-world courtesy (including addressing
me as 'dear boy') which by now has become a virtual cliché in
discussions of him.

So I went away a very happy customer. And I *did* pass on his love
to 'dear Joanie', who died the following February.

*   *   *

Naturally, I read *An Autobiography* at not much more than a single sitting. The story contained within its pages, so engagingly related by Cushing, remains a remarkable one, moving from childhood play-acting in Purley to a frustrating spell as a very minor Surrey civil servant and thence to a memorable audition for Allan Aynesworth at the Guildhall School of Music and Drama.

Cushing's account of his mangled speech at this early period ('I wanna gow onna styge') provides a striking contrast to the cultured actor who would gain fame 20 years later, an actor for whom the words 'impeccable' and 'immaculate' were routinely invoked. In 1954, film director John Paddy Carstairs, commenting on *Beau Brummell* as guest TV critic in the *Evening Standard*, prophetically noted that Cushing's 'impeccable diction would enthral American viewers.' And by the time *Star Wars* came around in 1977, Gordon Gow in *Films and Filming* was referring to 'the immaculately spoken Peter Cushing, who ... seems in effect to share with [Alec] Guinness a Movement Toward the Perpetuation of Clear Speech.'

Perhaps the most extraordinary feature of Cushing's early life is his quixotic decision, after less than three years in rep, to try his luck in Hollywood. The good fortune he experienced there – playing opposite such luminaries as Carole Lombard and Laurel & Hardy – was accompanied by the remarkable coincidence of working in two films for the expatriate English director James Whale. It was Whale, of course, who had been responsible for Universal's *Frankenstein* and *Bride of Frankenstein*.

Cushing's post-war theatre career, much of which he owed to the patronage of Laurence Olivier, seems to have contained several performances prefiguring his later films. How one would love to have seen his Faulkland in *The Rivals* or Joseph Surface in *The School for Scandal*, which may have influenced the submerged vein of Restoration Comedy that runs through his later Baron Frankenstein. And, in particular, what fun it would have been to see his nervous style translated into the manic farce of *The Proposal*.

This Chekhov one-acter was used as a prologue to Jean Anouilh's *Antigone* in 1949 and, among other things, involved Cushing 'sitting' on a chair that was actually part of a painted backcloth. Cushing's Lomov was described as 'galvanically funny' by the *News Chronicle*'s Alan Dent, while Harold Hobson came up with the following in the *Sunday Times*:

> *I expected the audience would listen to [the play] with*
> *about the same degree of attention as the Windmill patrons*
> *accord to the male turns before the girls come on. I was wrong.*
> *Olivier, as producer, has demanded a tremendous pace from*
> *the three players in it, and Peter Cushing ... brings off a*
> *farcical triumph.*

As we have seen, Cushing's subsequent entry into television rapidly transformed him into a household name, making him the only actor to rank alongside such instantly recognisable BBC personalities of the day as Gilbert Harding, Sylvia Peters, Wilfred Pickles, Isobel Barnett and Sir Mortimer Wheeler. In due course, he would have a memorable run-in with the irascible Harding on the panel game *What's My Line?*

> *'Very, very trying!' muttered Mr Harding – as Cushing, our*
> *top spine-chilling actor, clowned non-stop in 20 fake voices.*
> *I waited for Mr H to explode, with some justification.*
> *Instead, he alone guessed the teaser's identity – and*
> *complimented him gracefully.*

Thus the *Daily Sketch*, with *Reynolds News* adding the observation that the guest celebrity's 'versatile performance was a godsend to a programme dying of decay.' Cushing was in the midst of filming *The Revenge of Frankenstein* at the time, but this display of comic pyrotechnics didn't just come as a revelation to viewers familiar with his horror roles. It was also a shock to those who remembered his remarkable run of television drama earlier in the decade.

In the brave and extremely nerve-wracking new world of live TV, Cushing was seen as the natural successor to a wide range of theatrical giants. He accordingly reinterpreted roles originated on stage by John Gielgud (*Richard of Bordeaux*), Eric Portman (*The Browning Version*), Ralph Richardson (*Home at Seven*), Emlyn Williams (*The Winslow Boy*) and Michael Redgrave (*Uncle Harry*). He had *Nineteen Eighty-Four*'s Winston Smith all to himself, however – until a film version came along starring the apparently more bankable Edmond O'Brien.

Cushing's co-stars in the Orwell play were André Morell and Yvonne Mitchell, who later offered an intriguing insight into Cushing's methods in her 1957 book *Actress*.

> *He has a surprising approach to acting. In rehearsal he is meticulous. He writes down every note the producer gives him, every move, every thought. And yet he never refers to his notes again. He likes to work out to a millionth how he will be sitting or how he will say a line, and yet when transmission time comes all this detailed analysis and secure basis will be thrown away, and in its place will be a completely spontaneous performance. The work he has done has given him a rock-like foundation, leaving him free in performance to invent, feel and express anything the mood of the actual moment dictates.*

This freewheeling fastidiousness made him a natural for the sophisticated Grand Guignol provided by Hammer horror, which took the nation – and the world – by storm when *The Curse of Frankenstein* was released in May 1957. In a *Picturegoer* set report, Tom Hutchinson had already given warning of the film's content, as well as providing an indication of Cushing's personal brand of gallows humour:

They introduced me to Baron Frankenstein, the originator
of the do-it-yourself craze, who made his own monster
from dead bodies. They called him Peter Cushing. But
this wasn't the Cushing I knew. This was a sinisterly
handsome man with a laugh like ice breaking. Said he
happily: 'They gave me sheep's eyes to play with.
They're supposed to be a dead man's eyes. Funny thing:
the Creature has half his head shot away – with one eye –
and he still walks about.'

Soon enough, columnist Ivor Jay was able to title a Cushing piece *The Actor 'X'traordinary*. Other commentators, however, adopted a lofty tone of regret, evincing a form of cultural snobbery that hasn't completely died out even today.

A prime example appeared in *The People* in March 1958, with Kenneth Baily heading his piece 'HORROR FILM VICTIM – That is the fate of TV's greatest actor'.

I do not think I put it too high in saying that in his TV
work he has shown himself capable of reaching heights
equal to those attained by any living actor in theatre or
films. His rise in TV, a few years back, led people to suppose
that this exceptional talent would lift Cushing to the
Olivier-Gielgud-Guinness top rank. It has not happened.
The theatre has ignored him. Films have used him, but
only with his talent half displayed. There was The Curse
of Frankenstein, *then* Dracula *and again* The Revenge
of Frankenstein. *His only worthy film roles have been*
supporting ones in The End of the Affair *and* Violent
Playground … *The irony of it is that the cinema patrons*
know him, from TV, as a far better actor than the cinema
allows him to appear.

Cushing was returning to television at the time in *The Browning*

Version, and the same occasion brought forth the following from the *Daily Mail*'s Peter Black:

> *Cushing's last appearance was as the unpleasant*
> *Mr Manningham in* Gaslight. *Since then he has been*
> *occupied in a succession of horror films. His sense of humour*
> *is proof against the uncongenial chore, which is more than*
> *I can say of mine. I think it disgraceful that such a fine actor*
> *should be thrown away on this rubbish.*

Happily, Cushing's instinct for accepting iconic roles, in whatever genre, was proof against this kind of uncongenial snobbery. Even so, comments like these no doubt contributed to the discussions Cushing had with his wife Helen on the dangers of typecasting. But as the 1950s drew to a close, they may well have drawn comfort from the fact that Cushing was in the Guinness 'top rank' in at least one respect. He was reported as being one of only three British stars who was able to 'sell' a film in the USA. The others? His frequent co-star Christopher Lee and – yes – Alec Guinness.

In fact, Cushing made at least one attempt to break away from horror. Having made *The Brides of Dracula* early in 1960, he devoted himself to colourful period adventures that mirrored the tales of *Boy's Own* derring-do he had thrilled to as a child. *Sword of Sherwood Forest* and *Fury at Smugglers' Bay* were followed in 1961 by *Captain Clegg* (the latter flavoured, it must be said, with a heavy dose of Hammer Gothicisms). He also made a scintillating little 'B' film opposite André Morell called *Cash On Demand*, as well as essaying an appropriately 'lean and hungry' Cassius in the *Julius Caesar* sections of the BBC's 1963 Shakespeare marathon, *The Spread of the Eagle*.

There was also a fleeting return to the theatre, collaborating with farce masters ancient (Ben Travers) and modern (Ray Cooney) on a 1965 revival of *Thark* at the Garrick.

Peter **CUSHING**
Kathleen **HARRISON**
Alec **McCOWEN**
Ambrosine **PHILLPOTTS**

in

T H A R K

"I rolled in my seat."—*Evening News.*
"Very clean family fun."—*Daily Telegraph.*

Monday-Friday 7.45. Matinee Thursdays 3 p.m. Saturdays 5.30 & 8.40

GARRICK THEATRE
CHARING CROSS ROAD   TEM. 4601

For this one, Harold Hobson weighed in with another enthusiastically pro-Cushing review, noting that

> *In these grievous times we should reverence all actors who build up Britain's reputation abroad. Though they remain in Britain, they are cultural exports. Mr Cushing is the idol of the* Midi-Minuit Fantastique *mob, and the mere mention of his name, coupled if possible with that of Christopher Lee, is enough to raise spirits in the Rue du Cherche-Midi.*

Hobson was astute in his reference to the tremendous vogue British chillers enjoyed in France. For, despite these gestures towards diversity, Gothic horror had claimed Peter Cushing and would not let go.

It was, in a strange way, his true métier. His grandfather, Henry William Cushing, had acted with Sir Henry Irving – and there was perhaps more to this than the pleasing coincidence that Irving's right-hand man had been Bram Stoker, author of *Dracula*. Like Christopher Lee, Cushing was a fascinating paradox – an indisputably modern actor who was nevertheless a throwback to Irving's Lyceum.*

When Hammer first kick-started the horror boom in the late '50s, Cushing and Lee were without doubt the right men in the right place at the right time. British horror would not have achieved anything like the international impact it did without them.

* * *

'He does go to the Caprice sometimes,' Helen Cushing confided to *The People* in 1968. 'But it's only to sit at a corner table and have eggs and bacon, 15 shillings.'

The subject was her husband's complete lack of interest in showbiz socialising, and the wider context was his imminent return to the BBC as Sherlock Holmes. The reporter was Cushing's old antagonist Kenneth Baily, though Cushing, characteristically, appeared to hold no grudges.

Cushing's first go at Holmes had been in Hammer's lusciously Gothic rendition of *The Hound of the Baskervilles* in 1958. (Reviewing this film, Paul Dehn memorably pointed out in the *News Chronicle* that Cushing's 'questing hawk's-head so swivels in the throes of observation that one can almost hear the brain brought to a fine fizz inside.') Now, ten years on, Cushing had the opportunity to do another 14 Holmes stories, plus a two-part reprise of *The Hound*, and was determined to be as fanatically faithful to Conan Doyle as possible. 'I mean, I don't want to be a pest, dear boy,' he told Baily, 'but we do want the Holmes series to be right.' In the event, the

---

* Intriguingly, both Cushing and Lee were at different times courted to actually *play* Irving – Cushing in an unrealised BBC drama in the mid-1950s and Lee in an aborted Hammer project from 1972 called *Victim of His Imagination*.

series' budget and schedule proved unequal to the task, distressing its nervily perfectionist star considerably.

When his television Holmes came up for colour transmission in 1970, he was interviewed in *Radio Times* under the only half-joking title 'I'm a Bit of a Nervous Norah'. In the course of the interview, he made the rather surprising claim (aged 57) that 'I can play 40, with extra hair. That's no problem.'

Apparently said without irony, this assertion was particularly ill-timed, given that the television cameras used for the Holmes series were less flattering to him than the film cameras he was used to. And, even on film, the gaunt-faced Faustian villain he had played so brilliantly in the recent *Frankenstein Must Be Destroyed* looked anything but 40. Even so, Cushing's continued youthfulness was a popular topic in 1970; an interview in the *Kent Messenger* in June of that year was titled 'Why Frankenstein Looks So Young'.

Yet by the following March it was a conspicuously aged Peter Cushing who reported to Pinewood Studios to start filming *Twins of Evil*. His wife's worsening illness had forced him to decline several recent offers (most notably *The Abominable Dr Phibes*, in which his role was taken by Joseph Cotten), and her death in January 1971 produced a profound change in him on several levels.

The loss resulted at once in a new, and frequently harrowing, emotional fragility in Cushing's acting. Unlikely though the contexts may seem, his performances in *Tales from the Crypt* (persecuted widower) and *Asylum* (bereaved father) are especially upsetting to watch. And this new-found vulnerability was sometimes capable of blooming into all-out hysteria, as in *The Creeping Flesh* or *The Ghoul*. Helen's death also resulted in a tremendously prolific upsurge in his film commitments, for the melancholy reason that only constant work could blot out his bereavement.

Cushing's scrapbooks contain a nakedly confessional note, entitled 'My Prayer – 1972', dated 26 May (his birthday) and written on Brown's Hotel notepaper. It's addressed to 'my belovèd Helen' and concludes like this:

> *There is so much I wish to make amends for. So much*
> *I am ashamed of. God grant I can redeem myself in*
> *His and your eyes and heart. And make up for the times*
> *when you were so hurt by my foolish adolescence and*
> *made to feel insecure and – of all impossible things –*
> *inadequate. My dear one, I want to die, because that will*
> *be the continuance of our life – together – as it has been*
> *and always will be. God speed the day, I beg.*
> *Amen.*

What did Cushing mean by the phrase 'my foolish adolescence'? And what did he mean, in his later autobiography, when he wrote: 'There were many times when I had been human and erred: Helen was divine, and forgave, but I could never forgive myself'?

In a *Daily Express* interview in 1986, he clarified these cryptic observations, referring to 'two or three one-off temptations' with actresses of his acquaintance. These liaisons presumably answered a need not satisfied in a marriage that 'was a spiritual union, the physical element holding little importance.'

This aspect of Cushing's life is a useful corrective to a widespread misreading of his memoirs. In them he depicted Helen as a saint, yet many fans have somehow displaced this beatification process onto Cushing himself. Personally, I'm convinced that he would have thought it embarrassing and inappropriate to be regarded in such a way. He was not a saint; he was a fallible human being like the rest of us, and this in part is what makes his acting so compelling.

Whether or not unresolved guilt was a component of the nervous breakdown triggered by Helen's death, news of the breakdown itself soon appeared in the press. In April 1972, Ray Connolly visited Pinewood, where Cushing was filming *Nothing But the Night*, and his subsequent *Evening Standard* interview featured several starkly cheerless Cushing quotes like this one:

> *And sometimes one might think what is one doing here, and*
> *why one doesn't do what dear George Sanders did the other day,*
> *or what poor Tony Hancock did. But I know I've been left for a*
> *reason. There is no waste. No waste.*

I vividly recall stumbling upon a similar interview in the summer of 1974. I was in the Windsor branch of WH Smith, no doubt looking for the latest issue of *Legend Horror Classics*, or *World of Horror*, or maybe even *Monster Mag*. And to my surprise I saw Peter Cushing's face looking out mournfully from the cover of a quite different paper, *New Reveille*. I was even more surprised when I read the contents. 'What I am doing is merely existing,' Cushing said. 'I could not take my own life, but I would be so happy if I could die tomorrow.'

This kind of thing was very puzzling to an 11-year-old. Has this marvellous actor, I asked myself, gone slightly mad? Crude and unfeeling though these ponderings may seem, I wonder now if they weren't shared by many people in the film industry. How else – other than an unwillingness to deal with a person who was obviously damaged – can one explain the fact that in May 1976 Cushing spent a week at Elstree playing the suavely evil Grand Moff Tarkin in the epoch-making *Star Wars* ... and *absolutely nothing* came of it?

Cushing had pulled off a remarkable coup here. Having appeared in *The Curse of Frankenstein* 20 years earlier and thus revolutionised the horror genre, he was now appearing in a film that was to revolutionise science fantasy. (And cinema itself, come to that.) Yet, in its wake, this actor who hated to travel acknowledged ruefully that 'You have to go where the work is today' – and jetted off to Germany, Zambia and Spain for projects that virtually qualify as 'lost' films. Worse still, he declined a trip to Pasadena to appear in *Halloween*. Donald Pleasence took his place and the result was another genre-defining smash.

There were a few delightful gems to come – a marvellous Dr Manette in *A Tale of Two Cities*, a nostalgic reunion with Vincent Price and Christopher Lee in *House of the Long Shadows*, an autumnal return to Sherlock Holmes in *The Masks of Death*. But prolonged illness finally got the better of him, and in June 1987, aged 74, he announced his retirement.

* * *

By the time Helen died, a sea change had occurred in the attitude of many film critics, with older ones recanting their former views and a new generation seeing Cushing's achievements on film for what they were. In 1972, for example, Susan d'Arcy maintained in *Photoplay* that

> *The reason Peter Cushing and Christopher Lee lead the [horror]*
> *field is that they believe in what they do. Unlike young actors*
> *who romp through horror films with a slight smirk on their*
> *faces, Lee and Cushing play it as though it were Shakespeare.*
> *Their serious attitude is the only thing that could have kept us*
> *convinced for so long.*

By the time of Cushing's own death, on 11 August 1994, this kind of view had, happily, become the dominant one. His memorial service took place on 12 January the following year at the Actors' Church in Covent Garden and was a moving occasion. Christopher Lee and Ron Moody read the lessons and soprano Rosie Ashe sang Noël Coward's appropriately titled 'If Love Were All'. For me, the only disappointment was a presiding minister so ill-briefed he mispronounced Cushing's name – as in 'gushing' rather than 'pushing'.

In the years since, a sizable Cushing cult has grown up, with *An Autobiography* and *'Past Forgetting'*, despite their long unavailability, constituting twin pillars of that cult. The first is a slim volume, clocking in at not much more than 50,000 words, and is riveting when Cushing describes his long climb to fame and genuinely moving when he recounts Helen's death. In between, however, he loses a little bit of steam when discussing his film career, and it was to fill in a few more details of this that he wrote *'Past Forgetting'*. The result was even shorter (not quite managing 25,000 words) and almost stream-of-consciousness in its collage-style structure. But both books are invaluable for the insight they give into Cushing the man, and the very real old-world charm that radiates from every page.

For the 21st century reader, *An Autobiography* gets off to a slightly uncomfortable start, and *'Past Forgetting'* reaches a somewhat awkward conclusion, for reasons Cushing couldn't possibly have anticipated. His account of the Helen Cushing rose, which he calls 'a crowning glory to my career', reads uneasily because the rose was cultivated under the patronage of Jimmy Savile. In light of recent revelations, it's tempting, albeit glib, to suggest that Cushing's two appearances on Savile's programme *Jim'll Fix It* were the only occasions when cinema's most celebrated monster hunter shared the screen with a real monster.

Fortunately, there's nothing uncomfortable in the remainder, and indeed there are numerous sections that will make the reader laugh or cry, and sometimes both. My personal favourite might well be the section in *'Past Forgetting'* (on page 203) where Cushing offers a very entertaining digest of his 16 screen deaths, plus one 'Don't know' – *Asylum*. (And yes, he expired in that one, too – shot to death by a nervous tailor.)

Now here's a diverting little parlour game for all dyed-in-the-wool Cushing aficionados. For it's clear that the great man actually forgot about quite a few. I'll start the ball rolling by adding the following half-dozen, bringing the total to a tentative 23… Beaten to a pulp by his own charity patients in *The Revenge of Frankenstein*, roasted to death by extraterrestrial fried eggs in *Night of the Big Heat*, zapped by his own surgical laser in *Corruption*, submitted to a neo-Nazi death grip in *Scream and Scream Again*, decapitated in a Weybridge waxworks in *The House that Dripped Blood*, and exploded by holy water in *The Devil's Men*.

Can anyone think of any more?

Jonathan Rigby
London
April 2013

Jonathan Rigby is the author of English Gothic: A Century of Horror Cinema, American Gothic: Sixty Years of Horror Cinema, Christopher Lee: The Authorised Screen History *and* Studies in Terror: Landmarks of Horror Cinema.

PETER CUSHING

AN AUTOBIOGRAPHY

PREFACE

'Begin at the beginning,' the King said gravely,
'and go on 'til you come to the end: then stop.'

What better advice than Lewis Carroll's when attempting to write a life story? However, since my life as I knew and loved it ended with the passing of my belovèd wife Helen, I intend to take this narrative no farther than that fateful Thursday in 1971, January 14th.

I have in my possession a Birthday Book by Caterina, and printed alongside that date is a little homily: 'You cannot alter your fate at present, be content,' and beside the date of my birth: 'You will make a great friend of someone you least expect.'

Truisms, perhaps, but as Noël Coward said of cheap music, it is extraordinary how potent they can be. I have to accept my fate, but cannot pretend I am content. On the other hand, I have been blessed with so many great and good friends who have stood by me since '71, that I cannot let this opportunity pass without telling them how much I have appreciated their kindness, understanding and help. It is not possible to name them all individually – that could fill another volume – but I would like to mention those who so graciously and with such unstinting generosity gave permission for the photographs to be reproduced within these pages. The warmth of their letters, conveying the esteem in which I am held, astonished and overwhelmed me.

I would also like to thank my publishers, especially Mr David Roberts, for his patience, sagacity and enheartening enthusiasm; Kevin Francis, the film producer, who remembered me from his youth, and has since inundated me with kindness, benefaction and employment, and very dear friendship, when – morally – such things were most needed; also my dear friend Sir John Mills who, by his encouragement and example, finally persuaded me to take the plunge and record these memoirs, which I had started originally as a form of therapy, with no intention of making them public. He threatened never to work with me again if I didn't.

By the time this book is published, a rose will have been named after Helen, through the kind consideration of Jimmy Savile and his *Jim'll Fix It* colleagues at the BBC, cultivated by Christopher Wheatcroft in his Nottingham nurseries, thus keeping in perpetuity the memory of a very wonderful lady, Helen Cushing. I look upon this as a crowning glory to my career. My deep thanks, gratitude and affection to them – to you all, and may God's blessing be with you always.

In all sincerity,

Peter Cushing
Whitstable, 1984

I

MYSELF WHEN YOUNG

'HAVE YOU, BY any chance, found a little boy who is lost?'

It was my Father speaking anxiously over the telephone to the local police station.

'No, I'm afraid not,' the duty sergeant replied, 'but I see in our book we've found a little girl.'

A pause. Then, lowering his voice in case Mother should be within earshot – too delicate a subject for a woman born during Queen Victoria's vintage years to overhear – Father said, 'Look here, I wonder – would you … would you make *sure* it's a little girl?'

Another pause, this time on the sergeant's part. At last the penny dropped.

'Oh, I get you, sir. 'Ang on a minute.'

Father obliged, and presently the voice at the other end returned with apologetic surprise: 'You're quite right, sir – it *is* a little chap!'

My mother, having given birth to my brother David three years before me, and always longing for a daughter – wanting 'one of each' – had mitigated any slight disappointment in my arrival by dressing me in girls' frocks, and allowing my hair to grow in long curls, tied in bows of pink ribbon. Hence the temporary bafflement of the policeman and Father's embarrassment.

Eventually, he exerted his gentle authority and insisted upon a change of attire more in keeping with my sex, and also a haircut.

To this day, a golden hank lies curled in the Family Bible, together with a pressed flower – a sentimental souvenir kept by my mother of her unrealised yearning.

When I was a little older, I was to discover that Father's qualms about her overhearing his intimate conversation with the sergeant were quite unfounded. I had been invited to a mixed bathing party, which would involve changing from clothes into swimsuits in the cold light of day on an open beach. To ease my adolescent fears of any indecent exposure, Mother's remarkable advice had been, 'If you see anything you haven't seen before, dear, throw your hat at it.'

* * *

I imagine my father – George Edward – was of the upper class, and my mother – Nellie Maria, née King – of somewhat humbler stock, lower middle class, Mr King being a carpet merchant. I say 'imagine', because Father was a most reserved and uncommunicative soul, reticent to vouchsafe any information regarding his ancestry, and I never got to know him really well.

Born in 1881, he'd obviously experienced a very strict, conventional Victorian upbringing, and I always had the impression his childhood had not been a happy one, although he didn't ever admit it.

With great clarity, I remember the daguerreotype photograph of my paternal grandfather hanging in the dust-sheeted front parlour, flanked by aspidistras: the formidable face of a disciplinarian which petrified me, his stern eyes behind the pince-nez seeming to follow me about the room whichever way I went. But I never met him, and photographs have been known to lie.

What little I did glean about Father's past life and times was either winkled out of him by my inquisitive probings and, indeed, very real interest, or supplied by his sister Maude, my favourite aunt. She felt her brother had lowered himself by marrying 'beneath' him, and had, out of deep love and loyalty, given way in most things to his wife's wishes. It must be remembered that they had been brought up in an age of propriety, when great store was set upon what was regarded as 'doing the right thing'. 'For instance, my deah, I'm surprised you didn't become another Oscar Wilde – perhaps not in the poetic sense, but most certainly in the other, treated as you were – from the cradle – as a gel.'

Maude ('for Heaven's sake don't call me Aunt') Ashton had been on the stage, and played all the Gertie Millar roles during the halcyon days of touring companies to South Africa. She retired when I was very young, but before this I'd been taken to see her in a one-act drama, in which she played 'a lady of easy virtue', although I wasn't aware of such subtlety at the time. I just thought she was quite lovely and exciting, and was thrilled to have her as a relation.

She had married a professional soldier whom she met when abroad, Lt Col Richard Annesley West, VC, DSO with Bar, MC. He was killed during the First World War, awarded a posthumous VC for leading the tanks into action – 'on a horse of all things, deah! But then he was a mad Irishman – the British Army wouldn't have him at first – "too old" or something, they said, but as he threatened to join the Germans if they turned him down, they decided to accept him!' With deep sincerity she added, 'I loved him, very much.'

I asked her how she'd come by the name of Ashton. 'Oh, I saw it printed on the side of a passing pantechnicon, deah – and thought it most suitable!'

She presented me with some beautiful souvenir programmes of Sir Henry Irving's productions at the Lyceum Theatre, London, and as I browsed through them a name leapt out of a page at me. There, in 'The Dramatis Personae' of 'Shakespeare's Historical Play – *King Henry the Eighth*', presented on 5 January 1892, sandwiched between MR. REYNOLDS ('a scribe') and MISS ELLEN TERRY ('Queen Katherine'), was MR. CUSHING ('a secretary')!

I tore my eyes away from this magnetic name and read, avidly, the rest of the cast. What company he was in! Apart from Irving himself as Cardinal Wolsey and Miss Terry, there were such players as:

King Henry VIII	MR. WILLIAM TERRISS
Duke of Buckingham	MR. FORBES ROBERTSON
Cromwell (servant to Wolsey)	MR. GORDON CRAIG
Anne Bullen	MISS VIOLET VANBRUGH

Maude told me that my grandfather had been a more or less permanent member of Irving's Company, touring with him on numerous occasions in England and in America. My thoughts went back to that portrait on the shrouded parlour wall with a new respect – and something akin to awe.

This Mr Cushing was, by profession, a quantity surveyor – or so I had always been led to believe – who had said to his son George, 'When you leave school, I shall endeavour to find you some kind of employment. After that, you can expect no further help from me' – or words to that effect. So son, like father, became a quantity surveyor, remaining a highly successful and respected one with Selby and Sanders until his retirement at the age of 65.

I could never get a satisfactory explanation to my repeated questions as to how Grandfather managed to be an actor as well as a quantity surveyor, both professions requiring one hundred per cent of one's time, I should have thought. Perhaps he, too, had been equally unforthcoming, and it remained a mystery.

Quite recently, I had reason to go through a file of family documents, and came across a batch of Birth, Marriage and Death certificates. There seems to have been some discrepancy regarding Granddad's 'Rank or Profession'. Under that heading in 1866, Henry William Cushing is entered as a Civil Engineer. In 1881, he becomes a Vocalist; 18 years later a Brewers Architect, reverting once more to a Vocalist in 1907, and finally finishing the course – to me, triumphantly – in 1912 as an Actor (Tragedian). I liked that.

No mention of a quantity surveyor, but with that little lot tucked under his belt, it really didn't matter.

My step uncle – yet another mystery as far as I was concerned (obviously 'The Tragic Actor' had married twice, a topic regarded as unsuitable for my youthful ears) – was also in the theatre. He wrote as well, and took part in many of his own music hall sketches. He stage-managed and assisted in the original production of *Charley's Aunt*, by Brandon Thomas, which opened at the Royalty Theatre in 1892 and ran for 1,466 performances, a record which would remain unbroken until 1941, when Noël Coward's *Blithe Spirit* beat it by running for 1,997. (Of course, this record was later broken by such blockbusters as *The Mousetrap*, etc.)

In partnership with Mark Ambient, he had written *A Little Ray of Sunshine*, the only play which WS Penley appeared in following his enormous success as Lord Fancourt Babberley in *Charley's Aunt*.

He passed on in 1913, just before I was born. His stage name was Wilton Herriot, and I was christened after him – Peter Wilton Cushing.

*   *   *

Many years later, in an unguarded moment, my dear father astonished me with an intriguing titbit involving my antecedents. I'd just told him that I'd been offered an Old Vic tour of the Antipodes.

'Your Uncle Bertie was banished to Australia in 1901,' he said absentmindedly. 'We've never heard of him since…'

Uncle Bertie? Banished! I could hardly believe my ears … it was reminiscent of some romantic novel – and I'd never even heard of him until that moment in 1948.

What heinous crime could he have perpetrated to deserve such a fate? They used to send convicts there! My imagination boggled at this world-shattering statement, coming as it had from out of the blue, and I felt quite a wave of sympathy for this lonely, unknown exile. I managed to squeeze out the fascinating information that he was 'of artistic temperament' and 'a wanderer', but after these initial slips of the tongue, Father closed down like a clam, and I could see it was no use pursuing the subject. Here was a skeleton in the cupboard and no mistake – and likely to remain there!

*　*　*

Of my mother's father I have only one recollection, but it is extremely vivid: a kind-looking man, with grey hair parted down the centre, arranged carefully in quiffs on either side, and a grey moustache, the ends waxed into sharp-looking spikes, lying on a couch, wearing braces over a blue and cream striped woollen shirt, no collar – just a brass front stud.

He coughed, and expectorated into a large polka dot handkerchief, showing the sputum to his daughter with the words, 'That's what's killing me, Nellie.'

*　*　*

Born on 26 May 1913, my earliest memories of the 1914-18 war are watching German Zeppelins caught like giant silver cigars in the criss-cross of searchlights over Dulwich Village, where we were living, and the wonderful 'game' my parents invented in the hope of keeping their two offspring safe. They suggested we pretended to be Red Indians, using the stout oaken kitchen table, with a cloth draped over it, as a wigwam, and they made sure we got under its protective cover whenever they thought there was any danger of falling bombs, which were usually heralded by a policeman going around on a bicycle blowing his whistle.

How could that chubby little Cherokee, or Sioux, or whatever tribe I belonged to in childish imagination, know that Fate was already weaving her web around him? That, as he squatted there beneath a wooden tepee in a South London suburb, wearing his chicken-feathered headdress and smoking a chocolate Pipe of Peace, his 'squaw' to be, in the person of a beautiful girl, 12 years old, blonde and blue-eyed as an angel, was at that moment away on the distant High Seas, bound for England, fleeing with her family from a Russia racked by bloody Revolution? That their paths were destined to cross; that he would meet her some 25 years later during another World War? Meet her and love her, and lose her. Lose her? I do not think so.

However, that is far ahead in the future: we are but yet in 1917.

*　*　*

Whatever Father's early years may have been like, mine were indeed happy, except for a few isolated incidents. Some of these were to leave their scars, and have adverse repercussions upon my development.

I burst into this world on a Monday morning, weighing in at a record 10½ lbs, in Kenley, Surrey – then no more than a village but now, I imagine, all but swallowed up by the sprawling suburbia of the Great Wen. I was apparently ravenous from the word go, arriving in time for an early breakfast, and much of my childhood was spent foraging for food, to keep me going between proper meals. My mother maintained that I had hollow legs.

One of those supplementary snacks was raw bacon rind, which I would suck in the garden. Once, to Mother's horror, I came in happily sucking a long, juicy worm, having dropped the original delicacy and picked up the unfortunate invertebrate by mistake. I suppose I was about two at the time, my palate and perception not sufficiently developed to notice any difference.

When I was old enough, I would volunteer to go shopping for Mother, always with a wistful 'Can I keep the change?' – invariably granted, depending upon the amount involved.

'…and a penn'orth of broken biscuits, please,' I would add, after I'd given the grocer the official order. In those days, long before the era of pre-packaging, this was a most profitable purchase, being presented with a large paper bag full of every imaginable biscuit, which had not withstood the journey from bakery to retailer. These would be consumed on the walk back, but having a sweet tooth, I wasn't too keen on the cheese varieties, so they were scattered to the birds. Sometimes there was a preponderance of these, as they were less resilient to transportation than my favourites, but I lacked the courage to return and lodge a complaint with the shop keeper. And anyway, the birds were grateful, and made good company with their perky twitterings.

If there happened to be a freshly baked loaf on the list of family requirements, it didn't remain intact for very long, the aroma proving too much for my susceptibilities, and great hunks of the staff of life would be missing by the time I got home. I was always delighted if it happened to be a cottage loaf because the whole of the smaller bun could be removed and devoured, leaving the larger portion looking less as if mice had been at it.

I had a curious habit in my gastronomic feats at the dining table. Having a fully equipped doll's house – presumably a hangover from the days before I was 'defrocked' – I would eat my meals using the miniature cutlery, measuring approximately 1½ inches. My parents never objected to this eccentricity, unless there was company present, because – although it took me a considerable time to wade through my huge helpings (I was still on 'firsts' when they were tucking into 'seconds') – it meant I didn't 'gobble my food', which was rightly considered good for the digestion.

One Christmas, as a special treat, I was taken to a London theatre to see *Peter Pan*, and fell quite desperately in love with Peter. Since He was always played by a She, that really wasn't as bad as it sounds, although I'm sure Freud (perhaps even Aunt Maude) would have found something to say on the subject.

For many weeks after this enchanted evening, I would fling the window wide open when I went up to bed and kneel before it, cocooned in a counterpane, praying for him to come flying through, teach me how to fly and take me back to see the 'Never, Never, Never Land'. Mother often found me asleep in this attitude of prayer, the bedroom as cold as the outside of an igloo, and, like Puccini's Mimi, my tiny hands frozen.

It could well be that Peter Pan's desire to remain 'The Boy Who Wouldn't Grow Up' rubbed itself off on me, which I think becomes self-evident as my story unfolds…

* * *

It seems that I was always a great imperialist, parading up and down tram or omnibus gangways, with my tin seaside pail worn as a helmet, and spade held over my shoulder like a rifle at the slope, chanting 'I'm marching for my tin,' which was my nearest approach to 'King'.

Perhaps I was not paying too much attention when Mother had told me what to do whenever a funeral cortège passed by. Following what I thought were her instructions, at the first opportunity I took off my cap and twirled it enthusiastically above my head, cheering lustily.

'What *are you* doing?' she whispered, aghast.

'You told me to wave my cap.'

'I said *raise* it – not *wave* it!' she gasped.

My brother and I called ladies clothing stores 'rag shops', and, as such, they never appealed to me. But I often went with Mother on her shopping sprees, a never failing attraction being that they always ended with a slap-up tea in Alders or Kennards cafeterias, or at Wilsons in the High Street, Croydon. I was also fascinated by the system employed to convey money from the various counters to the Accounts Department. The banknotes were thrust into a small metal cylinder suspended on overhead wires, and at the pull of a chain, it was whisked away as if by some magic force. I yearned to become like Gulliver during his travels in Brobdingnag (which I'd seen in my picture story book) – small enough to get inside one and glide so effortlessly over the crowded floors, to be returned with the loose change, which came tinkling down a shoot at the assistant's elbow.

I had to find ways of augmenting my sixpence per week pocket money, the donor always reminding me that he only received a penny a week when he was my age. I didn't have the knowledge then that this amount could very possibly have had the equivalent spending power in that bygone time, and in any case, I doubt if I would have entered into an argument about High Finance with Father.

Expenditure was considerable. My literary taste had to be catered for. I adored the daily cartoon of Pip, Squeak and Wilfred created by AB Payne in the *Daily Mirror*, with the much loved catchphrase of the little long-eared rabbit set in a balloon – 'NUNC!' I joined his 'secret society' and became a 'Gugnunc', the password being, if I recall correctly – 'ICK ICK PAH BOO'. However, there was little else in the family papers to capture my attention, so every Wednesday I would collect *Puck* and *The Rainbow*. The former contained, among other exciting material, the stirring adventures of Rob the Rover and his wonderous amphibious aeroplane, and the latter an endearing family of animals led by Tiger Tim, with his inseparable friends Bobby Bruin and Joey the Parrot.

This feast of strip cartoons cost threepence – half my 'salary' gone in one fell swoop! The other half mortgaged for the ever necessary 'iron rations'. These consisted of the aptly – if crudely – named gob stoppers, about half the size of a golf ball, which miraculously changed colour as you sucked them, rather like a chameleon, plus a supply of pear drops, turning the tongue bright scarlet, and a deliciously sticky confection called coconut surprises. This supply of sweetmeats was always exhausted long before the next pay day.

Occasionally, largesse would be bestowed upon their readers by the publishers of those weeklies, and a sherbet dab (a packet containing a flat, circular piece of toffee attached to the end of a thin stick, which you licked and then dipped into that toothsome if hiccup-making powder) or some other delectable morsel would be given away – 'Free, Gratis And For Nothing' writ large on the front page – a gesture which met with my instant approval, and consumption; but, like Oliver Twist, I wanted more.

To meet my pressing demands, I hit upon the idea of becoming a pavement artist – in the safety of our hallway, I hasten to add.

When Father returned home from the office in the evenings, he would often discover me sitting yogi-fashion (I had observed the 'professionals') with a burnt-cork moustache smudged across my top lip, a woollen scarf around my neck, and one of his old Trilby hats upended before me, to receive any offerings he might make as a token of his appreciation for the works of art propped up alongside me. There was also a sign in a prominent position, bearing the legend:

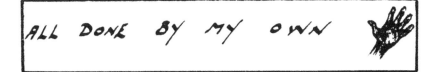

I refrained from adding 'Wife and three children to support', because, although I'd seen it used, I thought it was a little too advanced for me at the moment. My takings were on a sliding scale, with a downward trend, but every little helped.

As time went by, I graduated from my colourful comics to the now legendary *Gem* and *The Magnet*. The very titles fill me with nostalgia, evoking that pungent smell, a mixture of newsprint, peppermint and aniseed, which permeated the paper shops of yesteryear, where I bought those precious journals, and to which I had hurried with palpitating heart, lest they should all be sold before I got there. I recall the many hours of sheer serendipity spent up a tree in the summer – to escape any interruptions – or curled before the fireside in our play room during long winter evenings, with the ever present bag of sweets to hand, utterly engrossed in those splendid schoolboy stories.

There was also *The Popular*, which featured Jimmy Silver & Co, who ruled the roost at Rookwood. Harry Wharton and Co (plus the Fat Owl of the Remove, Billy Bunter) resided at Greyfriars, and Tom Merry and Co at St Jim's.

All this scholarly fiction was written by one prodigious author, Charles Hamilton, using several pseudonyms, and I owe him a great debt of gratitude, not only for the enormous pleasure I derived from his work, but also for his influence upon me as a person. Tom Merry was my hero, and I tried to mould my way of life according to his tenets.

This departure into the realms of past delights brings me – with a jolt – to the cause of my insolvency. Rising prices ('plus ça change…'), also the fact that I had furthered my fields of interest. Those 'penny dreadfuls', as my dear Dad called them, cost twopence each: there was the serious consideration of allowing for the appalling amount of fourpence a month, when *The Schoolboy's Own Library* was published (more escapades of those famous fellows) or even eightpence if there were two in this series which I desired.

Besides attempting to satisfy my insatiable appetite – an impossible task – I had now embarked upon collecting William Britain farm toys and model soldiers. These delightful figurines fetch fantastic prices in auction today, and are much sought after, but when I started my collection they were very reasonably priced – provided you had the means: for example, one lead chicken – one penny.

The situation was becoming desperate – bankruptcy stared me in the face. It was then I thought of my Punch and Judy set, and resolved to capitalise on this recently acquired Christmas present. There were many aunts and uncles, who often visited us for family get-togethers.

I threw myself into intensive rehearsals with my glove puppets, and brother David constructed a traditional marquee for the show I intended to put on for their benefit, and our gain.

It was Uncle George Gatenby who gave us the key to financial success with this venture into showmanship.

He was married to Mother's sister Rose, and it may be of some passing interest to note that he was the proud possessor of a 10 hp De Dion Bouton, vintage 1904. I am led to believe it still runs in the annual London to Brighton Veteran Car Race – they certainly made things to last, way back when! He often took us for spins, and I remember the little flight of collapsible steps which you folded down at the back, and climbed up in order to reach the rear seats, like chickens into their coop.

'Don't charge your customers to come in,' he advised, 'but charge them as they go out.'

I didn't quite understand his reasoning – but it worked. Bowing to his wisdom, I displayed a large board announcing 'Admission Free' and, ever optimistic, I envisaged 'House Full' notices as they filed dutifully into the billiard room where the performance was being held. A willing enough group, and I'm sure this was out of the kindness of their hearts not to disappoint the young entrepreneur on his First Night. But, quite understandably, they soon tired of my amateurish efforts, and one by one began to sneak out, only to be confronted at the door by an inexorable elder brother on guard duty, demanding payment before they could pass through the portals to peace, and a refreshing cup of tea. An entrance fee might have kept a few away, but now there was no escape.

Within my tent the 'auditorium' was hidden from my view so I was unaware of this exodus, and in blissful ignorance my version of Grand Guignol continued its squeaky course to the bitter end, culminating in poor Punch hanging on the gibbet, whacked heartily by the Policeman's truncheon – a somewhat macabre drama for the young, when you consider it.

I was most disappointed when the curtain finally fell, as the rapturous applause I had expected from an appreciative audience didn't materialise. It met with stony silence, until I heard the chink of coins as David started totting up what was in the kitty. That cheered me up no end! The day was saved, if only temporarily.

After this initial success in accruing wealth, further methods of ruthless extortion were levied on unsuspecting relatives, and any neighbours who happened to be on hand in times of pecuniary crisis, which was a pretty permanent state in my affairs.

One of these exploitation schemes took the form of 'bus rides'. Chairs were arranged in paired tiers with a gangway between them. When our passengers had taken their seats, I 'ting-tinged', and then demanded, to the manner born, 'Fares please!' And I meant it. Mind you, I had in all fairness dressed up for my role of the conductor, an old peaked yachting cap found in the attic, even if a trifle on the big side and somewhat moth-eaten, doing good service as the Thomas Tilling official headgear, and any dog-eared cigarette card 'swops' made very attractive tickets. I had no wish to take money under false pretences, or without giving something in return. David was at the driving wheel, which consisted of a seaside bucket placed over a walking stick, and he managed to honk most realistically.

But these static excursions didn't get us anywhere, proving unpopular with busy and long-suffering adults. Even a poster proclaiming 'REDUCED FARES' failed to attract custom, so that enterprise was abandoned as uneconomic.

I welcomed the seasonal tradition of carol singing, because this profitable business, with quick returns, often saved me from liquidation. Our vocal efforts were not of the highest standard and our repertoire very limited, alternating between 'While Shepherds Watched their Flocks by Night' and 'Good King Wenceslas'. We would tap on the doors speculatively after a few uninspired opening stabs, hoping to get our torturous harmonising over and done with as quickly as possible, and so move on swiftly to our next unfortunate victims. Obviously, the captive listeners were as anxious to terminate the cacophony as the 'singers' were to make off with their ill-gotten gains, and we found we could do whole streets in less than no time. Some of our sufferers offered us mince pies instead of cash – a little disappointing, but we ate them with relish.

'You should save your money, my boy. It doesn't grow on trees, you know.' Although I knew Father's oft-repeated reproach to be botanically sound, I couldn't comprehend how he expected me to hoard something I didn't possess…

* * *

My first seat of learning was a Dulwich kindergarten, where I also made my first appearance on the stage. For reasons which escape me, I was hidden within a wicker hamper, dressed in green rompers – representing some devilish little gnome or hobgoblin, I think, with lots of elves and sprites hopping about outside. It was not on the agenda, but to enliven the proceedings, I squeezed a hand through a gap in my 'cage', so that I could nip the passing bottom of a lumpy fairy as she teetered by on unsteady tippy toe, which made a complete mess of her already wobbly pas seul.

Only one other incident whilst there jogs my memory. No doubt because drawing was the only subject I was any good at, I became Suspect Number One for an example of graffiti discovered on a wall in the boys' WC. I was taken by the Head Mistress for a private view of this masterpiece, and in the confined space of the pedestalled show room, confronted with it and wrongfully accused as the perpetrator. I hotly denied the charge. Not only was I innocent, but the anatomical member so graphically depicted by some budding Leonardo da Vinci meant nothing to me, nor did the descriptive text beneath it. My plea of 'not guilty' was swept aside, and with an admonishing finger wagging under my nose, sentence passed upon me. 'Your pencil will be confiscated, and your parents informed of your disgraceful conduct.'

Back at my desk, I began to smart under this unjust indictment, and resolved to run away from school. Raising my hand and excusing myself for the usual legitimate reason, I hurried to 'Cloaks'. As part of my winter equipment, I wore a pair of long, tight-fitting boots, which had to be removed and replaced by plimsolls before entering the form rooms. This involved unlacing them completely from knee to ankle, and now the reverse procedure faced me. Instead of simple hooks they had eyelets, and as the metal rims around the majority of them, as well as the tags at the tips of the laces, had long since disappeared, the frayed ends needed frequent applications of saliva to produce the required point for easy threading. This exercise took time and patience, both at a premium in my present high endeavour.

Many minutes later, the tedious task accomplished, I was finally 'booted and spurred'. At precisely the same moment, the bell rang announcing the end of lessons for the day, and a swarm of infant prodigies, joyously let loose from stuffy classrooms onto a hitherto peaceful neighbourhood, enveloped me in a boisterous yelping multitude, and I was borne along in its wake, my bid for freedom foiled, my gesture of repudiation passing unnoticed.

I have forgotten the outcome of this 'mauvais quart d'heure' – my first experience of a wicked world's injustice – but I lived to tell the tale, and presently I was sent to the Shoreham Grammar School in Sussex.

Always prone to home sickness, the thought of being a boarder filled me with dread. Mother accompanied me on this journey into the unknown, and I can remember the abject terror which gripped me every time the slow train to the South Coast stopped, and crying out to her in anguish, 'This isn't the station, is it?'

My consternation affected her deeply, and in the event I was only to stay at Shoreham for one short – if miserable – term. I became practically a pathological case, incontinent in bed, and forever blubbing in the locker room. Father was all for my staying the course ('He'll get over it, Nellie') but Mother, as ever, won the day.

Walking to and from the football field on sports days, the route passed under a railway bridge, and I had heard the old superstition that if you stood under one of these constructions as a train thundered overhead and made a wish, that wish would be granted. So, if I saw an engine approaching in the distance, I used to pelt along the lane like one possessed in order to reach the sanctuary of

the arch in time to gasp out 'Please – I want to go home!' – a form
of prayer which was eventually answered.

I don't think my appetite was in any way impaired, however.
Whilst searching amongst those family papers, I came across a
'compulsory letter' which I'd written during those excruciating
weeks. These were devised by those in authority with a threefold
purpose in mind: to make sure the young kept in touch with home,
to put their grammar, spelling and general composition to the test,
and to improve penmanship. Our Mistress would read and censor
these epistles before they were sealed and posted.

I spread it out, and there before me, immortalised in wavering
script which barely succeeded in keeping within the bounds of
carefully ruled pencil lines, and with not a punctuation mark in
sight, was the poignant cri de coeur:

> *My dear Mother and Father Teacher is*
> *nice and nasty and looks like Man Friday*
> *please can I have some more cake from*
> *your loving son Peter*

The reference to Robinson Crusoe's savage companion on his
desert island stemmed from a visit to 'the pictures' with Mother,
when we had seen an exciting serial version of Defoe's classic story.
Poor 'Teacher' cannot have felt very flattered, whether she'd seen
the film or not, even though I do remember she had a head of
hair like my toy golly. To her undying credit, she left for posterity
my eulogy as it was originally conceived, adding in red ink, with
remarkable generosity, a footnote: 'Writing improving'. It needed to.
I'm surprised she didn't give me ten out of ten for innate honesty.

*   *   *

By no stretch of the imagination could I be called a good or
attentive student. Anything that didn't interest me had no chance

even of going in one ear, let alone coming out of the other. Even that passage was denied it. But I've always had an enquiring mind, pestering grown-ups with questions, some of which were impossible to answer. Witty Uncle George dubbed me 'the why's one'.

Having been told that cats always fall on their feet, no matter from what height they fell, I once pushed a tiny kitten off the kitchen table to prove the validity of this theory. It was not a premeditated act of cruelty, but a sincere desire to learn something. I was horrified when I saw the inert little body lying on the floor in a small pool of blood, and rushed to find Mother, seeking First Aid for the casualty. Fortunately, it suffered nothing more serious than slight concussion, plus a nose bleed, and my furry friend was soon playing happily with a ball of wool, having first lapped up a saucer of top-of-the-milk, which I had proffered as compensation for damages.

I was not punished for this experiment with the force of gravity. My contrition was obvious and genuine, Mother declaring that I had not tried to hide the deed from her, but owned up to it voluntarily. (Tom Merry's early influence!)

The rod was always spared in our home but she had, none the less, her own method of punishment which she would inflict upon me whenever I did anything naughty. I regret to say it had a disastrous psychological effect, leaving me with a morbid and quite unnecessary fear of death. Of course, this was not her intention – in fact I'm sure she had no idea it would cause such repercussions, and used to laugh at my concern.

Her tactics were to sing the first few bars of the refrain from 'Love Will Find a Way', made famous by José Collins in the romantic musical *The Maid of the Mountains*, fitting her own lyrics to its haunting melody – '…I'm going away, away, away, across the ocean blue…' – and then pretend to be dead, by sitting very still, eyes closed and head lying back on her easy chair.

I can still hear myself screaming 'No! No! Don't go away – come back! I won't be naughty any more, if only you'll come back to me!'

Of course, I was naughty again, and Mother would repeat her successful performance every time I erred, completely unaware of the damage she was doing. It preyed upon me to such an extent that eventually I confided in my brother. He assured me it was only an act, and his practical suggestion was that I should pinch her whenever she feigned death in the future.

I just could not bring myself to do this, but another way of proving his reassurance presented itself. On this particular occasion I was eating (naturally) a huge slice of bread and butter and marmalade. With heart in mouth, I stole up to the 'corpse' and gently but firmly plonked the sticky slab on the upturned face. The cure was effective immediately – and Mother's 'resurrection' permanent.

But the seeds of fear and doubt had been sown in the fertile soil of an impressionable child's mind. Even into adulthood, whenever I heard those strains on a gramophone record or from a wireless set: '...What ere befall I still recall, That sunlit mountainside...', I would hear Mother's version, and my plea, 'Don't sing that song, Mother – it's a horrid song!' Guilt and remorse would grip me like a vice.

Those seeds had germinated and were to propagate, not to be uprooted for many long years, and then by the tender pruning of a wiser and gentle lady who became my wife.

Another fear engendered by punishment was of being alone in the dark. This time it was administered by Father, who was equally unconscious of any side effect his disciplinary action would have upon me. I cannot recall what my misdemeanour was, but it must have been something extremely bad to merit so drastic a step. I was condemned to the cellar, to me a veritable Black Hole of Calcutta, dark and forbidding, with unspeakable horrors lurking in every nook and cranny. The door at the top of the stairs, which led down to those dreaded depths, was shut and locked, leaving me in total blackness, and I beat upon it with my fists, shrieking, 'Give me a knife so that I can kill myself!' – so great was my terror. Father must have realised I was not 'play acting' (to use his own expression) for, after a few minutes which seemed an eternity, the door was opened, and the blessèd light flooded in and shone upon his ashen face. It was evident that he had been badly shaken by my unexpected outburst.

'Don't be silly, boy,' he muttered, adding those three futile words – 'Pull yourself together.'

For many weeks after this incident, I was beset with frightful nightmares, culminating in beseeching my parents to allow me to sleep between them in their large double bed. They agreed to this, somewhat reluctantly on Father's part. I suppose, from a moral point of view, he regarded this threesome as unhealthy. I was nudging nine at the time, and quite soon I was relegated to my own quarters once more.

In later years, as a cure for my induced nyctophobia, I forced myself into taking solitary walks at midnight, purposely choosing byways which led through lonely labyrinths, beautifully bosky and dappled with dancing sunlight during the day time, and bright with butterflies flitting among the wild hedgerow flowers. But, at the witching hour, still, dark and mysterious.

Gradually, I began to enjoy these nightly jaunts, and even looked forward to them. Sometimes, the pale light from a shy moon would filter through the tracery of overhanging branches, and the occasional hoots and screechings of owls, mingling with other eerie murmurings and rustlings of the night, provided a certain romance, and a plaintive but not unpleasant accompaniment to my nocturnal wanderings.

Consequently I became rather a 'loner' at heart, and have remained one ever since.

But I was destined to share a partnership such as I had never dreamed of.

2

'BRIGHTEYES'

WHEN THE 1914-18 war ended, we left Dulwich, returning once more to Surrey. This time to Purley, immediately adjacent to Kenley, the village where I was born, living near the station to start with and subsequently at the top of Downs Court Road.

We had a rather odd maid with protruding eyes, who glared balefully through parted net curtains at all the tradesmen who called, before opening the door. Eventually she married one of them and had about eight children straight off, finally leaving her husband '…on account of I never reely liked 'im, mum.'

My brother and I put our Guy on her lavatory pan for fun one evening, and out of the dusk she announced to Mother in a pained voice, 'I'm leavin', mum, on account of there's a norful lookin' man sittin' in my toilet wiv 'is 'at on.'

Guessing the source of this unwelcome 'intruder', Mother replied, 'Well, before you go, tell him it's rude, and to take it off at once.'

She stayed with us. She was forever dropping things and, sweeping up the scattered shards of crockery or best china, would reassure her mistress with a mournful smile: 'It 'asn't cracked, mum, it's only broke.'

Because of my disastrous term at Shoreham, it was decided to send me to a day school for the next step in my education, the one chosen being within a few hundred yards of our house – from the ridiculous to the sublime! It was the Purley County Secondary

School, lying at the bottom of St James' Road, classified in those days as 'un-made'.

I soon had my standard togs, consisting of a crested cap, grey flannel shorts, blazer, navy blue mackintosh, and a bulky satchel, absolutely crammed to the brim with tuck.

Next to hunger, my worst enemy was time. I was always late, especially if I wasn't all that keen on the appointment awaiting me. Therefore I needed some form of locomotion which would enable me to reach my new alma mater at the approved hour, and for this express purpose, David made me a marvellous go-cart, using pram wheels and an old toboggan top. I would hurtle down the one in seven gradient at an alarming lick, the precipitous descent made all the more dangerous and exciting by the potholes and furrows in the uneven surface. Flushed with success and not always unscathed after these downhill plunges, I would proudly park my vehicle, followed by many an envious eye, amongst the more mundane mode of transport in the bicycle shed in the quad.

(Just for the record I would like it to be known that I now eat in moderation, am a strict vegetarian, and would rather be half an hour too early than a minute late for any appointment!)

*   *   *

For three successive years during my infancy, I was a victim of pneumonia, the third time developing double pneumonia, very often fatal in those days before the advance in medical science.

To keep me amused when convalescent after my third bout, Auntie Flo, one of mother's five sisters, made me a costermonger's barrow out of plasticine, filled with fruit and vegetables. The tiny bananas, apples, oranges, cabbages and cauliflowers all looked so tasty, it was the most natural thing in the world that I should eat them. This did not improve my condition one little bit.

Upon the doctor's advice, I was put out into the open as much as possible, and in the process became rather a 'fresh air fiend', very keen on keeping myself fit. I took cold baths every morning throughout the year, and indulged in many and varied exercises.

Under the expert supervision of our 'physical jerks' instructor, I added an extra one and a half inches onto my height, stretching my still 'green' vertebrae by hanging from the gymnasiums' overhead bars, and from any handy trees.

I managed to top six feet and weighed twelve stone five pounds. If I gained any distinction at all when I finally left Purley County, it was by virtue of the fact that I was the only pupil of such dimensions to attain the age of 19 and still be wearing short trousers. I spurned 'longs', because I liked the air to get at my legs.

I remained a dreadful student; apart from rugby football and general athletics, the only other things which interested me were art lessons and taking part in the annual play production.

I have already mentioned that my code of conduct was based entirely upon my youthful hero, honest Tom Merry in the *Gem* – 'true blue, eye-on-the-ball, no cribbing and no smoking' – and it was thanks to him that I eschewed this vice until I joined the theatrical profession, when a certain part required me to smoke a church warden pipe. As I had heard it could make me feel sick, and fearing I might disgrace myself, and at the same time upset the flow of the piece being performed by vomiting on stage, I thought it would be a wise precaution to taste the noxious weed beforehand, breaking myself in gently through the medium of cigarettes. So 'Lady Nicotine' wooed and won me, and I've been in her clutches ever since.

* * *

Providing the 'crime' was not a very serious one, the punishment to fit it was optional. You could either 'stay in' after school, writing out a hundred times 'I must not let my white mouse run over Sir's desk' or whatever the situation demanded, the alternative being six of the best administered by 'The Beak' in his study. I always chose the whacking – short, sharp and, if not exactly sweet, at least it was over and done with in a few stinging seconds, leaving the rest of the precious day free for more important matters. There was a bonus in this choice: the looks of respectful admiration from the less valiant, lurking outside the Head's door, as the victim emerged from the torture chamber, biting his bottom lip, but contriving a dignified if somewhat stiff exit into the sunshine.

Perhaps without knowing it at first, I always wanted to become an actor, and this preoccupation made me oblivious to anything that was being taught in the classrooms, with the result that homework was not only anathema to me, but also an impossibility. I would put it off until the last minute and then, after a few feeble and frustrating attempts, approach my brother, begging his assistance, looking up at him with large, appealing eyes, rather like a plump puppy.

'Alright "Brighteyes"', (as he had christened me) 'I'll do it for you.'

He had inherited Father's expertise with figures, which I most certainly had not. I like to think it was Tom Merryian honesty that prompted me to write 'helped' (in brackets) at the foot of whatever complex mathematical or algebraic mystery he had solved on my behalf, but I think there was more than a smattering of shrewdness behind this inspiration, realising that suspicious eyebrows would be raised the next day by my mentors down the road, who would undoubtedly question the extraordinary erudition I displayed at home, compared with my complete inability to cope with the most elementary problem put before me when at my desk amongst them.

'The boy's hopeless' was my father's comment upon reviewing my end of term reports, knowing that the brain behind any brilliance recorded therein didn't belong to his younger heir, and he gave me up in despair.

Tapping the offending sheets which he held in his hand, he rebuked, 'It is stated here that your rugby tackles "deserve to be framed". I wish the same could be said of your work, my boy, and that you could apply yourself with equal panache to that!'

* * *

As far back as I can remember, I had a passion for dressing up and playing games of 'Let's Pretend', which are, of course, the basic principles of acting, and if you are lucky enough, you get paid for so doing, hard work though it may be.

A confirmed picture-goer, I was enthralled by the exploits of my favourite cowboy star, Tom Mix, and his wonderful white horse Tony. I wanted to be like him when I grew up, unaware that this was my lineal blood stirring within me a latent desire to follow in the footsteps of Grandfather Cushing, Aunt Maude, Step-uncle Wilton, and no doubt those of the wandering Uncle Bertie with his 'artistic temperament'.

Returning from the Picture Palace, I would re-enact some of the deeds of derring-do which I had just witnessed, using our back garden as a prairie. It sloped down quite steeply towards the house, from the foot of a sharp angled railway embankment, and large trees screened my theatre of operations from Mother's view, if she happened to glance out of the windows. Which was just as well, because I'm sure the poor dear would have had a fit if she'd caught sight of what went on. I recall one occasion, during a summer holiday, when David was letting me down a cliff face on the end of a rope, so that I could inspect at close quarters a kestrel's nest on a ledge several feet below. As I disappeared over the edge, she gasped 'My *boy*!' and fainted.

That escapade was as nothing compared with my post-picture-show performances.

A Boy Scout's hat purchased at a recent jumble sale sufficed as a sombrero, although its colour didn't please me, my hero on the screen nearly always favouring a white 'ten galloner'. I tried dyeing it with Blanco, but this was only partially successful, the stuff flaking off onto my shoulders, giving the impression that I was suffering from severe dandruff. A pair of hairy hearth rugs purloined from the parlour made excellent chaparajos, lashed to my legs with string; a spotted 'kerchief knotted loosely around my neck after the approved style; and the addition of a cap pistol tucked into my belt lent a touch of authenticity to the tout ensemble.

Arrayed in this finery, I'd mosey down to the old corral (the 'cycle shed), mount my faithful steed (Mother's bike) and then gallop off into the sunset. It wasn't very far – just at the bottom of the garden. From the top of the incline, I whizzed full tilt towards a clothes line, which I'd stretched tautly between a couple of trees. The collision knocked me for six just as Tom Mix had been sent flying, when ambushed in similar fashion by the Redskins.

Bruised, battered and bleeding, but blissfully happy, I took encore after encore, until either the bike or I – or both – needed running repairs.

My next turn was a faithful reproduction of the lynching scene – a must in most Westerns. This was highly dangerous, and could have resulted in my early demise. I was virtually hanging myself by the neck, with that same clothes line from one of those same trees, dangling grotesquely for long stretches of time. Perhaps this assisted my efforts to add to my stature.

I also challenged myself to one-man wrestling contests, trying to throttle one or other of me. Then there was 'Bang! You're dead!' For this portrayal, my chaps were removed and turkey feathers replaced my skewbald hat, brown Cherry Blossom boot polish representing stripes of war paint on my cheeks, it now being the Indians' turn to 'bite the dust'. Whooping along the perimeter of the embankment as fast as I could go, I would reproduce – vocally – the detonation of a Winchester '73, and then fall, uttering a blood-curdling death cry, rolling headlong down the grassy ramp at breakneck speed, sustaining scratches and cuts on the way, from the flints and rubble embedded in its surface.

Mother had made the Red Indian outfit, and wanted a snapshot of me wearing her creation. 'Smile, dear!' she said brightly, focusing her Brownie. I remonstrated sternly: 'Indians never smile' – which was hardly surprising, considering how I was treating them.

I toyed with the idea of playing the feminine lead in *The Perils of Pauline*, tying myself across the railway track to await the oncoming express. But I had second thoughts, since it would involve my being dressed as a girl again. I wasn't awfully keen about that, and there was no guarantee that an heroic Mr Crane Wilbur would come dashing to the rescue in the nick of time, as he had done so often for Miss Pearl White. Wisely, I decided that this reconstruction would not be included in my repertoire.

These excursions into realism have stood me in good stead during my career, whenever I've had to take part in a fight or simulate falls in films or on stage. I'd become immune to physical damage.

I must admit, however, when I'm asked nowadays if I feel the type of part I play in certain films might have any adverse effect upon the adolescent, remembering how I had been influenced, I shudder to think of the number of embryo mad scientists I may have engendered, who could be skulking about the country in search of human limbs in order to string them together like some monstrous do-it-yourself kit. A hair-raising thought.

On the other hand, there could be some less gruesomely occupied, wearing deerstalker hats, smoking a pipe and carrying magnifying glasses…

*   *   *

'Come along, "Brighteyes", I'll teach you how to ride a bike,' said David, and he did.

I wanted to learn so that I could play those Tom Mix games in the garden. The go-cart was my pride and joy, but to my aesthetic eye it could not pass muster as a horse, whereas a bicycle could at least be mounted.

David had worked on the principle: 'What the eye doesn't see…' To start with, he held the back of the saddle to keep me on an even keel, as I wobbled about grinding away at the pedals. Persevering with this unsteady balancing act some weeks later, prattling away to him, I received no response to something I'd asked and, turning my head, saw him a quarter of a mile or so up the road, waving encouragingly. I promptly fell off.

But it taught me that I could keep my balance unaided, and very soon I was 'flying' solo, having mastered the technique from his clever use of psychology. He used the same method to teach me to swim, slackening the harness cord until, all unaware, I was doing the breast stroke under my own steam.

He also explained the intricacies of driving, using an old Tin Lizzie which he had borrowed from a friend of his. The engine was often reluctant to start, but invariably responded splutteringly to a smart kick up the bonnet. There were no restrictions such as driving tests or 'L' plates. You just went to the Post Office and bought a red cardboard-covered licence for five shillings, which qualified you automatically to become a latent Stirling Moss.

It was one of the very few cars to be seen on our particular roads. More familiar sights were muffin men wearing padded cloth caps on which they supported, at rakish angles, large wooden trays (loaded with those delicious freshly baked cakes), covered with a piece of green baize, clanging a hand bell to signal their welcomed approach.

There was still an ancient 'growler' in the station yard at Purley doing brisk business, and cheeky sparrows would pinch a share from the aged nag's nose bag. Milkmen, standing in beautifully painted horse-drawn floats, stopped at every house, their cheerful cry of 'Milk below!' echoing down the street, and busy housewives emerged bearing jugs, which would be filled from the large churns with a gleaming copper ladle.

The wooden paved roadways were rich with manure, which we gathered into sacks and sold to neighbours who had flowerbeds for a penny a pailful, proving the point made by those shrewd Northerners who say that 'where there's muck, there's brass'.

Having succeeded in making me mobile, brother David decided it was high time I learnt something about the Facts of Life, after overhearing me state categorically to Mother that there was absolutely no physical difference whatsoever between man and his mate.

'Come along, "Brighteyes", I want to show you something.'

'Brighteyes' dutifully followed him out into the garden.

Realising his axiom for my mobility could not be successfully employed in this delicate exigency, and that he must resort to visual aid, he had enlisted the services of a very young girl who lived next door, now awaiting us under the trees.

He dared her to shin up an elm, on the pretext to see if there were any baby birds in a mistle thrush's nest which we already knew was deserted. She accepted the challenge with alacrity, obviously delighted to be called upon to perform such a masculine feat. We stood directly underneath, looking up, presumably ready to catch her if she fell. She was a hefty child, and I didn't relish the prospect of breaking her fall should it happen.

But that was not the idea behind my brother's cunning scheme. Following the direction in which his index finger pointed, I was unimpressed by what I saw – or, rather, didn't see, deciding it must be some freak of nature, or caused by an accident at birth, although I admit, remembering my mother's early advice, I did reach instinctively for my hat.

I remained sceptical. Had not I been clothed and coiffured just like her in my pre-emancipation days? So how could there be any difference?

I heard him sigh, but refusing to accept defeat, David persevered with this most refractory pupil in his simple Biology class, and marched me off to a nearby farm over Riddlesdown way, where there was ample confirmation to support his claim and convince the most stubborn of unbelievers. Even so, I was still reluctant to accept the evidence of my own eyes.

'But they are *animals*,' I protested.

The wise one spoke: 'And so, "Brighteyes",' he said profoundly, 'are *we*.'

I hadn't thought of that. It clinched the deal. His patience and resourcefulness were rewarded at last. From that moment on, until I learnt otherwise, I regarded the entire feminine gender as 'soppy girls'.

Some long time after my 'awakening' and acceptance of the corporeal difference between the two sexes, my interest aroused, I advanced a few tentative steps into the mysteries of physical attraction, experiencing my first kiss. It was a mere platonic peck, planted upon some blushing maiden's lips. Stricken with horror and remorse, I fled home to seek my instructor, and found him in the bicycle shed, cleaning a stinking acetylene lamp. Bursting in upon him, I confessed all, ending with the impassioned cry, 'I've been a cad! I've impregnated her!'

I believe he sighed again.

*   *   *

As it became increasingly obvious to some of my exhausted and bemused form masters that teaching me was futile and unrewarding, they tended to give up their endeavours to pass on their knowledge to me, doubtless agreeing with Father that I was a hopeless case. So many of my 'working' hours being devoted to other diversions, it was hardly surprising that, when an examination paper demanded an essay on the subject 'Etiquette when travelling abroad' (mine were lavishly illustrated, leaving as little space as possible for the written word), I wrote, quite seriously: '…and when in Paris, do as the Parasites do.'

But my physics master, Mr DJ Davies, saw things in a different light. He was very keen on the theatre, always producing the school plays. Having detected in me some acting potential, he did much to foster my development in this field, and deciding – as his colleagues had done – it was a waste of his time and mine to attempt to instil my mind with any gems of scientific phenomena, he allowed me to be *absens* from his allocated hour, so that I could be more usefully employed in painting the scenery for our forthcoming presentation. Of course, I was as pleased as Punch with this arrangement and, bedecked in a pair of overalls, I would set about the congenial task with great relish. It also provided me with an unexpected opportunity to indulge in some knockabout comedy.

My scene painting activities took place on the rostrum in the Hall, which also served as an auxiliary classroom. The master in attendance would stand with his back towards me, and there in front of him – and, what was equally important, in front of *me* – sat a ready-made audience of attentive pupils. I seized this unexpected chance to test my ability as a comedian with both hands – and both feet – giving them an impromptu Fred Karno sketch.

Slapping away merrily, paint brushes charged with distempers of every hue, I would let the canvas 'flat' I was daubing fall gently away from the wall, at the same time turning round and walking downstage, ostensibly to pick up a carefully planted bucket, full of evil smelling size. With splendid timing, I twisted on my heels to catch the wooden framework just before the moment of impact, at the same instant contriving to get a foot wedged in the pail of glutinous gunge, and then clonking about like Frankenstein's monster. My performance was greeted with suppressed giggles and a few guffaws of ill-concealed merriment, but I regret to say it was not shared by the learned gentleman in charge of this responsive assembly. He was experiencing difficulty enough in cramming his charges, without any assistance from me to add to their lack of concentration. But when he glared over his shoulder to see what had been the cause of such unseemly laughter, I was studiously engaged in mopping up operations, after what was apparently an unfortunate accident.

Unwisely repeating my comic turn in his presence on a later occasion, I pushed my luck – he was too quick for me, and I was literally caught in the act. Not appreciating my efforts to entertain, he dismissed me to continue my work in the empty playground.

David had seen one of these ventures into slapstick and, to my delight, he declared during supper that '"Brighteyes" was jolly funny at school today!'

Father glanced up from my current academic report which he was perusing. 'Now make *me* laugh,' he said, wearily.

* * *

Although living as I did in a world of make-believe, I had many and varied interests in more earthly things, acquiring knowledge about them from cigarette cards, those beautiful little mines of condensed information which disappeared during the Second World War, but I'm glad to see have returned recently in one form or another.

The original output was immense, every conceivable subject being dealt with. Ogden's contributed five series about Boy Scouts, four of the 225 cards being devoted to the alphabet for the deaf and dumb. David and I studied these, and became quite proficient, enabling us to convey messages to each other when talking was forbidden, or if we had some secret to relay. We collected all the Natural History sets, disdaining to play 'flickums' with such treasures, keeping them carefully in albums especially designed for that purpose.

This hobby led us to explorations in the glorious surrounding countryside of Surrey, our happy hunting grounds chosen amongst the woods and lush meadows near Godstone and Dorking. We would spend whole days trying to learn some of Nature's secrets, setting off on our bicycles in the early morning, returning home in the dusk of summer evenings, David on his splendid three-speed gear-change 'jigger', with 'Brighteyes' trailing behind on Mother's less modern machine, which had no gears. The lack of a crossbar always made me feel rather self-conscious and I tried to ignore this deficiency by swinging my leg nonchalantly over the saddle in what I hoped was a manly fashion, and so dispel any inherent inferiority complex.

'Wait for me, Dave!' I would pant if he got too far ahead, but I was content enough, bowling happily down leafy country lanes, particularly as the basket attached to the handlebar, and the carrier on the rear mudguard, provided ample accommodation for our luncheon and tea. In case of any unforeseen emergencies, further supplies were packed into a whacking great rucksack strapped on my back, making me look like a miniature Quasimodo on wheels, en route for Notre Dame.

One by-product of my voracious appetite was a layer of blubber which enabled me to withstand the lowest of temperatures, and I was always detailed by my leader to swim the still, icy cold waters of some mere, in order to gather an egg – ('Only one, "Brighteyes", and *none* if the clutch is small' were my strict instructions) – of moorhen, grebe or coot for our collection, and scale dizzy heights to the haunt of rook or sparrow hawk: duties performed with great willingness, but always observing decorum when taking to the water, girding my loins about with a grubby handkerchief, emerging triumphant from my return journey, resembling some podgy naiad, disgorging the unbroken egg from my mouth, having retrieved it in the manner recommended by expert ornithologists.

'Jolly well done, "Brighteyes"!'

Jolly difficult, if it happened to be a swan's egg…

*   *   *

Eventually the day arrived when David had to 'go out and make a living for yourself, my son.'

Although he had prepared himself for a business career far better than I had, which is putting it more than mildly, his heart was set upon farming. It always had been, and it is nice to record that we both achieved our youthful ambitions in the long run – his much shorter than mine. But Father had no connections with that branch of the Yeomanry and persuaded his son to accept a post in the City with an Insurance Company, where he'd been able to use his influence in securing the position.

David did his level best, but loathed the work and London from the very beginning. 'I can't stand bricks and mortar,' he would growl, showing his dislike by refusing point blank to carry that symbol of the City, an umbrella, and ramming his bowler hat so well down on his head that it bent his ears.

After a few months of this torture, Father could see that he was really fretting for the open air life in the country and sent him to serve an apprenticeship on a farm near Pulborough in Sussex, and later set him up with his own small holding at Norwood Hill, near Leigh, in Surrey.

I have not seen him for many years now: but I look back upon those days spent together – and him – with nostalgia and affection.

*　　*　　*

Then came my turn. Poor Father. What could he do with me? Just consider my qualifications for the harsh world of Commerce and Big Business: top marks in art: nil for everything else: capped for rugger: Gold, Silver and Bronze medalist for athletics and swimming: played the lead in nearly all the school productions: able to tell the difference between a chiffchaff and a willow warbler without the aid of binoculars: an ability to fall down a cliff without breaking my neck: and just for good measure, an appetite like several horses.

When I ventured to suggest the theatre, he paled visibly. Considering his own family's background 'on the boards', it has always puzzled me why he was so averse to my continuing the tradition. Perhaps he still regarded it as full of rogues and vagabonds, beset with hoards of loose women waiting to lure his young hopeful, a penniless actor 'sansculotte', into their iniquitous seraglios. Good Lord! I might even become another Uncle Bertie, wandering about with my artistic temperament, and getting up to Heaven knows what! He perished the thought.

What strings he pulled I do not know, although I did hear him mutter to himself, 'I suppose the boy can draw...'

He must have fixed a hook to the end of one of them, and dangled this dubious piece of bait, in order to land me a job in the Drawing Office of the Surveyor's Department at the Coulsdon and Purley Urban District Council, for the fact remains that, in the summer of 1933, at a salary of 30 shillings per week, I became a Local Government Officer, NALGO No: 16851, complete with club blazer and tie: black, with thin red, white and blue alternating stripes, very patriotic – except for the black, which matched my gloom.

Forced into long trousers at last, and equipped with a papier mâché briefcase to hold my lunch, I reported for duty wearing my first suit, a Montague Burton's off the peg dark blue serge (DB), price 50 bob, soon to shine at elbows and seat like burnished metal, a pair of brown kid gloves, but no hat.

Thanks to my brother, I felt the time had come when I wouldn't need one any more.

3

'HOW NOW BROWN COW?'

MY OFFICIAL CAPACITY bore the imposing title Surveyor's Assistant, but I was really only a glorified office boy, remaining one for nearly three years – through nobody's fault but my own. Ever living with my dreams, I didn't want to spend the rest of my life in an office, and whilst less than half-heartedly carrying out some of the duties expected of me, that entire period was devoted and directed towards realising my ambition.

For six days of the week – mercifully only in the morning on Saturdays – I set off to work on my 'cycle, permanently borrowed from Mother, as I couldn't very well use the go-cart now – I didn't think 'they' would approve – in vain attempts to reach the offices in the Brighton Road at the compulsory clocking-in time of 9.00 am ('The 'bus won't wait for you, my boy.') I rarely succeeded in this praiseworthy aim but always clocked out slap bang on the dot of 5.00 pm, even earlier if it could be wangled. One hour was allowed for lunch, but I always stretched mine to two by the simple expedient of volunteering to take the first shift, 12 noon to 1.00 pm, which meant I had from 1 to 2 on my own in the Drawing Office, 'minding the shop' whilst my colleagues were having their break. Those extra, golden, stolen 60 minutes were put to good use, although perhaps not in the way my superiors would have wished.

Whenever possible, I prolonged any chores which took me outside, such as Street Numbering. In fact, I quite looked forward to this, since – with a little planning beforehand – a Cook's Tour could be made, even of the shortest journeys, and often, by adopting a solicitous demeanour to occupiers who were anxious not to be No 13, an invitation to step inside and partake refreshment would be extended to this ambassador of goodwill. Over cups of tea and seed cake, we would discuss – at great length – the possibilities of their being No. 12a instead. If shrewdly timed, these convivial talks could be judged so as to make a return to the office unnecessary. I went straight home by direct route to a more substantial meal.

Another task, if less edifying, but also requiring precise timing in order to avoid any mutual embarrassment, was collecting coins from Ladies' and Gentlemen's Public Conveniences – always a discreet 'rat a tat' on the door of the former, with a cheery query ('Coo-ee! Anyone at home?') before venturing into their inner sanctums.

The weekly office order of tobacco and cigarettes – picked up on pay days from a local tobacconist who offered cut prices for bulk buying – could pass a pleasant half hour or so. I would hover outside the shop until it was pretty crowded, and then tack myself on the end of a long queue, thus providing an excellent excuse for tardiness when I finally showed up, laden with tins of Players Navy Cut, cartons of Ardath (their coupons were very popular – I had an aunt who practically coughed herself to the grave collecting them), Craven A, and those packets with an obliging butler printed on them saying 'Your Kensitas, Sir'.

The only duty I performed with any relish – and the reason for my being employed in the first place – was drawing prospectives of proposed buildings, but these were always rejected on the grounds that they were too imaginative, too expensive, and having suspect foundations – a mere detail I never bothered about. Once I was instructed to trace on linen a very large plan, which contained a mistake. This had been 'scriggled' out with a pencilled flourish. I laboriously made the tracing in Indian ink, including the mistake

– 'scriggle' and all. No one had told me to do otherwise … my mind was just not on my work.

* * *

There was one aspect of this office life that really did appeal to me. A rota system was operated, giving each member a Saturday morning 'off' every month. Being so stage-struck, when my turns came around I would journey up to London's West End, into Theatre Land, where I contrived to sneak past stage door keepers, cosily ensconced in little cubby holes behind their counters, swiftly and upright when backs were turned, or on all fours if they weren't, just to revel in that intoxicating atmosphere and heady odour – a combination of dust, size, distemper and grease paint; to stand on the stage in the set that was prepared for the next performance, temporarily lit by a single working light, which somehow added an extra magic and mystery to those surroundings which I loved so much. Once I even dared to swing on the same rope I'd seen Laurence Olivier use for that purpose in Priestley's *Bees on the Boatdeck*.

On another occasion, standing entranced by the delicate beauty of Rex Whistler's setting for *Pride and Prejudice*, I was confronted by a suspicious gentleman who demanded to know what I was doing there. I had remembered seeing the names of a famous firm of Scenic Constructors, Brunskill and Loveday, stencilled on the back of a flat. Quick as a flash – first crossing my fingers, as Tom Merry plucked at my sleeve – I said I was waiting to see Mr Brunskill, hoping and praying he was still in the land of the living. It did the trick, and I was left in peace.

But these adventures in Wonderland were over all too quickly, alas, and it was back to the grind again on Mondays, so I had to invent other ways and means of making life tolerable until my next free Saturday.

The hand-numbering machine provided a certain relaxation. It was a small device, resembling a speedometer, with a sprung handle which, when struck smartly, impressed consecutive numbers ('In the top right hand corner, Cushing') on such items as letter copies to be filed. I had two variations on a theme when using this gadget. For the benefit of those musically inclined, my first 'Divertimento' was interpreted thus:

'PPP.' *PIANISSISSIMO* (as soft as possible)
'ADG.°' *ADAGIO* (slow)
'AND.' *ANDANTE* (moderately slow)
'ACCEL.' *ACCELERANDO* (gradually increasing in speed)
'CRES.' *CRESCENDO* (gradually louder)
'f.' *FORTE* (loud)
'ff.' *FORTISSIMO* (*very* loud)
'CODA' (a passage forming the end of a piece, giving it a
    rounded or dramatic finish – this came about the same time
    as No 50 appeared on whatever I was 'tattooing')
'fff.' *FORTISSISSIMO* (as loud as possible)
'D.C.' *DA CAPO* (repeat from the beginning).

I regret to say these performances were seldom appreciated by my fellow workers, but, if they were in the mood, they would join in my other – perhaps more subtle – musical caprice, which took the form of tapping out tunes in Morse Code fashion, and they had to guess what I was playing. Requesting everyone to stand, I always ended these recitals with a spirited rendition of the National Anthem. This last exercise was used recently in that excellent programme on BBC Television, *Face the Music*. I should have taken out a copyright all those years ago.

Whilst this humdrum routine went on ad infinitum, I was not letting the grass grow under my feet in the direction they wanted to go. I had by now acquired my first 'young lady', as we called them in my day, and I still appeared in the school plays, thanks to the connivance of my ex-physics master and friend Mr Davies, and also in local amateur productions which were put on at the

Church Hall. These latter pursuits entailed a great deal of study and rehearsal, denied me by the demands made upon my time by the UDC. I hit upon an idea to overcome this obstacle, by suggesting it might be a good thing if I put the old Ordnance Survey Maps into some semblance of order. They were stored in 'The Roof', a large attic approached by a ladder and trap door. Many blissful hours were spent up there nearer Heaven, in my private 'theatre', draped with cobwebs, and with spiders and mice as my silent spectators. Of course the maps remained in a state of wild disorder, but lines were learnt, and moves and 'business' worked out to perfection.

I remember doing WS Gilbert's *Pygmalion and Galatea*, a romance concerning an Athenian sculptor who falls in love with his statue of a beautiful woman. I had an idée fixe that all Greeks had hairless legs, and having spotted a jar of Veet at home, I applied the stuff lavishly from hip to ankle. The label claimed it 'removes unwanted hairs,' and I expected it to do so immediately, but it didn't. I soaked them in a tub of hot water, which turned the unguent into cement. This I had to hack off, using Father's cut-throat razor, lacerating my shin bones and making the bathroom look like an abattoir. My legs were things of shreds and patches by the time I appeared upon the platform that evening, wearing Pygmalion's mid-thigh length double girded chiton, causing one lady in the front row to enquire loudly of her companion, who must have been deaf, 'Lydia, dear, do you think shingles is catching?'

Every week I bought *The Stage* (price fourpence) and during that extra lunch hour I went through it with a fine-tooth comb, paying special attention to the 'Wanted' columns. In those pre-television years, there were repertory theatres dotted all over the country, and the various companies running them often needed additions to their troupes. Some of their advertisements were couched in such economic journalese that I could make neither head nor tail of them. Others were clear and to the point, and excerpts from a few of these etched themselves indelibly upon my mind. One in particular, recruiting members for a lengthy tour, concluded with the stern injunction: '…No brown paper parcels on train calls.' Yet another, which read 'Wanted: Juv. Char./ASM' (Juvenile Character Actor combined Assistant Stage Manager), also required the applicant to help paint the scenery ('…prepared to wk. all hrs…') and be general head cook and bottle-washer, and ended curtly with the dire warnings '…a lazy-bones won't last five mins … ask no fancy prices.'

One and all demanded 's.a.e. with all ENQS.', also 'state prev. exp.' This was my stumbling block. I could just about manage the s.a.e.s, but what to do about 'Previous Experience' stumped me, and I had a suspicion my Amateur Status would not be viewed in a favourable light. Hence I made no reference to this in my carefully composed letters, just putting 'very keen to begin', which could have been one of the reasons why my 'enqs.' never received any 'ans.'.

It was rather like being told you couldn't go in the water until you could swim, and having read a touchingly worded 'Personal Card' in that section of The Stage – 'Mr … finds himself unexpectedly vacant. Will accept any reasonable offer' – I was sorely tempted to insert a duplicate, omitting the final adjective.

I decided against this, however, feeling it would be lowering my standards before they were even raised.

Months went by, and it became increasingly evident that my offers of service were falling upon stony ground. For one reason or another, I thought a change of name might also change my luck. In the thralldom of puppy love, 'darling' played a prominent part in my vocabulary, and so I chose the last syllable of that endearment as my nom de guerre. This aroused some lively opposition at home, but I stuck mulishly to my choice until – at last – I received a reply to one of my applications.

With trembling hands I tore open the envelope, to read: 'Dear Mr Ling … I'm afraid there is limited scope for a Chinese actor in the Repertory Movement…'

I reverted – immediately – to the family name.

* * *

Although he had passed on in 1926, the impact made upon most female hearts by Rudolph Alphonso Guglielmi di Valentino d'Antonguelia was as strong as ever in 1933, and equally his influence on the hair-dos of the younger male generation of the late twenties and early thirties. Nearly all of us sported the Rudolph Valentino style, slicked down, shining like well polished shoes, with neatly trimmed sideboards of varying length.

I attended many a Tango Tea Dance, all the rage in my youth, not a hair out of place, plastered into position by Californian Poppy (solid) Brilliantine (it's a wonder I didn't become as bald as a coot at 20), and dressed to kill in the latest fashion: voluminous 'Oxford bags', 30 inches around the turn-ups, Fair Isle pullover and patent leather dancing pumps. (These alternated with white and brown 'co-respondent' shoes when not in the ballroom.) My partner and I would slink across dance floors to the tunes of such favourite numbers as 'Jealousy' and 'Softly as in a Morning Sunrise', under the bespangled revolving globe suspended from the ceiling – casting winking colours into the dusky gloom all around us.

We won a competition once, the ladies' prize being a half pound box of chocolates – Terry's (all hard) Spartan Assortment, which I thought a rather inappropriate choice. To my over-sensitive pride, it implied that my shunting of my partner about the floor had been a sort of test of endurance for her, feeling that a soft-centred selection with an Arcadian ring to it would have been more in keeping with our romantic mood. I was presented with a somewhat garish Tootal tie, which clashed sickeningly with my Fair Isle. But I wore it – proudly.

I always attended these soirées armed with a small packet of Sen-Sen or 'Phŭl-Nānā' cachous ('All the mystery of the Orient'). When I was much younger, an over-affectionate acquaintance of the family would clasp me lovingly to her ample bosom whenever she had the chance, crushing my ear agonisingly against an enormous cameo brooch in the process, and cooing "ow's my little darlin' today then, eh?' As her little darling was all but asphyxiated by her unfortunate and quite ghastly halitosis, I was unable to tell her, for fear of inhaling the deadly fumes. Lest I should similarly embarrass my fellow beings, I became very sensitive about dental hygiene, cleaning my teeth so often that Mother declared I would 'wear them away'. The cachous were an added precaution against such an anti-social condition.

In these modern times, with explicit love scenes proliferating on our screens, which can be very tiresome, I often find myself thinking – I *do* hope they've both brushed their teeth.

We also enjoyed regular Friday night treats to 'the Pictures', having a splendid 'set tea' beforehand on the mezzanine floor – (1s/6d each, 3d slipped under a plate for the waitress, who wore the smart black and white 'Nippy' uniform which was the current vogue) – at the Davis Cinema in Croydon. After the repast, at a charge of 4s/-d for both of us ('Seats in all parts 1s/-d before 2.00 pm'), there followed a programme which not only included two full length feature films, the News, Pathé Gazette, a comedy short – Laurel and Hardy or Charlie Chaplin – and a Walt Disney cartoon, but also a live stage show, Paul Whiteman ('The King of Jazz') and his orchestra, Mr Charlie Kunz dressed in immaculate tails at a white grand piano, and suchlike attractions. More often than not there would be a travelogue as well, nearly always ending with an exotic sunset scene, accompanied by the immortal words '...And so we say farewell to...' wherever it was we had been transported on the magic carpet of Filmdom.

For good measure, during the intermission, a mighty Wurlitzer arose majestically from the bowels of the orchestra pit, signature tune blazing away at full throttle, before merging into more dreamy and delicate airs, such as Mrs Amy Woodforde-Finden's 'Indian Love Lyrics', the organist casting a beaming smile over his shoulder as he entertained the assemblage, who retired to 'make themselves comfortable', or stretched their legs, purchasing ice creams or chocolates from spot-lit usherettes, displaying these goodies on trays hanging from straps around their necks. When the lights dimmed again, these same young ladies would glide discreetly up and down the aisles armed with spray guns, squirting a fine mist of perfumed disinfectant above the heads of the absorbed multitude, as if officiating at a massed baptism. And, of course, next week's tantalising trailers ('Coming Attractions') made eager our anticipation for those delights in store.

Total outlay for the evening's wealth of entertainment: seven shillings and eleven pence, including return bus fares, if we got off at the stop before the cinema and walked a few hundred yards. What value for money!

*   *   *

Such, then, was the pattern of my first year of office life, during which I spent a small fortune on stamps and stationery, writing beseeching letters, demanding letters, cajoling and almost threatening letters, long ones, short ones – and, with the single exception of that isolated reply addressed to Peter Ling, Esq – all to no avail.

I was deeply depressed. Apart from my failure to break through the 'sound barrier' of the theatrical profession, several other factors contributed to my depression: some tiff with my dancing partner; being inordinately upset upon discovering Father had scrawled some mathematical calculations all over a large watercolour I'd painted ('Sorry, my boy, I thought it was only a rough sketch...'); having been told I was hopeless – a family joke by now, but in my present mood I began to believe it was true.

I became secretive and solitary, withdrawing deeper and deeper into my world of dreams, building around myself a protective carapace.

In retrospect, but with no disrespect to my elders and betters, I do feel it was not very far-sighted of them to impose the learning of Shakespeare's speeches as a school punishment, destroying for many years the beauty and joy of those magical writings; likewise forced to go to church '…otherwise what will the neighbours think?' Surely this was no way to approach an understanding of His teachings and comfort, resulting subsequently in my rarely attending on Sundays, but seeking the solace of prayer and meditation in those serene sanctuaries during the week when they are empty.

And, listening to Beethoven, being requested to '…turn off that noise.' Beethoven – noise! Oh, dear! Oh, dear! – still, I suppose – 'one man's meat…'

My parents went down to David's farm every weekend, and always wanted me to go with them. Rather than cause hurt by a flat refusal – also fearing their persuasions might force me to accompany them – I would hide up a side street near our house on my way home from the office at lunch time, until I saw them pass by in the car. This filled me with relief, knowing I had the rest of Saturday and all Sunday until they returned in the evening, alone to dream and scheme.

One day, I decided to end it all.

I chose a Bank Holiday for my coup de théâtre, taking advantage of a cheap day Excursion ticket. A suitable suicide note propped against the clock on the mantelpiece, I entrained for Exmouth. Looking at the jubilant 'trippers' in the compartment, I thought to myself – with a fine sense of drama – 'Little do you realise what you will read in your newspapers tomorrow!'

Upon arrival at my destination, I made my way to the cliff path, walking along it above Orcombe Rocks towards Straight Point, on the look-out for a good spot to drop off into oblivion.

It was a glorious day – cloudless, the sun sparkling on deep blue and emerald green waters, still as a mill pond, and so clear, I could see the sea bed of rippled sand and rocks, the clinging sea wrack undulating in the gentle currents beneath the translucent surface. Overhead gulls squawked raucously, beneath my feet and all about me a profusion of nodding 'totty' grass and soft cushions of thrift, bedecked with Chalkhill Blue butterflies basking in the warmth, and Six-Spot Burnets flying their warning colours.

Here and there larks ascended like tiny stringless kites, hovering high in the sky, trilling their joy of living, and then – along the track ahead of me, a shy but friendly Wheatear suddenly appeared. No doubt remembering that its ancestors were regarded as delicacies on Victorian menus, it was cautious and kept its distance, but nevertheless seemed pleased to have company, dipping along jerkily, close to the ground, stopping every so often to cock a beady eye in my direction, as if to make certain I was following and then, reassured, taking off again. Fascinated by these antics, I ignored my original intention and followed the bird instead, presently finding myself in that delightful little coastal resort, Budleigh Salterton.

There was the very wall where the youthful Raleigh might well have sat, gazing out to sea, and dreaming, too: his dreams had been fulfilled – some of them, at any rate – so why not mine, one day? Life was good, and a delicious Devonshire cream tea amongst the garden hollyhocks of a thatched cottage added to its pleasures. Counting my change – and my blessings – I reckoned it was a toss up between leaving a tip or taking the bus back to Exmouth Station. The waitress won. I was glad. I might see that Wheatear again.

In the train puffing back to London, I was glancing through a periodical someone had discarded on the luggage rack, when I came across an article dealing with Drama Schools. There was mention of scholarships available at the Guildhall School of Music and Drama, adding that former pupils had enjoyed successful careers after their training. Vaguely thinking a course or two might be accepted as that elusive 'experience', I determined to apply and, a little while after my day by the sea, received a letter requesting me to go up to town for an interview with one of the adjudicators.

It was Allan Aynesworth, who belonged to the Old School of Thespians. He rose to his feet when I was ushered into his dignified presence, and, having shaken my hand, asked, 'Well, laddie, and what can I do for you?'

According to an eye- (and ear-) witness, my reply sounded something like 'I wanna gow onna styge.'

The worthy gentleman uttered a cry resembling a wounded stag, clasped his hands to his ears and fell back in his chair. 'Take him away!' he cried. 'His voice offends me!'

Bewildered and somewhat shaken by this sudden and unexpected outburst, I found myself in the corridor, being comforted by the kind and understanding secretary. She advised me to wait until the other applicants had been dealt with, and then she would try to persuade him to see me again…

I entered warily. This time he remained seated, raising his hand in an imperious gesture, compelling me to keep silent and listen. 'Your diction, which I can only liken unto that of a costermonger, will not do for the Theatre.' He handed me a piece of note paper, covered with neatly printed words. 'When you have mastered these basic vowel sounds you may return – but not before.' I opened my mouth to mutter thanks but, noticing he blanched, I shut it again. Bowing in grateful acknowledgement, the mute withdrew – backwards, as if from Royalty – clutching his homework.

The sympathetic secretary had given me a booklet which illustrated the correct shape the lips should form for certain sounds, and every evening during the weeks that followed I marched over the North Downs, enunciating loudly and repeatedly through contorted mouth, 'How Now Brown Cow', 'The Moon in June is Full of Beauty' and 'Who's to know Small Frogs Pass Up where Landsmen Fear to Wade', much to the surprise of courting couples, their heads popping up out of the long grass, seeking the source of these strange pronouncements. Doubtless they thought I was some fanatical Jehovah's Witness with a nervous twitch, but their suggestions to 'put a sock in it' were ignored, as I persevered with my lazy lips and tongue.

I had been completely unaware of my slovenly speech and deplorable accent. But I do recall that when trundling our Guy along the pavements, cadging pennies to buy fireworks, I would chant the traditional doggerel of 1826:

Please to remember the Fifth of November
Gunpowder, Treason and Plot…

my version of the last line being:

Gunpowder, Trees and Per lot…

And when listening in to *2LO Calling* on the wireless, hearing the Savoy Orpheans Dance Band, I always felt so sorry for all those poor musicians, thinking they had no mothers or fathers. Reading about the emancipation of women, I thought it meant they'd all gone thin.

My efforts to master the King's English were hampered further by my associates, who 'chi-iked' me mercilessly – but good humouredly – for speaking 'posh'. Embarrassed and self-conscious, I would steal up to my refuge in the roof whenever I could. Gradually, *very* gradually, some small improvement was achieved, and when next I reported to the Guildhall, I was accepted – although a great deal of polish was still required to reach any sort of perfection. In this I was most ably assisted by the diligent Mr Cairns James, a former member of the D'Oyly Carte Opera Company, and his colleague Mr Horace Sequeira, who also taught me the rudiments of make-up.

Never did a more ardent and punctual pupil attend these classes – so different from the slacker at those other schools – going up to town twice a week immediately after office hours. Happy times they were, too: I felt I was at last making some headway towards my ultimate goal.

In 1935, I took part in two end of term plays, Ben Lorris in *The Red Umbrella* by Brenda Girvin and Monica Cosens, and Mr Frederick Towers in George Kelly's *The Torch-Bearers*. Inserting these in my circular letter under the non-committal heading '…appeared in London as…', I redoubled my onslaught upon the impregnable fortresses of the provinces, supplementing my meagre armoury with some portraits, which I had taken at a 'passport photograph while you wait' kiosk. Although these made me look like a glassy-eyed juvenile delinquent in the last stages of degeneracy, I hoped they might add weight to my attacks.

The Connaught Theatre, Worthing received my heaviest bombardment, because we'd spent many enjoyable holidays in that Sussex town, and I loved the South Downs and surrounding countryside. A salvo was directed at this objective once every three weeks, and after six months of intensive fire, to my utter joy and amazement, they surrendered, the White Flag fluttering through our letter box, requesting me to go down and see Mr Bill Fraser.

In a fever of excited incredulity, I burnt my boats behind me with gay (I use the adjective in its original context) and almost unseemly abandon, handing in my fortnight's notice there and then. Having recently caught me playing darts with an expensive precision instrument, the Chief Surveyor couldn't help but show a certain understandable relief when he heard of my decision, but they had all been extraordinarily kind and tolerant and, despite the lack of interest I had shown in local government administration, seemed genuinely sorry to see me go.

After what seemed eternity, the Saturday of my departure arrived: my few belongings packed and ready long since, I set off immediately the office closed down for the weekend, arriving at the theatre in between the matinée and evening performances.

The stage door keeper directed me to Mr Fraser's dressing room. I tapped and entered. Mr Fraser was having his tea, and enquired politely who I might be. (Obviously those photographs had not done me justice.) I told him.

'Ah, yes!' he exclaimed, 'very good of you to come. I cannot help but admire your persistence, but I do have other things to get on with besides reading letters all day, and I thought the only way to discourage you would be to ask you, personally, please – PLEASE – do stop writing to me!'

I was utterly shattered. The sun which had shone so brightly clouded over, and all was grey again. Tears of frustration stung my eyes.

He looked compassionately at the dejected wretch standing near the door, noisily blowing its nose. Heaving a little sigh, he asked, 'Do you know Priestley's *Cornelius*?'

I shook my head, not daring to speak.

'Well, that's the play we're doing tonight,' he continued, 'and there's a scene where a group of creditors come into an office. Since you're here, would you like to be one of them?'

The clouds lifted – I could almost see a rainbow through the moisture in my eyes! I nodded, whispering, 'Yes, PLEASE.'

'Very well, you can walk on. Just stand in the background and listen to what's being said. You don't have to do anything – just stand there, that's all. Here – you can wear this.' He helped me into a huge Teddy bear overcoat, which reached down to my ankles. 'Never mind – keep behind the others – you've nothing to say, and you won't be seen so much.'

After the jubilation of the last two weeks, it seemed rather an anti-climax. After all, this was to be my professional debut, and since I had no lines to speak, at least I wanted to be noticed. At last the great moment came. During the dialogue, I cautiously edged myself downstage towards the footlights, and once there, I proceeded with a routine I'd often seen performed by my favourite comics in the cinema, pretending to take a wodge of chewing gum out of my mouth, getting it stuck on my fingers, and finally transferring it to the instep of my shoe.

This execrable interpretation raised a few titters from the audience, and I felt quite pleased with myself, hoping it had made a favourable impression upon the producer, Bill Fraser, who was also playing the leading role. I stole a look in his direction, and his expression told me all was not well. I froze on the spot. The tabs were lowered at the end of the Act, and showing admirable self control, he beckoned me to his dressing room. Behind closed doors,

Above: George Edward Cushing, 1905.

Above right: Nellie Maria Cushing on her
wedding day, 3 July 1907.

Below: Mother's 'little girl', 1915.

Right: David and Peter Cushing, 1922.

Turning 21 and wearing plus-fours, 1933.

Below: As Lt Archie Forsyth with Dorothy Primrose as *Marigold*, an 'Arcadian Comedy' presented at the Theatre Royal Rochdale, 1937.

Bottom: Advertising for Merton Hodge's play *The Island* at the Theatre Royal Nottingham, 1938.

PETER CUSHING
who plays " Lieut. Simon Savil, R.A."

Above: With Peter Gray (in deck chair), taking a breather from rowing up the Trent – Nottingham, 1938.

PETER   CUSHING

IN HOLLYWOOD 1939
' MY FIRST CAR ! '

Above: With Louis Hayward – Brentwood Heights, 1939.

Right: Posing with the Hudson, 'my first proper car' – Hollywood 1939.

Above: Stan Laurel and Oliver Hardy, with Wilfred Lucas and Frank Baker, look down on supine students Peter Cushing, Gerald Fielding, Victor Kendall, Gerald Rogers and Charlie Hall in *A Chump at Oxford* – Hollywood, 1939.

Left: With Carole Lombard and Anne Shirley in *Vigil in the Night* – Hollywood, 1939.

Below left: As the young Clive of India in *The Hidden Master*, part of MGM's *Passing Parade* series – Hollywood, 1940.

Below: As Captain Evans in *Women in War* – Hollywood, 1940.

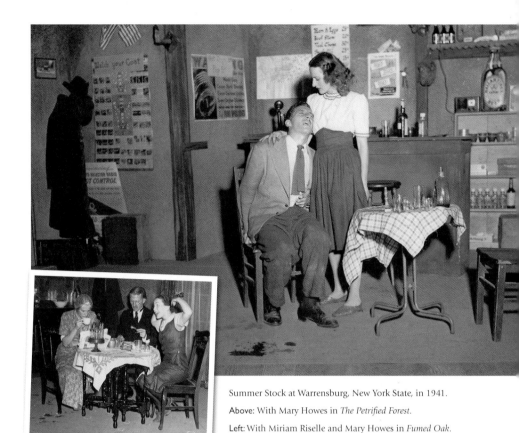

Summer Stock at Warrensburg, New York State, in 1941.

Above: With Mary Howes in *The Petrified Forest*.

Left: With Miriam Riselle and Mary Howes in *Fumed Oak*.

Below: With Elmore Mackee, Gloria Hope, Miriam Riselle, John Ireland and William Rykey in *The Ghost Train*.

Above: Hanging a
pastel of himself as Mr
Faulkland in the HM
Tennent production of
The Rivals (Criterion
Theatre, 1945-46). The
other pastel on the bench
is of Private Charles in
Happy Few (Cambridge
Theatre, 1944).

Right: Terence Rattigan's
While the Sun Shines at
the 'Q' Theatre, with Ann
Bennett – October 1946.

As Joseph Surface in *The School for Scandal* – Old Vic West End season, 1949.

As Valentine in *The Gay Invalid* (a musical version of Molière's *Le Malade imaginaire*) – Garrick Theatre, 1951.

Left: As Lomov in Chekhov's *The Proposal* – Old Vic West End season, 1949. Note the 'furniture' is painted on a back cloth.

Below: Helen, 1950s.

At home, sorting through
photos of his role as Osric
in Laurence Olivier's
1947 film, *Hamlet*.

he gave me the biggest 'dressing down' I had ever experienced: but it taught me my first invaluable lesson in keeping still on stage.

When the show finished a party was held, to which I was invited and asked if I would help serve the liquid refreshment. Desperately anxious to make what amends I could for my terrible faux pas, I was most liberal with the libations, but being a teetotaller then as now, my knowledge of alcohol was limited, although I had observed its effect upon those who imbibed not wisely but too well. Since I couldn't get near the taps at the wash basin in the crowded confines of the dressing room, I was rather nonplussed when asked for 'Whisky and water, please', so I added a generous slug of gin instead, which it resembled. Drinking nothing but tonic myself, I was soon the only person left standing. It was in the early hours when I finally escorted Mr Fraser to his house – fortunately nearby – where he cooked some delicious scrambled eggs which we scoffed together in the kitchen.

'Tomorrow's Sunday,' he yawned, as he made his way upstairs to bed. 'See you in the theatre on Monday.' I spent what was left of the night happily asleep on the sofa.

In the morning I acquired some 'digs' and duly presented myself at the Connaught the next day. When Bill Fraser saw me, he blinked and said, 'What! are you still here?' which completely took the wind out of my sails. Seeing my crestfallen face, he added, 'Oh well, I suppose we'd better put you to work – we do need an ASM. Fifteen shillings a week – is that alright? The Stage Manager will show you the ropes.'

Thus, in June 1936, after almost five years of 'blood, toil, tears and sweat', I entered the ranks of the profession – with a 50 per cent drop in salary, but a 500 hundred per cent rise in morale.

* * *

An Assistant Stage Manager's job in weekly rep is excellent training for any would-be actor. It is a gruelling occupation, especially when you are called upon to play parts as well – so many lines to be committed to memory before turning in for the night, rehearsing during the day, and performing the current production in the evening.

One of my many duties was to 'beg, borrow or steal' from the local shops all the furniture and 'props' required for each play, making sure they were returned safely and in good condition when no longer needed. I became an inveterate note-maker, a habit which remains with me to this very day. My cigarette packets are covered with 'don't forget to's...'

Being employed for the best part of the day on these tasks, or busy inside the theatre, there was no such thing as regular meals, and since I gave the landlady my full salary each week for Bed and Breakfast, I had nothing left to pay for them anyway. Consequently, I often felt pretty peckish when I finally got to bed, so I was always delighted when a script needed food to be served, because this meant I could have a jolly good 'tuck-in' from the left-overs after each performance. Noël Coward's *Hay Fever* was a great favourite of mine – all those lovely tea and breakfast scenes! Not many people realise how difficult it can be for actors to 'time' their lines, so as not to have a mouth full of food when it's their turn to speak, and, of course, it is most unconvincing if the meals remain untouched.

These comestibles were usually provided gratis, by courtesy of Sainsbury's, in return for a credit to that effect printed in the programme, plus a couple of complimentary tickets for the show. (Likewise 'Cigarettes by Abdulla' – a welcome sight, keeping me well supplied with 'gaspers'!)

For many obvious reasons, it was not practical to cook 'the real thing', and necessity became the mother of many culinary inventions in the prop room. Tinned half-peaches were an excellent substitute for the yolk of fried eggs, but I couldn't think of anything better than damp cotton wool for the white, which didn't go down too well with the cast; but thinly sliced bananas, judiciously daubed with redcurrant jelly, proved popular, and made passable and very edible rashers of bacon. My inner man was not quite so satisfied when *Anthony and Anna* by St John Ervine was presented, because the only character in that play who ate anything was a dyspeptic American millionaire – on a strict diet of soda water and charcoal biscuits. A week of those put me off them for life.

During the last weeks of the Summer Season, Bill Fraser had a short holiday, and in his absence Peter Coleman, who ran the Southampton Rep, took over. Before he left, he invited me to join his company there at the Grand Theatre, as ASM and to play small parts. He was a dear person, and I was delighted to accept his offer, but ever grateful to Bill Fraser for giving me my first opportunity.

* * *

The stage carpenter at my new job – Harry, if I remember aright – was full of cockney charm and capers.

On the billboards outside the theatre, I had seen the name Walter Plinge prominently displayed, amongst the rest of the permanent cast listed in alphabetical order, but could not recall ever meeting the gentleman. I asked Harry if he could enlighten me. 'Ah! yer wants ter keep yer mincepies peeled fer 'im, guv'ner, 'e's bin missin' fer mumfs. Big feller 'e is, wiv ginger 'air and a moostarch like 'itler's. I reckon 'e dun a bunk wiv the petty cash.'

Such a vivid description should have told me that it was a leg pull, but I was too keen and eager to suspect, and, ever anxious to prove my worth, I did indeed keep my eyes open, thinking what a feather in my cap it would be if I could find him. I could see the headline in the local paper – 'New recruit at Grand Theatre finds missing link!' But I never did, simply because he didn't exist. After several weeks of eagle-eyed searching, I found out that this appellation was used to make the marquee more impressive, and if an actor was playing two parts in a play, it would appear in the programme as well.

Before I made this discovery, the same worthy joker handed me 'the Key to the Grid', laying great stress upon the grim consequences if it were lost. It was a massive affair, like one of those used to lock dungeon cells in mediaeval castles, and weighed a ton. Bursting with pride to be so entrusted, and put in sole charge of such an important article, but apprehensive of losing it, I hung it round my neck on a leather thong, and slept with it under my pillow in great discomfort.

The grid in a theatre is the vast, doorless open space above the stage, surrounded by catwalks, where scenery is 'flown' when not in use. One day I explored that region, and began to 'smell a rat'.

Bill Waddy, a character actor of great charm, put me wise to these time-honoured theatrical gags, which are tried out on all beginners, and for which, like any innocent, I had fallen – hook, line and sinker. I was glad to get rid of the thing – it was beginning to hunch my shoulders.

One of the more painful pranks – albeit unintentional – played on me was when I had to wear a large beard and moustache for a cameo role. I had run out of spirit gum, and Harry told me to use Whitehart Varnish instead. 'It won't corst yer nuffink neither – there's bottles of it in the painting dock.' It certainly did the trick, but when I took it off, a thin layer of my skin came away with it, leaving that part of my face permanently allergic to any form of gum. Nowadays, if ever I need facial whiskers, I have to be warned well in advance, in order to allow them to grow. Alternatively, special pieces have to be made for me, with double-sided adhesive tape.

There was not an ounce of malice in 'Arry-boy and had he known his suggestion would backfire in this way, I'm sure he would never have made it.

The following snatch of his cockney wit remains engraved on my memory:

'Hey – Peter – yer laundry's back.'
'Oh, good!'
'Yus – they've refused it.'

*　*　*

Doreen Lawrence (who later married Jack Hawkins) was the juvenile lead, and we became good friends. She came to tea at my lodgings one day, to run through a scene we had together, and was horrified when she noticed the walls of my bedsit were oozing with moisture, and tiny fungi sprouting on the ceiling. The house possessed no bath, and the loo was at the bottom of a long, narrow garden. She lived with her parents in Southampton, and they most kindly insisted I stayed with them until I could find less damp and more convenient quarters to lay my weary head.

Bill Johnson, the stage manager, was also a very dear friend, and helped me a great deal. He left the business soon after the war, and became the manager of Dudleys – a large store in North London. A small booth was erected in one of the show rooms, where he exhibited a model I had made (the interior of an old country house). An entrance fee was charged in aid of SSAFFA (Soldiers', Sailors' and Air Force Families' Association), and this raised a tidy sum for that worthy cause.

*　*　*

Towards the end of each season, I scanned the 'vacancies' column in my old stand-by *The Stage*, and applied for any 'Juv./Character Leads' that were advertised. I was by now in the more satisfactory position of being able to state – without fear or favour – my 'prev. exp.', which had so eluded me during my 'salad days'.

'Special Weeks' came my way, in Burnley and other North Country towns, playing all manner of characters in all manner of disguises. I also enjoyed an engagement in Rochdale with the

William Brookfield Players, and subsequently went to Scarborough with the same company.

Of course, it was inevitable that I should fall in and out of 'love' with practically every young lady I worked with. I did, with unfailing regularity, but never had the time to pursue these romances. In any case, none of them could quite compare with my new Idol of the Silver Screen – Loretta Young, who had displaced my old hero Tom Mix in my fickle affections.

On one occasion Mother travelled up to see me, and was taking tea in my dressing room after the matinée. This was before the Tannoy system was installed, and a call boy would go round knocking on all doors, calling the half hour, quarter, five minutes – and finally 'Overture and beginners, please' – before each performance.

As I was 'on' at the start of this particular play, I got up to make my way down to the stage, whereupon Mother said indignantly, 'Don't you go, dear. You are not a beginner – you've been an actor for quite some time now.'

Where ignorance is bliss, indeed! – and it reminded me of an earlier misapprehension, when I arrived home after a game of rugger and announced proudly I'd dropped a couple of goals. 'What a pity, dear,' said she sympathetically, 'but never mind – perhaps you'll do better in your next match.'

* * *

During that heyday of repertory theatres, Harry Hanson was the doyen, and it was the ambition of most young actors to get into one of his companies, which were called the Court Players. His headquarters were in Hastings, but he also held sway in many other towns. Eventually, I was selected to join his elite society, at the princely salary of £2.10s per week, which enabled me to open my first Post Office savings account, managing to put away as much as half a crown on rare occasions.

This was in Nottingham at the Theatre Royal, and it was there that I met Peter Gray, who was to become one of my oldest and dearest friends. He proved a marvellous companion. He taught me to scull, and we spent many happy Sundays on the 'smug and silver Trent', pulling ashore to partake of tea in some sequestered inn and hear each other's lines. He weaned me from my schoolboy literature which I was still reading at the advanced age of 25, stirring my interest in more adult spheres with JB Priestley's *The Good Companions.* I still have this book on my shelves, and on the flyleaf he had written 'Dear Old "Pal and Friend" – with all my good wishes for Hollywood and many joyous memories – Yours ever – Peter.'

Little did I dream – when all but killing myself with my lasso – that one day I would actually meet the man who had inspired those reckless activities – no less a person than the great Tom Mix himself.

The house of varieties was adjacent to the legitimate theatre, and he was on one of the bills with his splendid white horse Tony, descended no doubt from the one he rode with such skill in those early films. I called in to thank him for all the pleasure he'd given me. 'That's real nice of you,' he said. 'I wonder if you'd do me a favour – will you witness my signature on this contract?'

It's rather a nice feeling of basking in reflected glory to think that perhaps there is yet a musty old document hidden away in some agent's files, bearing my autograph under his!

There was another attraction which drew me to that stage door. A turn entitled *Hollywood Star Doubles* was featured, and, of course, I fell for Loretta Young's. She and her friend, the spitting image of Zasu Pitts, joined Peter and me on many an outing, rowing up the Trent, and showing them the sights in general. They were enchanted, and enchanting.

Later Peter and I went to Peterborough under the same banner of Court Players, and then came the parting of our ways.

At least eight turbulent and eventful years were to elapse before we met again. I remember standing at the open window of our shared 'digs', looking out over the darkened rooftops of the town, each wondering what the future held in store for us. It was midnight, in the autumn of 1938.

Peter joined the Navy soon after the 'balloon went up', where he remained as a 'Jimmy the One' for the duration. Years later he was to suffer one of Fate's cruel blows – he became totally deaf. A severe enough handicap for anyone, but for an actor, it meant the end of his career.

Although he never admitted it, I'm certain this distressing condition stemmed from the constant battering his eardrums must have taken during the din of naval bombardments.

He bore his affliction with infinite courage and dignity and never a word of complaint, even managing to record many Talking Books for the Blind. But the theatre was his first love, and this being denied him, he decided to leave London. Devonshire born and bred, he retired to his beloved West Country where, judging from the tone of his letters, he is enjoying life immensely with his dear and devoted wife, Daphne Newton.

*   *   *

For many years, I had a hankering to try my luck in Hollywood, and having saved a small sum during my time in Rep, I asked Father if he would assist with my passage to the States. He did so, presenting me with a ticket. I noticed it was only one-way, and the old Music Hall patter, concerning a family on a low budget vacation, ran through my mind:

> *'How much farther is it to England, Dad?'*
> *'I don't know, son – keep swimming!'*

So engrossed with what I was doing, I had become oblivious to what was going on in world affairs, and scarcely aware that war was not only inevitable but also imminent. I had heard Neville

Chamberlain broadcast his speech on the wireless during the Munich Crisis, and seen him on cinema newsreels, stepping from the 'plane holding up that famous – or, in the light of what was to come – infamous piece of paper: 'I believe it is peace for our time – peace with honour,' he had predicted after the Munich Agreement in October 1938. In my ignorance, I took his word for it, and got on with the job in hand.

I derived great comfort some time later when I learnt I was not the only person to be so isolated from reality. I read an article by Emlyn Williams, in which he declared that he, too, was astonished when war was announced, being completely out of touch, wrapped up and absorbed in his work during all those ominous rumblings.

At 10.00 pm on Wednesday 18 January 1939, full of high hopes and the abounding impetuosity of youth, I boarded the SS Champlain at Southampton, outward bound for America, in search of fame, fortune, and – who knows – with a little bit of luck – I might just catch a glimpse of my heart-throb, the real Loretta Young…

I did.

4

CALIFORNIA ~ HERE I COME...

I SHARED A cabin with a young man who spoke only Afrikaans and seemed to exist entirely on biltong. He had bags of the stuff and offered me a slice, which tasted like brine. We tried to communicate with each other by sign language, but it wasn't very satisfactory. I thought some of his looked rather rude.

The voyage was uneventful otherwise, although I was agog with excited anticipation, and most touched to receive letters from my loving parents, who had left a batch of them with the purser to be given to me day by day.

The renowned silhouette of New York City as you approach Manhattan Island from the Hudson River has been eulogised so often, but never exaggerated. It really was a superb and breathtaking sight. I felt a trifle small and insignificant when we slipped into our berth, standing beneath all those towering blocks of skyscrapers, but I soon became accustomed to these strange surroundings, and stimulated by the electric atmosphere.

Having worked out a plan of campaign during the days at sea, I set about putting it into action. I knew it was imperative to live as frugally as possible and to start earning as soon as I could. My decision was to stay for seven days in the city, making the rounds of all the film company offices, which I would look up in a telephone directory, and ask if they could oblige me with letters of introduction to the casting directors in the corresponding studios on the coast.

I settled into the YMCA, paying a week in advance, also buying a train ticket to Los Angeles, making sure these necessities were at least accounted for, although this expenditure made quite a nasty dent in my capital.

I met a great number of polite but unforthcoming individuals during my tramping of the Great White Way, but one in particular lived up to his name, Larney Goodkind of Columbia Pictures, Inc. He knew someone connected with Edward Small Productions who might be useful to know, and gave me a note, as requested, warning me that I was not alone in my quest, and my chances were pretty slim. According to him, about one in five of the whole population of the USA wanted to get into the industry, but my English accent could be an asset, and give me some slight advantage over the host of other hopefuls.

I had never met Robert Morley, who was making his first appearance on Broadway as Oscar Wilde, but – nothing ventured, nothing gained – I went to see him at the Fulton Theatre to ask if he had any advice to give me, and any contacts that could be helpful. He was most kind and hospitable, but when I told him of my intention, he said, 'It's very crowded, you know, dear boy. Why don't you just go there for a holiday? Have you brought your bathing costume with you?'

*　*　*

The Challenger pulled out of Grand Central Station with me aboard, starting its five-day haul to Los Angeles, passing through the States of New York, New Jersey, Pennsylvania, Ohio, Indiana, Illinois, Iowa, Nebraska, Wyoming, Utah, Nevada and finally California, reaching our destination at 8.35 am on Friday 10 February 1939, in a cloudburst.

When evening approached on the first leg of the trek westward, a coloured attendant came down the aisle with pillows, to make the night pass more comfortably. I accepted one gratefully, but upon being asked politely for three dollars, I handed it back as if it had suddenly become red hot. There were three college students in my compartment, who strolled up and down the train, entertaining the other passengers delightfully with close harmony singing, to the accompaniment of a ukulele. We became 'buddies', but although I have a great love for music, I possess no talent in that branch of the arts (discounting my Council Office concerts) so I went along carrying the hat. There was an equal share-out of its contents at the end of each tour, which was most generous of the troubadours, considering my silent contribution. 'Mexicali Rose' was a big hit, followed closely by 'Mr Franklin D Roosevelt Jones', both songs being in today's parlance 'Top of the Pops'.

The sweet citrus scent of orange groves was intoxicating, as we sped through them on the last lap of our journey, but having always heard of 'Sunny California' I was a little dismayed when I stepped out into the teeming rain.

In the interests of economy, I chose to walk from downtown LA to Hollywood, wearing a thick tweed suit and lugging two bulging bags. It was a four-mile trudge, and very sultry. Quite soon I was perspiring like a pack horse.

Nothing daunted, I presented myself to the astonished clerk at the reception desk in the YMCA, North Hudson Avenue, and standing there in my steaming tweeds and an ever increasing pool of rain water, delivered my well-rehearsed speech:

'I've just come from England to get into films. I have 16 dollars and an Ingersoll watch, cheap but reliable. Would you please accept these as a deposit, until I am in a position to settle the bill for my room and board?'

He stared at me blankly, and – as if hypnotised – handed me a key without saying a word. Some weeks later, when we'd got to know each other better, I asked him why he had accepted me on such slender security.

'You were so plumb British,' he replied, 'and so honest, I just hadn't the heart to refuse.' (Tom Merry to the rescue again, I thought.)

Within 15 days of my sodden arrival, I was able to vindicate his trust, which was much sooner than either of us had expected.

*   *   *

That I should turn up at this precise moment was one of those extraordinary lucky breaks which we all need at some time or other during this life, but don't always get.

Armed with Larney Goodkind's note, I made my way to the Edward Small Studios and, at the outer gates, was confronted by a massive commissionaire, absolutely 'bristling with guns' as Noël Coward, 'The Master', once put it. I handed him my precious entrée, waited patiently, and presently he led me to the Casting Director's office.

A film entitled *The Man in the Iron Mask* was to commence shooting within a few days, starring Joan Bennett and Louis Hayward. The two leading male roles were twins, and he was cast as both of them. This would involve the split-screen process, and James Whale, the director, wanted an actor who would be willing to play all those scenes with the star, knowing he would never be seen by the public. In editing the final products, the film would be slit up the centre, the two Louis Hayward sections stuck together, giving the impression he was playing opposite himself, and the other two sections discarded.

This engagement was offered to me, at a salary of $75 a week, which represented a small fortune in my present circumstances, with a guarantee of at least two months' employment. I could hardly believe it, as I signed on the dotted line at the foot of my contract.

There is a note in the diary I kept during this period which reads: 'Returned to "Y" wondering if I really *HAD* got the job' – as well I might. Apart from easing my immediate financial anxiety, here was a Heaven-sent opportunity for someone who had never set foot inside a film studio before, to observe and learn how such old hands as Joseph Schildkraut and the rest of the distinguished cast set about the method of acting in this very technical medium, so different from giving a live performance in a theatre. Furthermore, I would be able to see the daily 'rushes', and correct the many faults I was bound to commit, and so gradually improve.

My confidence grew day by day, and to compensate for all my footage which lay cluttering the cutting room floor, I was given a small part, the King's Messenger, which involved me and my attendants in a sword fight with D'Artagnan, played by Warren William, and the Three Musketeers, played by Alan Hale, Bert Roach and Miles Mander.

'Ever done any fencing?' asked James Whale.

'Oh yes, sir,' said Peter Cushing, 'quite a lot'.

'Good. Go along and see M'sieur Cavens – first class swordsman. He'll take you through the routine that's been mapped out.'

M'sieur Cavens laid the blade over his left forearm, offering me the hilted handle, which I grasped.

His eyes narrowed as he peered at me shrewdly.

"Ave you fenced before?' he asked.

'No,' said Tom Merry, 'but I needed the job so badly, I had to say "yes" when the director asked me.'

'So! If you 'ad said yes to me, you would 'ave insulted my intelligence as well as my art. You took the sword from my 'and as if it were a carving knife. But since you speak the truth, now I teach you to be the best swordsman in the 'ole of 'ollywood. En garde! I show you 'ow.'

I didn't attain that dazzling peak of perfection, but he taught me enough to hold my own against Warren William when the time came.

The costumes for this early 18th century drama were magnificent – flowing, wavy wigs worn under gorgeous plumed hats, breeches, doublets with slashed leg of mutton sleeves, lace collars, cuffs and furbelows, gauntlets and long, floppy leather riding boots. I was much taken by a pair of spurs and asked the Wardrobe Master if I might wear them. They were very large, and made a most satisfying jingle as I proudly strode about, feeling I cut rather a dashing figure in my 'fancy dress'.

But pride came before a fall.

My riding experience was as wanting as my sword-play, all my previous horses having been Mother's bike, but no one queried this. I was given a splendid steed, with a saddle resembling a small armchair, and stirrups like backless clogs. I had to ride into the courtyard of an inn, and say to one of the Musketeers, 'The King wants to see you.'

On the command 'Action!', I must have inadvertently stabbed my mount's flank with the sharpish rowels of my coveted spurs. The beast took off like a thunderbolt, leapt over an oak table, scattering extras and their pewter tankards of ale in all directions, charged into a section of the scenery which came crashing down, stampeded wildly around and around, my sword sheath swinging of its own free will like a flail, thwacking its side which encouraged even greater displays of frenzied rodeo-like acrobatics. Suddenly it jerked to an abrupt four-hoofed stop, depositing me in a dazed heap on the studio floor. As I lay there, befuddled and dusty, it began to paw the sawdust and straw, then bent over and nuzzled my neck. For one horrible moment, I thought it was going to eat me.

When all the commotion had died away, I heard the director's plaintive voice calling anxiously, 'Is the horse OK?'

What price actors, I reflected ruefully.

Next morning, the damaged section of the scenery as good as new, I was ignominiously de-spurred before being allowed to mount, and the scene was re-shot without further mishap. During a coffee break, I gave my now docile charger a lump of sugar and, d'you know – I could swear that animal winked at me... It had given me an extra day's work while the set was being rebuilt!

All in all, I learnt a great deal from my first steps into the world of motion pictures.

* * *

I count myself very fortunate to have been domiciled in Hollywood during the golden days of its zenith. Like all 'rubber necks', I was thrilled to see so many of those legendary beings who had become such a part of my life, but whom, until now, I had never thought of as mere flesh and blood: just magical and mystic images flickering across a screen, giving untold pleasure to millions like me, who sat in darkened cinemas, silently worshipping at their feet.

A list would be tedious and the names could fill many pages of this chapter, but there they are, in my diary, and, like today's trainspotters, I had put a tick against all those I either saw or encountered.

I got to know Louis Hayward very well while we were working together, and we were firm friends. He struck me as a somewhat sad and lonely soul, disenchanted with the film business, who seemed glad to have someone to talk to about 'the Old Country'. He was married to Ida Lupino, and living in a delightful villa on the Brentwood Heights, about halfway between the film capital and Santa Monica, a profusion of scarlet poinsettia enriching the garden with their flaming beauty. I spent many enjoyable weekends there, and finally they kindly invited me to stay with them for as long as I wished. Like the man who came to dinner, I did.

Louis and I went to visit Ida on location at Big Bear Lake when she was making *High Sierra* with Humphrey Bogart. He was a most charming and intelligent person, and, upon my request, demonstrated his superb marksmanship and quick draw with a revolver, tossing coins high up into the air, nine times out of ten scoring a bull's eye before they reached the ground!

*　　*　　*

I think it was Bernard Shaw who wrote, 'England and America are two countries divided by a common language', or something very like that. I was given a splendid illustration of this aphorism when I went into Schwab's Drug Store, famous as a meeting place for actors, writers, and all the other aspirants seeking a livelihood in that land of dreams, where so few come true.

I had a sore throat, and asked the assistant if they sold gargles. 'Yes, *sir*,' he said, and obligingly offered me a large selection of sun glasses to choose from.

A few days after completing my stint on *The Man in the Iron Mask*, I was at that rendezvous again, enjoying a milk shake, and it was there that I heard Hal Roach was needing English-type actors for a Laurel and Hardy film, *A Chump at Oxford*.

I lost no time in making contact with his studios, and was accepted. My part was little more than an extra's but I was so proud to be with two of the greatest comedians the cinema has ever produced. Both were perfectionists, Stan Laurel thinking up most of the gags and routines, and then discussing them in detail with Oliver Hardy and the director, Alfred Goulding.

Olly was a key chain swinger, twirling it round his forefinger until it formed a huge ring, and then reversing the process, all the while humming a little tune. He was followed everywhere by a small black boy, who pushed a trolley groaning with coffee and doughnuts. 'I have to keep eating these things,' he once enlightened me, 'in order to keep my weight up. Try one?'

In that sunny clime, daytime was extremely hot, but there was no twilight, the sun sinking swiftly below the horizon, making the drop in temperature considerable. There was an evening sequence where several undergraduates had to fall fully clothed into a swimming pool. Both the stars made quite sure there were towels, blankets and hot drinks available for all of us, when we climbed out of the water, shivering in the chilly air. Such was their thought for others.

Mr Goulding wanted a bird's eye view of the famous pair, staggering about carrying a vast portmanteau, seeking the exit from Hampton Court Maze. As their faces would not be seen, he used 'doubles'. When Laurel and Hardy saw the rushes, Stan said, not unkindly – 'Olly and I must do that ourselves – those two are *trying* to be funny, and it shows.' Such was their professionalism. I was only with them for a week. It is one that I treasure.

* * *

The hospitality of our American cousins and British expatriates was overwhelming. I was a guest at many tennis parties, and swimming gatherings in private garden pools of cerulean blue, and every imaginable shape and size, or on the beaches at Santa Monica and off Catalina Island, which meant trips in various seagoing craft, finishing the day with a barbecue.

That grand old stalwart of the British theatre, Empire and cricket, C Aubrey Smith, invited me to play in his Eleven, which included Basil Rathbone, David Niven and William Pratt. (The movie moguls thought this a rather ordinary name, so they changed it to the more exotic-sounding Boris Karloff.) I was bowled out first ball, and missed several easy catches when fielding at mid-on, being so distracted by all those luminaries surrounding me. My services were not called upon again, but I attended several matches as an onlooker from the pavilion.

Ida and Louis took me to dinner one evening to Ella Campbell's Restaurant on Sunset Boulevard, which was run by that very English lady, who specialised in the traditional fare of her homeland – Roast Beef of Olde England, Lancashire Hot Pot, Steak and Kidney Pudding and Shepherds Pie, with Sherry Trifle for 'afters'.

We were among the first patrons to dine in this new establishment, and she requested us to sign our names, with a poker-work pen, in the centre of a large piece of three ply fixed on one of the walls. By the time I left Hollywood, it was completely covered, ours being surrounded with the autographs of practically every star who shone so brightly in that firmament of celluloid.

I caught my glimpse of Loretta Young that night – indeed, more than a glimpse, because I was introduced to her by my hosts. She was as gracious and beautiful off the screen as on. I kissed her hand in greeting, which was more than I had ever hoped for or expected.

There was one invitation I wished I had not accepted. Adolphe Menjou was taking a group of friends to a bull fight in Tijuana, south of the border down Mexico way, and asked me to join them.

The pomp and ceremony of the entrance of the toreadors was most impressive and full of atmosphere. The procession was led by two constables on horseback in 17th century costume, followed by the matadors in their resplendent garb, and the full panoplied entourage of various other fighters, who took their positions behind the wooden barricades. When this pageantry ceased, the arena stood empty and still. Then suddenly, to a loud fanfare of trumpets, the magnificent shining black bull charged into the ring, blood already oozing from wounds caused by the decorated darts piercing its neck, thrust in to weaken and infuriate the tormented creature. It came to a halt, sending up a spray of hot sand, as it stamped at the ground with its forefoot.

I was sickened and appalled by the cruel spectacle that ensued. When I could bear it no longer, I left as quickly as possible, feeling sullied and unclean, and made my way to a tiny Mexican Mission. Kneeling down, I asked that they might be forgiven: '...they know not what they do...' I also offered up a prayer for the bull.

*   *   *

Robert Coote, whom I had met at one of those cricket sessions, was involved in some pre-production work on an RKO film, *Vigil in the Night*, based on a hospital story by AJ Cronin. He thought I would be good casting for Joe Shand, a lad from the North Country who worked as a motor mechanic. He suggested this to the director, George Stevens, I was given a screen test, and to my delight, it was successful. This was an important role – the second male lead, and to have landed it in such a comparatively short time was most satisfying.

Carole Lombard had the leading part. She had made her name as a splendid comedienne, and this would be a change for her to appear in something more dramatic. Brian Aherne was cast opposite her, with Anne Shirley and Julien Mitchell playing the other main characters.

Shooting was due to start in July, but, ironically, Miss Lombard had to undergo surgery for acute appendicitis. This delayed commencement for about six weeks, but it helped her a great deal with her part as a nurse, as she was able to observe closely the daily routine in a hospital ward.

I had bought my first car (on the 'never never') – a Hudson – so during this enforced 'rest' I drove to Palm Springs, where the Haywards were taking a vacation. I was delighted to discover a Summer Stock theatre there, and to learn they wanted someone to play Bruce Lovell, the leading part in *Love from a Stranger* by Frank Vosper, for two weeks. Ever hopeful, I asked if I could oblige, and was surprised and gratified when they said, 'Yes, please.'

Taking the script to study my lines, I walked up into the mountains and enjoyed a swim in a natural pool amongst the rocks, which had been one of the location sites for Shangri-La in *Lost Horizon*, starring Ronald Colman. I made my way down again, by leaping from boulder to boulder in the middle of a gushing stream.

It was essential to the plot of the play that Bruce Lovell had blonde hair, so I purchased some 'gold lustre' from an art shop and used that. It was most effective. It also turned my scalp bright green.

The living quarters provided by my employers were somewhat primitive, to say the least. They were small wooden huts standing in a sort of sandy kraal, the inside walls made of whitewashed plywood, with nails driven in to hang your clothes on. Mine were constantly working loose, depositing my wardrobe, such as it was, on the dusty floor, so in the end I left it there, neatly folded. The furniture consisted of an iron bedstead with questionable sheets, a handy 'Jerry' underneath, except that the handle had been broken off, an upright rather rickety wicker chair which I imagine had seen better days, and a marble-topped wash-stand complete with china basin and jug, plus a cracked, fly-blown mirror. Nothing else, just a notice pinned to the back of the door (which, incidentally, jammed whenever it was opened or closed) which read: 'Please leave these premises as you would wish to find them.' Any water required was drawn from an artesian well in the centre of the compound.

No charge was made for this accommodation – it was considered part of my salary.

I see another note in that diary of mine, dated 10 August, which states bleakly, 'Feeling very lonely for England and home.' Perhaps these surroundings didn't help, but I was getting homesick. I tried to comfort myself by reflecting it was all part of life's rich pageant, and – like some latter day Gauguin – painted a view of Devonshire on the wall opposite my bed, so that I could look at it before I fell asleep.

* * *

We commenced filming *Vigil in the Night* towards the end of September, the majority of my scenes being with either Carole Lombard or Anne Shirley.

Having previously seen them only from a seat in the 'one and nines' at my local cinema, I was mesmerised in the presence of these fabulous creatures, regarding all film stars as not of this world, and verging on the sacrosanct. Before starting my first 'take' with Miss Lombard, I whispered to the director, 'Am I allowed to touch her?'

He looked at me in astonishment before replying, 'You can do what you like with her, so long as you cause no bodily harm.'

They were wonderful to work with, and George Stevens most helpful, encouraging and complimentary.

One morning, I saw a prop man carrying a succulent side of bacon into the operating theatre set.

'Lunch?' I enquired, hopefully.

'Nope,' he replied laconically, 'operation'. And there it was, slapped onto the stomach of an extra, so that the actor playing a surgeon could make a realistic incision with his scalpel. Just like rep, I thought, remembering the peaches doing such good service as eggs.

The shooting wound up on 30 November, and in typical Hollywood fashion, a party was given for the cast and crew, all the food and drink being served from hospital utensils by waiters dressed in clinical gowns and wearing rubber gloves. Rather than go into sordid detail, I leave it to your imagination what was used for 'bangers', curry and the like; toilet rolls were provided as serviettes. Suffice to say, it rather took the edge off my appetite. Clark Gable, who was Carole Lombard's husband, came along, took one look at the spread, smiled his famous smile, and said, 'Gee! am I glad I'm slimming.'

* * *

War had been officially declared on 3 September 1939, and all British subjects were ordered to report for a medical. Due to a couple of injuries sustained during my rugger-playing days – torn ligaments in my left knee and perforated left eardrum – I was given a low category, 4C, and told to 'stand by'.

'They are not in need of cannon fodder yet,' the cheerful MO informed me.

Some time after this interview, a blister on my heel burst and turned septic, coinciding with a severe case of athlete's foot, caused by contact with contaminated water in a shower bath. The infection increased rapidly, giving great discomfort, so I went to a clinic for treatment. A scalpel-happy surgeon was all for amputation, but after seeking a second opinion, I'm glad to say some less drastic measures were taken, the poison being drained away by a system of rubber tubes. Although infinitely preferable, it was a lengthy and uncomfortable process, and also very costly. When I was at last discharged, I returned my car, as I was unable to keep up the monthly instalments.

I managed to get a few more engagements, working once again with James Whale in *They Dare Not Love*, which starred George Brent and Martha Scott (no horses this time).

MGM were embarking on a series of shorts, under the general heading *Passing Parade*, following their earlier success with a similar programme, *Crime Doesn't Pay*, in which I'd seen an excellent performance given by Spangler Arlington Brough – another name that was to be changed, this time to Robert Taylor.

I was offered one of these, entitled *The Hidden Master*. My part was the young Clive of India, who – in a state of black despair – tried to blow his brains out. He put the pistol to his temple, and twice it refused to detonate: the third time, he aimed at a pitcher of water, which was shattered by the weapon suddenly responding. Clive regarded this as an omen, and history records the mark he made in an outstanding career.

The powers that be were pleased with this mini picture, and there was talk of grooming me for stardom. But it was now 1941, and I had become desperately homesick. I wasn't all that keen to kill anyone in conflict, or to be killed for that matter, but I did want to get home, back to England. My heart and mind set upon this desire, I declined MGM's proposal, and with a longing to get a little nearer to the United Kingdom, I decided to go to New York City, and work my way up to Canada, which was, at least, a British Dominion. I reckoned that 'standing by' on the move would prove less frustrating. Even if I could have afforded the fare, it was not possible to book a boat or 'plane passage to England, all transport being commandeered for war requisitions.

Having barely enough money left to get me halfway to the East Coast, I had written to the Office of the High Commissioner for the United Kingdom in Ottawa, and the Department of National Defence in Regina, Saskatchewan, explaining my circumstances, both replies stating that '...no provision exists to cover the cost of transportation from an individual's home to the point of enlistment. Yours truly, etc...'

With extreme generosity, Louis Hayward kindly lent me the sum, so that I might have some cash in hand during my travels. I had been treated with the utmost kindness and consideration during my two years in Hollywood, and was deeply grateful, also, for the experience it had taught me. And now, on 18 January 1941, I set forth on a pilgrimage, little knowing that another 15 long months lay ahead of me before I was to reach my journey's end.

*   *   *

One of the first things I saw upon my return to New York City was a banner stretched across the portals of a hospital, bearing the request in bold letters: 'GIVE BLOOD FOR BRITAIN!' Well, that's all I've got to give at the moment, I mused, so in I went and offered a pint, which was taken. I walked out, fell flat on my face on the sidewalk, and was carted in again to have two pints pumped back into me. They kept me there for a couple of weeks, apparently suffering from nervous exhaustion. I cannot call my first war effort an outstanding success.

The YMCA was full, and upon their recommendation I booked a room at the Hotel St James, in West 45th Street, just off Times Square.

My immediate concern was to earn some money in whatever way I could, to pay my fare to Canada. I scanned cards in shop windows, looking for any jobs which might be in the offing. One required a car park attendant on Coney Island, so I made a beeline for that popular summer resort in Brooklyn, Long Island, with its fine beach and countless amusement arcades.

The owner resembled Edward G Robinson – as a gangster – to a remarkable degree, his yellow teeth perpetually chewing a damp unlit cigar butt.

'You a Limey?' he asked when I introduced myself. I nodded. He looked doubtful, and with deadly precision, squirted a thin stream of nicotine into a brass spittoon, shrugged, and said, 'Okay. Get movin'.'

The customers drove their automobiles to the entrance, leaving them there with the engines ticking over. Then I took charge, carefully parking them in whatever space was available, making sure not to scrape any paint in the process. It took quite a lot of manoeuvring, and ten minutes went by before I succeeded in getting two stowed away.

Later in the day, 'Edward G' poked his head out of the window of his pay cabin and yelled, 'Hey, Buster, whaddaya think you're doin'? There's a queue stretchin' back to Brooklyn Bridge!'

I explained that I was trying to avoid any damage. Smacking his forehead with the palm of his hand, he proceeded to demonstrate the correct method, which looked to me as if he was behaving like some demented driver let loose on a dodgems circuit at a fun fair. Before I could say 'Jack Robinson', he'd shunted about six cars in line abreast, and squeezing himself between the tightly packed vehicles, puffed, 'That-away, see?'

I protested rather primly, pointing out I had a certain respect for other people's property.

He spat once more, and said, 'Aw – what the hell! I gotta make a livin'. You're fired.'

So that was that. I collected my few crumpled dollars and left.

The next card I spotted – 'Illusionist needs assistance' – sounded more like my cup of tea, although I was wary about the last word, hoping this was merely mis-spelt, all he wanted being someone to assist in his act, and did not imply that he, too, was 'skint' and in need of financial aid. Anyway, I thought it worth investigating, so went to see him in a rather sleazy night club off Broadway.

He was exceedingly slim, just the teeniest bit cross-eyed and, I think, a little 'pink around the edges', but we got along very well. He taught me some of the tricks of his trade: the different ways to hold playing cards, with their backs toward him, so that he knew what they were, and certain phrases to use when he was blindfolded and asked by the audience what I was holding in my hand. The engagement lasted for three weeks, four half-hour shows nightly, the last finishing about 3.00 am.

That added more grist to my mill, but I was still a long way from my target, and when the contract terminated, I went card-spotting again.

I could find nothing suitable until, while reading a copy of *Variety,* the American equivalent of *The Stage,* I saw that a radio network wanted actors to read commercials, and I did quite a few of these.

I remember two of them. One was spoken rhythmically to a sort of 'pom-tiddilly-om-pom, pom-pom' beat: 'Comes out a ribbon, lies flat on the brush (pom-pom) Colgates' Dental Cream!' The other, urging the use of a laxative, declaimed stentoriously over a roll of drums: 'Take YAW SERUTAN daily and be a regular guy – it's NATURES WAY spelt backwards!' and ended with a resounding clash of cymbals.

One Sunday, I was taking a constitutional in Central Park, feeling very disconsolate. An old rowing boat lay partly submerged under some trees by a lake, and I sat in it for a spell. Noticing a screwed up, sodden piece of coloured paper lying in the bows, I picked it up and began to unravel it. Lo and behold! a ten dollar bill appeared before my eyes. It was added to my emergency fund, but I spent 25 cents on a 'blue plate' lunch at a cafeteria, which made a speciality of this economic and tasty 'set' meal.

I had often frequented a small café run by an elderly Greek, where you could have two doughnuts and as much coffee as you wanted for only ten cents. I was in there one evening during May, and instead of bringing my usual order, he appeared with a sumptuous meal on a tray, complete with a vase of red, white and blue flowers. 'Tonight,' he said, 'I would be honoured if you will be my guest.'

Hitler's forces had invaded Crete, and the British Army was fighting side by side with his countrymen to repulse our common foe. This was a gesture of his gratitude. I was deeply touched.

Standing in Times Square after yet another unsuccessful round of shop windows, I was contemplating what to do next, and wondering vaguely how the enormous smoke rings were blown out of the open-mouthed effigy of a GI's head, advertising some brand of cigarettes, when I felt a tap on my shoulder and heard a voice asking, 'You are Peter Cushing, aren't you?'

Delighted to be recognised, I shook hands with this stranger. 'My name's John Ireland,' he added. 'I've seen some of your movies.'

He was trying to make a name for himself on Broadway, and with his wife Elaine, an actress, had just moved into the same hotel where I was staying. Like mine, their funds were low, so we pooled resources as far as meals were concerned. He made the most delicious porridge I had ever tasted, which he cooked on a gas ring in their room. After several weeks of this staple diet, he suddenly asked if I collected my Social Security. I didn't know what he meant, and he explained that a certain amount of my earnings in Hollywood had been deducted at source, and therefore I was entitled to 18 dollars a week unemployment benefit. We were able to supplement our oats for quite a few weeks following that most welcome information.

By this time, *Vigil in the Night* had been shown, and greeted with a favourable press and public reaction, so my name meant a little more than it had when I arrived in 1939.

Looking through *Variety*, I read that a Summer Stock company was being formed, and pulling the very slight rank I now held, applied for an interview, which was granted. Elaine and John went with me, resulting in the three of us being accepted.

The venue was a holiday camp called Green Mansions at Warrensburg, in the Adirondack Mountains, which form part of the border line between the States and Canadian territory.

A diverse programme of entertainment had been planned for the fortnightly guests, including a selection of plays to be directed by a gentleman who delighted in the name of Wilbur Sparrow. No salaries, but the company paid all expenses, plus a hundred dollars to each of us at the end of the four months' season.

The plays chosen were Robert E Sherwood's *The Petrified Forest*, Arnold Ridley's *The Ghost Train*, SN Behrman's *Biography*, a double-bill comprising an Irish one-act comedy called *Pound on Demand* and Noël Coward's *Fumed Oak*, and a modern dress version of Shakespeare's *Macbeth*.

Compared with the prison-like austerity at Palm Springs, the log cabins allocated to us here were spacious and beautifully appointed, situated amongst pine trees near a large lake, where canoes and rowing boats rocked gently at their moorings. Refreshed and invigorated by the clean mountain air, after the fetid atmosphere of summer in the metropolis, we could use these craft, or swim if so inclined, to reach the theatre complex which lay on the farther bank.

It was grand to be acting on the stage again, in such pleasant conditions, and I enjoyed the comradeship of my fellow actors. Under normal circumstances it would have been an idyllic existence, but four months seemed an awfully long time, and the financial side of this deal would not improve matters to any great extent. Still, it was better than the alternative of hanging around the stifling city, and at the back of my mind lay an idea to cross the border when we finished. The company having paid my fare thus far, it seemed the logical thing to do.

But – the best laid schemes o' mice an' men gang aft a-gley – and mine did.

Toilette items, cigarettes and the occasional round of milkshakes or coffee with the rest of the cast were not regarded as legitimate expenses, and quite rightly deducted from the hundred dollar bonus, leaving me with only about 25 when the time came to collect it – very little to swell 'the Fund', which was now reduced to square one.

On top of this, talent scouts had come to see some of our shows, and I received two offers to appear on Broadway; one from Gilbert Miller, who was presenting Hughie Green in *Golden Wings*, the other from Theatre Associates for their production of *The Seventh Trumpet* by Charles Rann Kennedy.

After much cogitation, I decided to accept this unexpected sidetrack, reasoning that, with any luck, the plays' run should consolidate my savings, and raise the sum I needed to make my next step towards home.

I had to take my pick, because the dates of the productions clashed. The part of a London 'Bobby' wounded in the Blitz appealed to me, so I plumped for *The Seventh Trumpet*.

Gazing wistfully at the distant mountain range, with Canada just the other side – so near yet so far – I resisted a wild temptation to climb over 'them thar hills' and, instead, joined my good companions on the long coach ride back to New York City.

*   *   *

I made the right choice with *The Seventh Trumpet* – we ran for two weeks, *Golden Wings* romping home in one.

We played at the Mansfield Theatre, with Carmen Mathews and Ian Maclaren in the cast. He had appeared as Osborne in the film version of my favourite play, *Journey's End*, by RC Sherriff, directed by my old horse-mate James Whale.

There was a current vogue amongst the newspaper critics for those clever if somewhat unkind one-line notices, such as 'Loved BEN – hated HUR.' They were known as 'The Butchers of Broadway', and a recent presentation of Shakespeare's *Antony and Cleopatra* received the following accolade from one of them: 'Miss –– as Cleopatra sailed down Broadway in her burnish'd barge last night, and sank.' I imagine it was the same gentleman of the press who wrote: '*The Seventh Trumpet* opened on Broadway last night and blew its last blast.'

We were lucky to survive for as long as we did, because after a critique of that nature, it usually meant the curtain fell never to rise again.

Meanwhile, the 'concrete jungle drums' had throbbed out a message regarding *Claudia*, Rose Franken's very successful play, which was enjoying full houses, starring Dorothy McGuire and Donald Cook. That excellent English actor John Williams was also in the cast, playing Jerry Seymour, but he was leaving soon to join the Royal Air Force. I fixed an appointment with Miss Franken, in the hope that I might replace him.

'We are set for a long run,' she said during my interview, 'and you are absolutely right for the part, but will you be leaving us, too'?

'Certainly not,' I lied. She smiled politely, and promised I would be hearing from her shortly.

Her letter arrived a few days later. Being an ardent Anglophile, she was saddened and disappointed by the fact that I did not wish to return and 'do my bit', and felt she could not offer me the part.

Honesty really is the best policy, I ruminated. Hoist with my own petard, I had let myself down in her estimation, and forsaken Tom Merry into the bargain.

But my object all sublime I did achieve in time, and on 8 February 1942 I caught the Iron Horse northbound for Canada. At long last, I set foot in Montreal, where I was treated with the same extraordinary kindness that I had encountered throughout America.

* * *

My next objective was to reach Halifax, Nova Scotia, so I set about raising the fare for that penultimate journey.

The YMCA needed a night porter, and in lieu of salary I was given a small room and two meals a day. One of the staff told me that Loew's State Cinema were short of an usher for the afternoon shift, and thought this would help to tide me over for a spell, still leaving the evenings free for my duties at the 'Y'.

I wore a pale grey pill box hat and 'bum freezer' uniform to match, which must have been made for a pygmy. It was terribly tight under the armpits, forcing my shoulders up, giving me elbow-length sleeves and a gait like a gorilla, similar to an American football player in that protective leather armour they wear under their jerseys. I was unable to do up the fly buttons, hoping this would pass unnoticed in the dark, but just to be on the safe side, I held the torch there. I think the effect was worse.

A nice perk which went with this assignment was the patrons' gesture of 'tipping' those who showed them to their seats. These gratuities were gratefully accepted, and I always contrived to get courting couples next to each other, by asking single customers if they would 'Kindly move along one, please', accompanied by a sibilant demand to 'SHUSH!' from the rest of the captivated audience.

One of the attractions shown was James Cagney in *Captains of the Clouds*, and years later, when someone asked me if I'd ever seen this film, I was able to reply in a manner worthy of 'The Master' himself.

'Yes,' I chirruped succinctly, ' – 45 times.'

To keep my mind occupied during the many idle hours forced upon me over the years, I often turned to painting or building small models. I was currently making a miniature Bechstein, using odd bits and pieces of balsa wood and card. It was only in the early stages of construction, as yet unrecognisable to the untrained eye, and I had left various sections on top of the chest of drawers in my room, so that the glue would be set by the time I got back from work.

When I returned, they were missing. Thinking they might have been swept aside as rubbish by a diligent chambermaid whilst dusting my minute domain, I went in search of her, and there she was – busy in the corridor.

She gave me what Mother used to call 'an old-fashioned look' and hurried off with her Hoover. I heard her mutter to a passing colleague, 'Glory be! 'tis a mad man we've got stayin' in Number

42. There's hardly room enough to swing a cat, and he's after asking me what I've done with his grand pi-ano!'

I had made contact with a local film studio, where some inserts and special effects were being shot for a picture in production back home – *49th Parallel*, starring Eric Portman. They required some flags depicting the Red Rising Sun of Japan and the Black Nazi Swastika – half a dozen of each. Short of draughtsmen, the Art Director kindly entrusted me with this task, suggesting I could do them at the 'Y' during any free time. I made a few that evening before desk duty, and after a cat nap, finished the remainder next morning, pinning them to a board in a neat row. I left the board on the chest of drawers and, after taking an early lunch, went off to work.

I should have known better.

Having watched Cagney up in the clouds all afternoon, I was brought down to earth with a bang when I entered the lobby of the YMCA and saw two gigantic Mounties standing there, looking as if they had just stepped out from the chorus line of *Rose Marie*. They grasped me under my armpits and practically frogmarched me to their Headquarters, where I was grilled.

That Irish cleaner-up of unconsidered trifles had seen the flags where the piano used to be and, with commendable if somewhat over-zealous patriotism, reported me as a suspect spy.

A 'phone call to the studios soon put me in the clear. I was released and, cavorting gleefully to freedom, slipped on the icy road, and lay there concussed.

The first thing I remember was standing in a snowdrift somewhere out in the 'sticks', having wandered about in a semi-conscious state for several hours. On the opposite side of the street was a flea pit showing Arthur Askey in *The Ghost Train*. Something so English I just had to see. Buying the cheapest available seat, I went up into the 'Gods', sat down, and promptly fell asleep.

* * *

By mid-March, the proceeds from my various activities provided just enough for my ticket to Halifax.

I covered the waterfront, mingling with the Merchant Navy lads, trying to find out how I could get aboard any ship bound for the United Kingdom. On Sunday morning, 15 March, I was rewarded with the information that the SS Tilpala, due to sail that night, was minus a deserter, and if he didn't show up, I could take his place.

He didn't – I did.

She was a 5,500-ton banana ship of the Fyffe and Elder line, designed and equipped for tropical climes and seas, hardly ideal for the North Atlantic in wintry conditions, and even the issue of heavy jerseys and sou'westers could do little to keep the cold at bay. We were instructed to remain fully clothed throughout the voyage, in case we had to take to the lifeboats in any emergency, or if we suddenly landed in the drink. I needed no encouragement to comply with this command. I did find the obligatory 'Mae West' a bit of a bind at times, although I knew that I might have occasion to be very, very glad of her bosomy company before we caught sight of the White Cliffs of Dover, or wherever we were destined to disembark.

The ever-present danger from lurking submarines, and the knowledge that the dreaded Tirpitz was on the prowl, kept everyone alert as we put to sea in convoy, a complement of about 50 craft, mostly oil tankers, all sailing at the top speed of the slowest ship. Just prior to the point of no return, our 'greyhound' escorts had to leave us without their protection for 24 hours, until similar vessels out from Great Britain could pick us up and nurse us safely back to Blighty. When we eventually docked in Liverpool, I learnt that, under sealed orders, the Captain had been told to take the peace-time route, as it was considered unlikely that the enemy would have laid mines in such an obvious shipping lane. The Admiralty were right in this conjecture, or we were lucky, making the crossing without loss in 12 days.

They were not without a few contretemps as far as I was concerned, apart from the fact that I was beginning to pong like a polecat and could lose all my best friends. I was very nearly knocked out of my bunk every time our depth charges were dropped, and had fallen a little foul of a rather belligerent young 'snotty', who saw me one evening, leaning on the rail, lighting a cigarette. Sweeping it from my mouth, he snapped, 'Put that thing out, man! Don't you realise the glow can be seen for miles? You are putting us all at risk.'

He was quite right, of course. We sailed 'blacked out' at night.

I was then appointed as look out, and watched the duffle-coated deck hand I was relieving descend from his swaying perch. As he passed me, I said uncertainly, 'It's rather a long way up, isn't it?'

Teeth chattering, and blue with cold, he grinned at me from under his hood. 'Wotcher want, mate?' he asked. 'Wings?'

Climbing the angled ratlin wasn't too bad, but where it joined the mast was a different kettle of fish altogether. Here the climb became vertical, then out and under the base of the barrel, which served as the crow's nest. This was a most hazardous manoeuvre, and I was absolutely terrified, my icy fingers unable to grip anything properly. To avoid slipping on the frostbound rope ladder, I had donned a pair of plimsolls, and when at last I managed to scramble over the edge of the contraption, my feet sank into about 12 inches of broken ice-cold rain water.

Looking down, the deck seemed impossibly narrow, and all around was a vast expanse of grey and menacing rolling ocean.

Since I gave no apparent signs of life when my regulation period of watch ended, my fellow mariners below guessed something must be amiss. I was frozen stiff, incapable of movement or speech, and a bosun's chair had to be rigged, so that I could be lowered to comparative warmth and safety, like a carcass of mutton taken from a refrigerator.

My second attempt to help win the war was no more successful than my fiasco as a blood donor.

When the Skipper heard that I was an actor, he muttered some uncomplimentary expletive, and put me in charge of the ship's cat for the rest of my service at sea. I enjoyed this assignment, and other lighter moments, too; drinking large mugs of steaming hot cocoa with the cat purring on my lap, and after supper, playing endless games of Monopoly with members of the crew, when I seemed to spend my entire time going to jail, heavily mortgaged, and never collecting two hundred 'smackers'.

* * *

On Friday 27 March 1942, under a festoon of cabled barrage balloons, hoisted to hinder attack from the air, we steamed slowly up the River Mersey, making way carefully between the hulks of sunken ships. Jutting from the graveyard of murky water, the silent sentinels of gaunt masts and criss-crossed spars resembled uneven rows of broken crucifixes – fitting memorials to mark their final resting place.

It may not have been as imposing as the approach to Manhattan, but the sight of the grimy and bomb-scarred Royal Liver Building and Dock Board Offices held more magic for me than all the skyscrapers in the world, and I was filled with overwhelming joy as I walked down the gangplank and stood in England once again.

Like the Pope, I knelt and kissed the ground. I was so glad, and so thankful, to be home at last – and all in one piece.

5

ENGLAND'S GREEN AND
PLEASANT LAND

'WOULD YOU CARE for some tea, sir?'

I was occupying a third class compartment, when the door slid back and there stood a restaurant car attendant, immaculately attired in a white jacket.

When in New York City, I was under the impression that such luxuries were just fond memories over here in wartime. I had visited a large store which had generously devoted its entire space and energies to collecting 'Bundles for Britain', anything from clothing to foodstuffs, and on one of the walls an enlarged clip from a newsreel, showing St Paul's Cathedral engulfed in flames and smoke, was projected continuously in order to give the citizens of that country some idea of what was going on a few thousand miles away on the other side of the Atlantic.

It was therefore a lovely surprise to hear this more than welcome suggestion. After nearly three and a half years in the wilderness of coffee, I was simply longing for that panacea for all British ills – a good old cup of strong sweet char. My wages as a very un-able-bodied seaman had covered my train fare to Reigate via London, with a little left over. Unable to resist the temptation, I lashed out and accepted this indulgence, by way of celebration. It was served on a tray, with a slab of saffron-yellow cake, a single cherry peeking out from its centre.

Having seen so many vast areas of arid wasteland in the States, it was sheer bliss to sip my tea, and watch the panorama of our beautiful Shires unfold itself and pass peacefully by the window: neat hedgerows, skeletal trees sparkling with rime and black with rooks cawing noisily amongst their nests, ploughed fields and pasture land, revealing patches of verdant grass where the snow had melted, studded with cattle and sheep gently grazing, beside meandering rivers and streams. It was a wonderfully soothing sight, and the cake was delicious.

A mess mate on the Tilpala had given me his family address in Ealing, where I could break my journey and spend the night before proceeding next morning to Reigate Station, the nearest to my brother's farm in Surrey, where my parents were living.

As I crossed London from Euston to Ealing, I saw signs of the appalling devastation the capital had endured during bombing raids, but with the inspired leadership of that great British Bulldog, Winston Churchill, the indomitable character and unquenchable cheerfulness of the British in adversity was evident wherever I went, their stoicism filling me with pride.

I enjoyed the first hot bath I'd taken for over a fortnight, wallowing in five inches of water, this being the standard depth following an appeal from the Government to economise and save fuel.

My luggage was now reduced to a sailor's ditty bag, as I had been reluctantly compelled to jettison whatever I could in my wake, but I still retained a few precious books and my paint box. The bag was pretty heavy, so I telephoned from a kiosk to let the folks at home know that the 'prodigal' had returned, and perhaps get a lift in the car. I had written from Canada, telling them I was on my way, but my movements and everything else being so uncertain, I couldn't let them have a specific date. Conscious of their concern, I also wanted to be quite sure I was safe and sound, and within 'spitting' distance, before arousing any false hopes.

Getting no reply, I guessed they were all at work out in the fields, so, slinging the pack across my back, I walked the footpathed way under an English sky, through woods and meadows, already showing signs of an early spring in these warmer southern regions.

Arriving at the cottage, I knocked on the door. Mother opened it, took one look at me, and fainted again.

*   *   *

Entertainments National Services Association, abbreviated to ENSA, and translated by His Majesty's Forces as 'Every Night Something Awful', had its headquarters in London at the Theatre Royal, Drury Lane, under the directorship of Basil Dean. Henry Oscar was head of the Drama Department, and within a few days of my homecoming, I arranged an appointment to see him.

Fate's guiding hand was drawing her strings ever tighter, and this was another case of being in the right place at the right moment.

Noël Coward's *Private Lives* was currently touring all the Navy, Army and Air Force stations in the British Isles. The actor playing the leading part had been called up, and would be leaving very soon. When Mr Oscar asked me if I could be ready to take over such a lengthy role in so short a time, I said yes. Later, he told me he thought I was mad.

I learnt the lines walking over Salisbury Plain near Stonehenge, for I was billeted at Devizes, Wiltshire, with the rest of the small cast, and in five days I was playing Elyot Chase opposite Sonia Dresdel's Amanda Prynne, with Yvonne Hills and Humphrey Morton completing the complement of leading players, in a production stage managed by Joan Craft.

To confound the enemy, should he invade, and make life more difficult for him, all signposts and railway station name plates had been removed, so we seldom knew where we were, except for the cities and country towns where we lodged. In remote rural areas, stately country mansions had been requisitioned and stripped of all valuables, which were stored away in safety for the duration.

Looking dwarfed and very out of place in bedrooms more accustomed to imposing four posters, folding army camp beds had been installed with short blue-grey blankets, which either kept your feet warm or your shoulders, but not simultaneously.

Ten pounds per week was the statutory wage for all performers, three pounds being handed over for whatever the accommodation, as were our ration books.

Apart from the satisfaction of giving a certain pleasure to the troops, or at least relieving their boredom for a few hours, it was a wonderful opportunity to visit quaint villages and see countryside entirely new to me, and I revelled in this delightful bonus.

Sonia Dresdel had been on the road with this play for over a year. She was completely exhausted, and needed a rest. So a new leading lady had to be found to play Amanda.

*   *   *

…From the stage door stepped a vision, and my heart skipped a beat. I had never met him, yet I knew, deep in my deepest heart, we had been together before. Tall and lean, a pale, almost haggard face, with astonishingly large, blue eyes: on his head an old grey velvet hat, with a hole between the dents of its crown, a jacket beyond description and repair, spotless white shirt badly frayed at cuffs and collar, a pair of once dark blue corduroy trousers, most of the nap long since worn away through constant wear, down-at-heel shoes of grey suede. Later, I was to discover the soles were as worn down as the heels, and had holes as large as half crowns in their centres, also woollen stockings that have never known the comfort of a darning needle. He walked with a slight limp, using an ash walking stick, the ferrule now a mere useless ring of metal around its tip, on his back a huge and obviously heavy kit bag, such as sailors use.

There was an aura about this 'belovèd vagabond'. His hands told me he was either a musician or an artist – they reminded

> *me of those drawn by Albrecht Dürer – and when he bent*
> *over one of mine to kiss it, a faint and quite delightful waft of*
> *tobacco and lavender water hung upon the air. I knew I would*
> *love him for the rest of my days – and beyond…*

It was in the month of May 1942, and Helen was outside the Theatre Royal, waiting to join the rest of the company in the coach which would take us to Colchester. She had been engaged to replace Sonia Dresdel, and that was how she described her first sight of me in a letter to a friend, when I came down from Henry Oscar's office.

We sat together in the front seat, so that we could run through our scenes during the journey. She was word perfect, and soon we began to talk of other things…

The little Red Indian chief from the Dulwich Village reservation of 1917 had grown up and met his squaw.

Her father, Ernest Beck, hailed from Lancashire, and was the proprietor of the James Beck Spinning Company, at one time the largest firm of cotton spinners in Russia. Whilst there, he married the daughter of the Polish Baroness Bronikowska and General Carl Enckell, who was Swedish.

Helen was born on 8 February 1905 in St Petersburg, now Leningrad, and became multilingual, speaking fluent English, French, Russian and German, and possessed a profound love for, and knowledge of, classical music and literature. By way of contrast, she also adored whodunnits and Jimmy 'Schnozzle' Durante.

With such a pedigree, I often introduced her as my very own petite League of Nations.

When Tsarist Russia crumbled under the Bolsheviks, the family – mother, father, three daughters and two sons – fled to England, taking only such possessions as they could carry between them, and leaving behind a large fortune, which they never recovered.

Having been brought up in the lap of luxury, with personal maids and servants in constant attention for all their needs, they were now compelled to fend for themselves, even having to learn how to cook. Helen adapted herself to this new way of life, with the result that she did everything superbly, including her darning, which resembled the finest embroidery.

She worked in André Charlot's revues, and became one of CB Cochran's 'Young Ladies', as his showgirls were called. He considered this title more dignified, and added refinement to his glamorous presentations. Helen appeared in several of them with Anna Neagle, and went to America, under his management, with Gertrude Lawrence. In 1926 she took part in *What Price Glory?*, made in Hollywood, starring Dolores del Rio, Victor McLaglen and Edmund Lowe, directed by Raoul Walsh.

Back in England, she was selected as English tutor to Mme Yvette la Brousse, who was soon to become the Begum Aga Khan. When she left for Egypt, she offered Helen a permanent job in that country, but Helen did not wish to leave her parents or England, and declined the invitation. Instead, she performed secretarial duties for Jessie Matthews and Sonnie Hale, who were married at that time, and then started a career in various repertory companies, helping to support her family in any way she could.

Her brother, Reginald Beck, became a most skilled and successful film editor, working in that capacity on many productions directed by Laurence Olivier and Joseph Losey.

Helen had endured the humiliation of a disastrous marriage, her husband eventually deserting her, and when hostilities began she was in repertory at Bath, and left to join the Civil Defence in London, living with her mother and father in Kensington. When the Blitz was at its height, she spent three successive shifts close to an unexploded bomb. With a thoroughness typical of her self-taught domesticity, she gave it a good polish every evening.

* * *

A few camps had Garrison Theatres, properly equipped, but for the most part our stages were mock-up affairs in drill halls or vast, cold and draughty aeroplane hangars. One of these had no rostrum at all, so long and flimsy trestle tables had been placed end to end, which made us bounce through the performance as if on a trampoline, taking care not to fall through the ever widening gaps between the tables, as they gradually shifted apart owing to our movements.

Although we never witnessed such mortification, we were told that reluctant servicemen were sometimes marched in at gunpoint by heartless sergeant majors, determined that the 'concert party' should have an audience, even if under duress. Without doubt, this was apocryphal, but we did overhear an enlightening conversation between two 'erks', contemplating the noticeboard in the NAAFI canteen, where *Private Lives* was billed for their evening's delectation.

'You goin' ternite, Bert?'

'Nah! I ain't gonna bovver. 'Sonly anovver of them plays orl abart VD.'

However, Noël Coward's elegant romp was usually received with great enthusiasm, the fight between Helen and me in the second act, ending with a gramophone record being cracked over my head by an irate 'Amanda', always proving very popular – doubly so on one memorable occasion.

Our ASM had obtained a job lot of old discs from a junk shop, and amongst them was one of the unbreakable kind. Helen was not to know this – nor was I – until she came to use it. She kept whacking my napper, and soon the record was U-shaped and I was rendered punch drunk. Her unsuccessful efforts to smash the wretched thing were so prolonged that when she paused to take a breath, a helpful piece of advice came from somewhere in the back row: 'Why don't you sock 'im in the jaw, girl!'

To ensure that I would last the course, this particular prop was carefully vetted from then on, to avoid any repetition.

Another incident of such joyous 'audience participation' took place when we were entertaining the Navy in Dover, and the

Luftwaffe decided to attack the harbour at the same time.

Towards the end of Act One, Sibyl, played by Yvonne Hills, and Elyot have an altercation. Reaching a peak of exasperation, he snaps, 'Don't quibble, Sibyl.'

We heard the drone of 'planes, and shortly after this unwelcome sound, shells started to whine down, and our own anti-aircraft guns went into action. We had to shout in order to make ourselves heard above the racket.

At the conclusion of the scene, Sibyl drinks a cocktail. The combination of fear and vibration made poor Yvonne shake so violently that she was incapable of holding the glass steady, spilling its contents down her décolletage as she attempted to take a sip, whereupon a voice, again from the rear of the hall, yelled out, 'Don't dribble, Sibyl!'

That resolute and witty rating brought the house down in a far nicer way than any bomb would have done, and relieved the nervous tension which was beginning to grip us all.

In September, we were in Wolverhampton, and I received instructions to attend a Medical Board. Again classified as Grade 4, I was declared exempt.

Helen and I continued with ENSA, which included hospitals in its itinerary. Because of the nature of their injuries, the patients of an orthopaedic ward in Oxford were compelled to lie completely prone. Their beds, with large looking glasses attached to the ends, were arranged in serried ranks, the heads toward the stage, so the invalids watched us as if looking into the rear view mirrors of so many stationary motor cars. They were a most appreciative audience, and being unable to clap, they cheered to the echo at the final curtain. It was a deeply moving experience.

Throughout our first five months together, I had become acutely aware of Helen's painful cough. The damp atmosphere which prevailed in many of our 'digs', and the general climate of England, aggravated this disturbing condition. One night, during an uncontrollable spasm, I noticed some blood on her handkerchief, and went immediately to call a doctor. Unable to rouse him by telephone, I borrowed a bicycle and pedalled to the village of Bridge, near Canterbury, where he lived. Getting no response from my repeated knocking on his door, I waited outside until he returned in the early hours of the morning, having been out on another case.

When we got back to Barham Court, where Helen and I were staying, he saw at once that she had suffered a haemorrhage...

This was the first indication I had of things to come.

Towards Christmas time we were stationed in a hostel at Taunton, Somerset, where I was laid low with congestion of the lung. The doctor was informed of my susceptibility to this ailment as a child, and warned Helen I would need nursing night and day until the crisis was over. She insisted upon undertaking this task, and took to it as a duck to water, passing her long night vigils in knitting me a beautiful, warm pullover and shawl. She concocted the most appetising dishes from powdered egg and spam, and whatever else she could lay hands upon. A coal fire in the bedsitting room was also stipulated – a luxury unheard of during the war, and greatly appreciated.

After his final examination the doctor pointed to Helen and said, 'You owe your life to this young lady.'

The show was cancelled until I was convalescent, and then Helen had to continue with another actor playing Elyot before I was fit to resume. I missed her dreadfully, and as soon as I could move, I joined her in Oswestry. She had arranged for me to stay overnight with her parents in their Kensington flat, because the journey was too long to accomplish in one day. They were enchanting, her mother reminding me of that diminutive Russian actress, Maria Ouspenskaya.

Amongst the family, Mrs Beck's malapropisms were legendary. She never quite understood the English idiom, speaking with an endearing accent, and had an individual way of pronouncing certain words.

Once, she declared that her son Reggie had many 'iddy-oz-knee-*krazz*-knees,' which was the nearest she could get to 'idiosyncrasies'. When I arrived at tea time, she greeted me with regal dignity, saying, 'Sit down, I worship you,' and, offering me two plates of wafer-thin cucumber sandwiches, enquired 'Would you prefer the bread white, or wholesale?'

While I was there she had an unexpected visit from her son in law, Graham Sutherland. A charming city gentleman, very correct and abstemious, he carried a furled umbrella, and was neatly dressed and groomed, not a hair out of place, brushed with pomade which gave it a sheen.

'Ah, here's dear Gramoshka!' she exclaimed, 'plastered as usual.'

In the New Year I was back at work, but the stress and strain of this arduous tour gradually took its toll on us both, and, in the end, we were 'invalided out' of ENSA.

We went for a week's holiday to Sussex, staying in Bramber at Lavender Cottage, which was entrancing. We were highly amused by some young honeymooners, who regarded us as a mature married couple, asking for any advice we might have to offer, in our wisdom, to establish a lasting and successful marriage.

From its beginning, our relationship had been unique, as though we were continuing something that had begun in another age. It was a spiritual union, the physical element holding little importance. We just had a mutual desire to spend the rest of time together.

In Ashton-under-Lyne, before the war, the company Helen had been with folded, leaving her almost penniless, and she had been reduced to sleeping between sheets of newspaper to keep herself warm in an unheated room. She became desperately ill, and in her delirium, imagined she saw the Angel of Death standing at the foot of the couch, beckoning. She had cried out, 'No! Not yet – there is something left for me to do.'

'Now I know what it was,' she told me, when I asked her to be my wife. 'I was spared to look after you, and that is all I ever want to do. But you are a young man – I am eight years your senior. You must be free. I don't want you to feel possessed. I shall always be there when you need me, for whatever reason.'

I say, with Milton, 'Love, sweetness, goodness in her person shined.'

It is a well known fact in our circle of friends that I married Helen for her money: she had 30 pounds and I had about 23. We did so quietly on 10 April 1943, at the Royal Borough of Kensington Register Office, Helen having bought the ring for nine shillings off a stall in the Portobello Road. It adorns my watch chain now as I write. Her parents acted as witnesses – I had not told mine, in case there was any opposition.

We experienced no difficulty in finding somewhere to live in London, so many people having left to escape the incessant bombing. We settled in Airlie Gardens, Campden Hill Road, taking a garden flat at three pounds per week, not far from Mr and Mrs Beck. We had little furniture – an unwanted divan bed and two armchairs given us by Helen's married sister. The rest had been converted by Helen from wooden crates and boxes found on bomb sites, which she padded with newspaper and covered with material. They looked very presentable, and were indeed serviceable.

On my behalf, Helen had long since pawned, and finally sold, her remaining pieces of Fabergé-delicate gold and enamel Russian Easter eggs plus some exquisite jewellery, saying it was me that mattered, not possessions. There came a time when our finances reached zero, and I had to apply for National Assistance. When the inspector came to view our premises, checking we were genuinely in need of help and had nothing we could sell, he raised an eyebrow at the apparent splendour of our surroundings, until he lifted one of the coverings and saw 'Johnnie Walker, born 1820 – still going strong' stencilled on the rough wooden side of what looked like a dainty foot stool.

He left us with a cheque for £50.

I had to do the same sort of thing at a later date, this time seeking aid from the Actors Benevolent Fund. The official asked me if I'd ever contributed to any charities, to which I replied I had never been in a position to do so.

'But you've given your services free for midnight charity matinées, haven't you?' he asked.

'Oh yes, several times,' I answered.

He gave me a cheque for £40.

The audiences for those shows consisted mainly of fellow professionals, whose support and reception made them joyous affairs.

* * *

If we pursued individual careers, we knew there would be inevitable separations, which neither of us wanted, so we decided that I should remain the breadwinner, with Helen contributing her wealth of experience and knowledge to help me in the struggles ahead. I started to construct a model tithe barn, and Helen – always so ready to admire, encourage and compliment – exclaimed, 'How typical, building something while others are destroying.'

All places of entertainment had been closed when war began, but their doors were soon opened again, despite the danger from air raids.

I had joined Al Parker's agency, and he contracted my first appearance in the West End, playing two roles, Alexander I, Emperor of Russia, and Captain Ramballe, a French officer, in a mammoth production of Tolstoy's *War and Peace*, directed by Julius Gellner and presented by Tom Arnold. We went on a prior to London tour, opening in Blackpool and then moving on to Manchester, where we had splendid 'digs' in that well known Mecca for all strolling players, Ackers Street.

There were 56 in the cast, among them a most talented playwright, Ronald Millar, now Sir Ronald, with whom we spent a lot of time.

His lodgings were quite disgusting, so he joined us in ours, sleeping in the bath, which we stuffed with pillows and a quilt.

Like everyone else who met her, he adored Helen. He read one of his plays to us, and found her observations and suggestions invaluable, and continued this ritual for many years to come.

We opened at the Phoenix Theatre, London, in September 1943, the first night lasting nearly five hours, by which time most of our patrons had left, or were fast asleep in their seats. The spectacle did not survive, and all too soon I was 'resting' again – that discreet expression always applied to out of work actors – and paying weekly visits to the Labour Exchange.

My next engagement was even shorter, because we never opened. The title eludes me, but I remember Bernard Miles was involved, and the director a refugee from Hitler's purge of the Jews. The part assigned to me was a Civil Engineer, and I had that sinking feeling we were doomed from the start when he asked me quite seriously, 'Doz this mean you are polite viz zer machines?'

After a few days' rehearsing, the piece was abandoned.

Once upon a time, nestling beside the River Thames at Kew Bridge, Chiswick, was the 'Q' Theatre, supervised by Beatrice and Jack de Leon, and I worked for them quite often. Their policy was to present weekly revivals of successful plays and also to 'try out' new ones, in the hope of transferring to the West End. The top salary was ten pounds, which included ten days' rehearsal. Not lucrative, but a useful 'shop window', because London managements would come down to see if there were any pickings.

I was performing there with Sonia Dresdel and Renée Asherson in The Dark Potential, by Joan Morgan, when Helen was taken ill. She had been looking very wan, suffering from severe abdominal pain, and was admitted to the Samaritan Free Hospital for Women in Marylebone Road. There was a coffee stall directly opposite, and wanting to be near at hand in case of bombing, I spent every night there after the show, drinking tea and munching stodgy macaroon tarts with shredded coconut decorating their tops.

Helen had to undergo major surgery for an hysterectomy, and a lifeless foetus was discovered within her womb.

The Dark Potential, renamed *This Was a Woman*, transferred to the Comedy Theatre where it ran for nearly a year. I didn't go with the company, being reluctant to leave Helen alone in the evenings and during matinées, when she was convalescent after her dismissal from hospital.

With hindsight, it was just as well. Fate was up to her tricks again.

*   *   *

The next play I was in did not last long, but it had a most rewarding sequel. Written by Paul Anthony, *Happy Few* opened at the Cambridge Theatre in October 1944. I was cast as Private Charles, a Free Frenchman.

Concurrently, Terence Rattigan's *While the Sun Shines* was a tremendous success at the Globe Theatre, Shaftesbury Avenue, with Jane Baxter, Michael Wilding and Hugh Wakefield. There was yet another French character in this play, Lieutenant Colbert, played by Eugene Deckers. Deckers had been ordered to rest by his doctor, and Elsie Beyer, General Manager of HM Tennent Ltd, the presenters, came to see the play I was in, and took me for a real Frenchman. I was invited to fill the impending vacancy.

I have no languages, experiencing enough difficulty in learning my own, and it was ironic that my initial incursions into the West End should all be as foreigners. Helen had taught me the accents by rote, and it was a tribute to her splendid tuition that Miss Beyer should have been so convinced by my portrayal in *Happy Few*. Four years later, Lieutenant Colbert and my 'command' of his lingo were to crop up again to our subsequent advantage.

Rattigan's comedy opened in December 1943. Ronald Squire had been the original Duke of Ayr and Stirling, the role now taken over by Mr Wakefield.

Brenda Bruce, who played Mabel Crum, brought her spaniel to the Globe each night, keeping it locked safely in her dressing room during the show.

Michael Wilding, with roguish humour – and to dispel the inevitable boredom of a long run – would shape brown paper soaked in water into 'naughty Fidos', and placed these lifelike replicas in strategic positions about the stage. His unsuspecting fellow mummers often encountered them on their exits or entrances, and would take involuntary high steps over rather than tread in what they thought was doggy 'No 2', muttering muffled profanities about people who dared to allow their pets to run amok in the theatre, fouling the pitch.

After a year non stop, Ronnie Squire had a short break, and when Eugene Deckers returned to the Globe Company, he went on a provincial tour with the play, and asked if I would go with him, still playing the Frenchman. Of course, dear Helen came with me, and the break from household chores helped her recuperation.

London and the South of England were now having to contend with the first of Germany's secret weapons, the V1s, pilotless flying bombs, christened 'doodle bugs' by the British. They were beastly contraptions, and when you heard the engine cut out you waited in dread, not knowing where they would land. These were followed by the V2s, explosive rockets which fell out of the sky unexpectedly and, until the last moment, unheard.

It was a relief to get away from this new menace for a spell.

On 8 May 1945 we were in Bolton when we heard the news that the European war had ended, so Ronnie arranged a celebratory dinner for all of us, the menu consisting of whale meat steaks and Woolton Pie, the only available fare. The country as a whole had been living on its nerves for so long, and now we were too exhausted to feel any real jubilation – just a heartfelt thankfulness that it was over, but knowing we still had to face the hardships of the aftermath of war. The encounter with Japan was still going on, lasting until 9 August, when it finished with the catastrophic horror of the atom bombs dropped on Hiroshima and Nagasaki.

Our tour was nearing its end, and in the last week Ronnie met an old friend of his, Edith Evans. She had been requested to re-open the Criterion Theatre in London, after its occupation by the BBC throughout the years of conflict, the chosen play being Sheridan's *The Rivals*. She asked him if he had any ideas for someone to play the melancholy lover Mr Faulkland, and he suggested me.

Oliver Messel designed the most exquisite décor, Anthony Quayle made a splendidly dashing Captain Absolute, Edith Evans was Mrs Malaprop, co-directing with William Armstrong, who complained rather pathetically that he couldn't see what was going on 'from under Edith's thumb'. That superb craftsman Tyrone Guthrie was then enlisted to act as arbitrator, and added his magic touch to the production. We always knew our performances were below par if he popped his head around the dressing room door and said, 'Loved your hat, dear'.

The play enjoyed a highly successful run, which enabled me to settle a few of my outstanding debts.

Ronnie Squire was a dear man, and very popular with audiences and his fellow actors. He had known my Aunt Maude in the old days, and often tried to persuade her to make a comeback in 'Mother' parts, but she never did. 'Such a waste of talent,' he lamented. 'She was a very fine actress. I'm glad you're following in her footsteps.'

He delighted in pulling people's legs, and whilst on the road he teased the company unmercifully, saying I was the only one who showed the proper respect due to him and, unlike them, had not become over-familiar! If I continued to be respectful, and called him 'Sir', he assured them that, when we parted, he would see to it personally that 'Cushing was well placed'. I played along with this charade, and it appealed greatly to his wry sense of humour when the joke paid off so handsomely.

After the feast, the reckoning, and mine took the form of a long spell of unemployment.

The rent for the flat had risen, ten per cent of all earnings went to my agent, and I was now just inside the Income Tax bracket, resulting in our bank statements – and me – looking red with embarrassment.

Not having enough to buy Helen a Christmas present, I painted a scarf, depicting characters from the novels of Charles Dickens, on a square of silk her Mother had rescued from Russia.

My solitary engagement in nearly nine months was a week at the 'Q' in Priestley's *They Came to a City*. Helen attended the first night wearing the scarf, which was much admired by Roberta Huby, who was in the cast. She asked if she might borrow it to show a friend of hers, a North Country textile manufacturer. Helen was reluctant to part with it even for a short time, but her instinct, which saved us on numerous occasions, made her feel this contact might prove useful, as indeed it did.

Mr X, an outspoken, self-made man if ever there was one, telephoned from Macclesfield, saying bluntly, 'Coom oop and see me. Roberta told me you're broke, but 'ave you got enoof for your fare? I'll reimburse you when you get 'ere.'

I spent a few days at his mills, learning the process of screen printing. As he showed me round, he began to expound. He told me how he had gone about raising the extra 'bit o' brass' he needed when wanting to expand his premises.

Waving a hand towards piles of silk bales stacked in a store room, he said, 'One way or t'other, this material practically spends its life in liquid, what with dyes an' all, but the Insurance boogers weren't to know, were they? Ah filled me basement wi' rolls of the stoof, then flooded it wi' water, and poot in a claim for t' damage. Ah built me new wing out o' that,' he added with pride.

He took me into his office, hung from ceiling to floor with fabric samples, ablaze with every imaginable design and colour, which was most impressive.

'Do you have any preference?' I enquired.

'Yes,' he replied, 'plain bludy white.'

I stayed in his house on the outskirts of the town, and in the evenings friends came to dinner, playing cards afterwards in the withdrawing room. It was like a hot house at Kew Gardens, with a large jardinière in one corner, full of white and blue hyacinths, filling the air with their fragrance, which even overpowered the aroma of Havana cigars.

When we were seated at the green baize table, he took a bundle of pound notes from his pocket. As he did so, one fluttered to the floor, and I bent to retrieve it.

'Leave it be,' he commanded. 'Maid'll pick it oop int' mornin',' and slapping a fistful in front of me, continued, "ere, you can play wi' these.' Seeing I was about to protest, he went on 'Don't worry – I'll win it back', and he did. I simply could not concentrate on the game, what with the hedonistic atmosphere and that 20 shilling note lying temptingly at my feet.

'Reet, lad,' he said when I departed, shaking my hand in a grip of iron. 'Now go back 'ome and start designing. I'll pay thee enoof to keep wolf from t'door. Like the Good Lord, you'll never know when I'm goin' to turn oop, so always 'ave summat ready t'show me.'

I did this for the next ten months, culminating in one scarf being accepted by Her Majesty Queen Elizabeth, now the Queen Mother.

I was to see that scarf again in the future, but under very different circumstances.

6

'FORTY AND A FAILURE'

'CAN YOU SPEAK with an American accent?'

It was autumn 1946, and *Born Yesterday* was being presented.

Al Parker had put my name forward for the part of Paul Verrall, played by William Holden in the film version of Garson Kanin's play, and I had gone to keep my appointment at the Garrick Theatre with Laurence Olivier, who was directing.

I had dreaded this question, hoping Paul could be portrayed as an Englishman, so I shook my head.

'But you've been to America,' he said.

I muttered something fatuous about having also been to Scotland, but I still couldn't speak Gaelic.

'That's not quite the same thing, boy.'

Desperately as I needed the job, I could never abide phoney accents, and, rather self-consciously, quoted the Bard: 'To thine own self be true...'

Laurence smiled at me quizzically, saying, 'Well, I appreciate your not wasting my time. I shall remember you.'

Regarding this as another version of the usual fob-off, 'Don't call us we'll call you', I went out into the cold of Charing Cross Road, feeling deflated. Several months were to pass before I found out how wrong I had been in this assumption.

Apart from looking after me and her parents with tender, loving care, Helen had taken in sewing to help make ends meet. I was worried about her persistent cough, as there seemed to be no cure for it, and concerned that she was doing too much for everyone else, to her own detriment.

The work provided by Mr X had been a godsend, and through his good auspices I had been similarly contracted by 'Sammy' scarves, who supplied Marks and Spencer with that merchandise, but the remuneration only covered our weekly overheads, and the bank larder was beginning to look distinctly bare.

This anxious period of the doldrums was lifted briefly by one of those unsolicited gestures of thoughtful generosity that touch the heart far deeper than the pocket.

Michael Wilding spoke a little Russian, and loved to keep in practice by chatting with Helen in this tongue. I would listen enraptured, not understanding one single word of their conversations. He came to tea one day for his 'lesson', and our impecunious existence must have been pretty obvious to that sensitive fellow. When we retired to bed that night, we found an envelope lying on my pillow containing £100, and a note from Michael saying, 'Just to tide you over until your boat comes in...'

Whilst designing head scarves, I still kept an ear to the ground as to what was going on in the theatre world, and had accepted another week at the 'Q' Theatre, playing Lieutenant Colbert yet again.

Laurence Olivier's right-hand man was Anthony Bushell, who had been present at the Garrick when I was interviewed. A book entitled *The Film Hamlet* was published in 1948 by the Saturn Press, and the following extract written by Bushell, in a chapter dealing with the casting of that film, describes the fortuitous consequence:

> ...Osric, that sinister Beau Brummell of the Danish Court,
> fell pat into place. Casting our stage production of Born
> Yesterday, in the autumn of 1946, Laurence and I had seen a
> clutch of young actors for the juvenile lead, among them a
> striking looking character, Peter Cushing, who stuck in our
> minds by a frank refusal even to attempt an American accent.
> Weeks later, watching another actor at the 'Q', I was struck by

a performance of the Frenchman in While the Sun Shines, *so true in style and accent that I looked for a French name on the programme. It was Mr Cushing, and he speaks no French. Here evidently was an actor, and his test for Osric disposed of the last of our problems on the male side...*

I started letting my hair and beard grow immediately, as required by the designs of Roger Furse, and soon reached that scruffy stage when it begins to look like sheer laziness. Walking in Holland Park studying my lines, the sky suddenly opened, and I quickly sought shelter from the downpour in the ruins of a bombed building. Squatting on a heap of rubble, deep in Shakespearian thought, I gradually became aware of two figures, standing with hands in pockets, staring at me intently.

Deserters from the armed forces were being rounded up, and they suspected I was one. They accosted me with a quickfire interrogation, random questions which utterly confused my Osric-ridden brain. The only one I remember answering without hesitation was 'What's your wife's name?'

Oh, dear! I thought – it's going to be a repeat of Montreal, except it was raining instead of snowing, and these chaps were much smaller, wearing Humphrey Bogart-type raincoats as opposed to magnificent uniforms, and bore no visible weapons.

In the war years, everyone was compelled by law to carry their identification card, and as the inquisition continued, I recalled I still had mine in my wallet, so I produced it. After a glance of verification, one of them said, 'We knew you were on the level – the guilty always have answers ready. You didn't even know what time of day it was,' which I accepted as a sort of backhanded compliment.

The other detective stretched up his hand to an overhanging branch and, plucking a sprig of early lilac, said, 'Give this to your missus – and get yourself a shave some time.'

* * *

Sitting in the make-up chair at Denham Studios about 6.30 one
morning, I saw Laurence reflected in the mirror as he came into
the room.

Putting his hands on my shoulders, he said, 'Peter boy, I'm
taking an Old Vic company to Australia later this year, and I'd love
you to come. Will you give it some thought?'

I assured him I had no need to think, my only concern being
that I didn't want to be away from Helen.

'There were enough separations during the war,' said Laurence.
'Of course your Helen shall be one of us. I'm delighted! See you on
the set,' and, kissing the top of my head, he left.

My hair was quite long by this time, and tidy. Impudent errand
boys would giggle and jeer, 'Wot-o, Paganini! Still on the fiddle,
are yer?' Laurence was also using his own hair, cropped and dyed
blond, for his portrayal of the Prince of Denmark, and remarked
it was a funny thing that we were the only two in the cast who
looked as if we were wearing wigs.

One of the scenes involving Hamlet, Osric and Horatio, played
by Norman Wooland, took place as we walked down a wide stone
spiral stairway. This created some technical difficulties for the sound
department, and the whole scene had to be post synched when the
shooting of the picture was completed. This process requires each
actor to synchronise his words with his lip movements, watching a
continuous loop of the section of film concerned.

During the interim of my finishing the photography and
waiting for this session, an abscess erupted in my hard palate, and
the only way the dentist could drain the poison was by extracting
three perfectly good front teeth. Helen in her wisdom realised this
bothered me a great deal, and eased my agitation by saying that if
I'd lost them playing rugby for England I'd be very proud, and that
I was the only person she knew who managed to look younger
instead of older without his false plate! Love is blind, they say:
but Helen saw everything with infinite clarity, and beatification. To
humour me she reminded me of something Gilbert Harding once

said: '"Like children, false teeth should be seen and not heard." Yours are very well behaved!'

When I reported for the post synching, Laurence detected something odd in the way I spoke, and asked what was the matter, so I told him.

'I know one thing that's worrying you, boy,' he observed. 'You are not using your lips, because you're afraid you might spit when you speak.' Putting his face within a few inches of mine, he continued, 'Now drown me. It'll be a glorious death, so long as I can hear what you're saying.'

He once confided in me how lonely it was when you reach a pinnacle, and how no one dared to approach him regarding his performances. 'One cannot be good all the time, and it would be so helpful if someone told me when and where I was going wrong.'

Helen's brother Reggie was Associate Producer, and supervised the editing. It was most satisfying for me to repay a loan he had made some time ago, and also dear Michael Wilding's contribution to our welfare. I had – and always have had – a horror of debts. Helen said I was apt to settle accounts – when I could – even before I received any invoice...

With my abiding love of cigarette cards, I always wished I could have been featured on one, but they had disappeared long before I was in any position to be considered for such an accolade. But, to my joy, I did become a toy! As a boy, I made a model theatre from large sheets of thin card, which I bought at a harberdashers in South Croydon. They cost twopence each, and were covered with colourful figures and scenery depicting melodramas and pantomimes. My favourite was *Robinson Crusoe*, followed closely by *Black Eyed Susan* and *Sinbad the Sailor*. I cut them out, and spent many happy hours producing these lavish spectacles in our play room.

Soon after *Hamlet* was released, Benjamin Pollock published a small cut-out book of this film, and there I was – twice! – a 2½ inch tall Osric! – one solo, and the other with Laertes (Terence Morgan) dying in my arms.

In that same year, JB Priestley wrote *The High Toby* especially for Puffin Picture Books, exquisitely designed by Doris Zinkeisen, and a single performance of this little piece was given at a large London store – Heal's, in Tottenham Court Road. The actors were hidden behind a curtain which enclosed the miniature stage, where they manipulated the figurines fixed to long-handled wire stands, whilst reading their lines, like a play on the wireless minus a microphone. I was invited to take part, surrounded by a cast as distinguished as Grandfather Cushing's had been in 1892! – headed by Sir Ralph Richardson and his wife Meriel Forbes, Joyce Redman and Robert Speaight, produced by his brother George. All the proceeds were donated to a charity.

Noël Coward had invited the Oliviers and us to see a show. Heating restrictions were still in force, and the theatre box we occupied was like a fridge. Vivien kept her mink coat on, but Helen didn't have such a thing, and her low-cut backless evening gown – the only one she possessed, which she had worn for Amanda – offered no protection. Her flesh was covered with tiny mountains of goose-pimples, as she sat there shivering. Noël stealthily removed one of the plush curtains from its brass rings and wrapped it around her, saying in that clipped voice we all knew and loved so much: 'That will keep you warm, dear – you look as if you've just been plucked, ready for the oven.'

* * *

Rehearsals for the three plays which comprised the Old Vic programme started in a Camden Town warehouse, which had been used by a bankrupt theatrical management as a store for scenery, furnishings and the usual bric-à-brac associated with some long forgotten offerings. The damp hit us like a body blow as we trooped into this erstwhile Aladdin's Cave, and our leading character actor, George Relph, said it was the result of all the tears shed by actors over the years who had never been paid for their services.

Laurence Olivier had been knighted in the Birthday Honours of 1947. Some 12 months later, he led a 'band of brothers', 38 strong, through a year's trek to the other side of the world, 'down under', with his lady Vivien Leigh.

We sailed from Liverpool on a chilly winter's day, and after five weeks the coast of Western Australia hove in sight across our bows, in sweltering weather. Anchored outside Fremantle Harbour, awaiting high tide, we felt embalmed by its intensity, and a humid offshore breeze, laden with the acrid, oily perfume of Eucalyptus trees, added to this discomfort.

Having unpacked, Helen and I went for a stroll in the cool of the evening, which was still as hot as a heatwave back home. We sat down on the sward of a park, and presently had a sensation that the ground was on the move. Putting my hand to the grass, it came into contact with a swarm of large horny beetles. The whole area was thick with the things, so we left them to get on with whatever they might be doing, and retired to our hotel, scattering a trail of insects behind us as they dropped off our clothing.

The Commonwealth Season opened with *The School for Scandal* at the Capitol Theatre, Perth – a cinema of such colossal dimensions it resembled Vespasian's amphitheatre in Rome. When Sir Laurence first surveyed the interior, he said we'd better forget all about Richard Brinsley Sheridan's intimate little comedy, dress up as early Christian martyrs instead, and throw ourselves to the lions.

This could have come to pass at our next scheduled stop, Adelaide, when a freak storm struck the zoo one night, the hurricane-force wind tearing down some of the cages. The following morning, those big, ferocious cats roamed the streets, and the populace were told through police car loud hailers: 'Unless you want to be eaten alive, shut all doors and windows, and remain inside until further notice. You have been warned.'

We took the hint.

Our itinerary covered Melbourne, Sydney, Brisbane, and then we went by flying boat to Hobart, Tasmania, before proceeding to New Zealand, where we played the four principal cities in the North and South Islands – Auckland, Wellington, Christchurch and Dunedin.

Shakespeare's *Richard III* and *The Skin of Our Teeth* by Thornton Wilder had been added to our repertoire early in the season, and the pavements outside the theatres and agencies were thronged every night with people bivouacking, to ensure they would secure seats when the doors opened at 9.00 am. Some had travelled hundreds of miles from the 'outback' to see a single performance, and tickets were sold on the black market at exorbitant prices.

All three plays were greeted with tumultuous applause at curtain fall, but we were mystified by the complete silence during the interpretations.

Sir Laurence had been told before setting out that Australasia was starved of live shows, films being the main source of entertainment. He and Vivien were held in such high regard that audiences considered it wrong to give vent to their emotions whilst those theatrical giants were actually performing, sitting in reverential quietness as if attending a church service. Sir Laurence decided to educate and put them at ease by giving a little lecture in front of the tabs before we began. He asked them to let us hear they were enjoying themselves by laughing or crying, or whatever else they might feel like doing to express their reactions, rather than leaving it all until the end, because that would add to their own pleasure and to ours, by letting us know as we proceeded that we were succeeding in our endeavour to please.

We were a very harmonious, close knit group, and our leaders went to great lengths to keep us happy and content throughout the tour. There were few real theatres, most of our playhouses being cinemas which contained limited accommodation for our personnel. The managers always provided large dressing rooms of some kind for our two stars, leaving the rest to fend for themselves as best we could. But the Oliviers would not hear of this, insisting we shared their commodious compartments, whilst they made do with makeshift affairs rigged up in the wings of the stage, comprised of tables and chairs, screened off with curtaining to provide some privacy.

All our birthdays were remembered, and celebrated with parties and presents. On free Sundays, they took us on sightseeing trips by coach, river trips by motor launch, and surf riding at Bondi and other beaches. We played cricket once or twice on the Test ground at Melbourne, and I did a little better than when I was 'capped' for C Aubrey Smith's Eleven.

Of all the weird and wonderful fauna we saw on these excursions, our favourite without doubt was the duckbilled platypus, a quite adorable creature. Helen thought it looked like an animated rubber hot water bottle wearing a fur coat. The birds of paradise certainly looked the part, fluttering their feathered finery like aspens quivering in the breeze, and we were most intrigued by the behaviour of brush turkeys, with their red and naked topknots. They built nests, sometimes reaching seven feet in height, with a vent near the base, and the birds poked their skinny bald heads through this aperture from time to time, checking that the temperature was right for incubating the eggs, which lay under those conical mounds of rotting vegetation. There were flocks of wild parrots and parakeets everywhere, looking to us as if they'd escaped from some menagerie, accustomed as we were to seeing them only in cages.

Sir Laurence also found time to see that a 'local boy made good'. He was most impressed with the talent and personality of a young amateur called Peter Finch, and, concerned that he might be lost to the world if left where he was, brought him to England when we returned.

Many functions were held in Sir Laurence and Lady Olivier's honour, but the combination of their names, plus the Old Vic and Vic Oliver, the violin-playing comedian who had been entertaining in Sydney, caused some confusion when their entrance was announced: 'Ladies and Gentlemen, allow me to introduce old

Vic himself, Sir Larry Oliver and Lady Lie' is a fair example of the attempts made by perspiring, harassed officials.

Arctic conditions prevailed in Hobart when we appeared at the delightful Georgian Theatre, built by convicts years ago. I played Joseph Surface in *The School for Scandal*, and during the famous screen scene, the action required my character to steal a glance behind it, signalling Lady Teazle not to make any noise. There she was, as portrayed by Vivien Leigh, looking perfectly exquisite in Cecil Beaton's delicately designed late 18th century creation, the tip of her retroussé nose tinged slightly pink by the cold, warming her hands and her tummy – with a large beaker of Ovaltine, and her feet before a very modern- looking electric fire. I wished I could have joined her.

The triumphant tour had been a most worthwhile experience, and we had been showered with hospitality and enthusiasm. But we were not sorry when it finished for there is no place like home, and we were wanting to get back to where our hearts belonged.

On the outward voyage the ship had stopped for 24 hours, to refuel and victual, at Cape Town. Table Mountain was laid with a billowy white cloth of cloud, so we didn't see much of that famous geographical landmark, but – which was more than the next best thing – we saw Ivor Novello in one of his delightful musical romances, *Perchance to Dream*, which he was touring in South Africa, and afterwards he invited us all out to supper.

Homeward bound, the captain made a slight detour, so that the passengers could visit Pitcairn Island in the South Pacific, where the descendants of Fletcher Christian, the leading mutineer of *Bounty* fame, rowed alongside in native boats, filled with their handicrafts and colourful lei's, which they sold as souvenirs, to the accompaniment of Hawaiian music and songs.

(In all those past months I never caught sight of wandering Uncle Bertie...)

* * *

We had a short break before rehearsals started for a limited Old Vic season at the New Theatre. *The Skin of our Teeth*, having enjoyed a successful West End run in 1945, was replaced with Jean Anouilh's *Antigone*. On the tour, Helen had been understudy to Eileen Beldon and Mercia Swinbourne, and made herself generally useful in the wardrobe and helping the ladies of the company with any quick change of costume. She continued understudying in London, and in addition played Eurydice in this production. It was preceded by Chekhov's three-handed one-act comedy *The Proposal* as a curtain raiser, in which I was cast as the desperate hypochondriac, Ivan Vassilyevitch Lomov.

I gave my hair a centre parting for this characterisation and, to my dismay, revealed a small bald patch at the back of my head. Having lost those teeth, I reflected gloomily upon this further evidence of advancing years, and pointed it out to Sir Laurence.

'I shouldn't worry,' he encouraged me. 'People will think it's a wig.'

Oh well, I philosophised … che sarà … what are a few non-existent hairs between friends…

Peggy Simpson and Derrick Penley (who was descended from the great WS Penley of *Charley's Aunt* fame) were the other players involved in *The Proposal*. Its normal running time was about half an hour, but Sir Laurence suggested we performed it in the fashion of a speeded up Keystone Kops car chase, and once we got into our stride it was all over and done with in 19 minutes flat. It took me another 19 to recover.

We had been working consistently for quite some time, but subsidised theatre salaries were notoriously low, and after we closed in February 1949, apart from the odd week at 'Q', I had no engagements worthy of note until early 1950, by which time Helen and I were close to insolvency once more.

I was – and indeed still would be – amongst the world's worst at auditions, not once getting the part I had read for at those, to me, humiliating sessions.

A certain well known and influential management invited me to a first night 'stag' party which I attended, but, not being of that persuasion, I refused to join in the paederastic fun and games which was expected of me after the buffet supper, and paid the penalty. ('...Nor hell a fury, like a woman scorn'd.') I was never asked to work for them again.

Sir Laurence had entered a new phase in his career by becoming an actor-manager, using the St James's Theatre for his presentations. One of these was *The Damascus Blade* by Bridget Boland, a drama dealing with the French Resistance during the last war, in which John Mills was set to play the lead. Sir Laurence was producing, and offered me the part of a Free Frenchman. I wasn't feeling at my best, but concerned about our status quo, naturally I accepted.

In 1941, the 'V for Victory' campaign had been launched, using the letter V in morse code ($\cdots —$) as a recognisable signal, which resembled the opening thematic statement of Beethoven's Symphony No 5 in C Minor.

At the first rehearsal, I gave a conventional rap on the door prior to my entrance.

Sir Laurence called from the stalls, 'Why not use the Victory signal?'

My mind not functioning properly, I withdrew, and entered again repeating the same knock as before.

'Haven't you heard of Beethoven's Fifth?' he asked with a touch of asperity.

In my overwrought state, this slight rebuke was the last straw, and I disgraced myself by dissolving into tears, the prelude to a nervous breakdown which was to last for six months.

He was at my side immediately, consoling and compassionate. He told me to go home to Helen, and get some nice, soft healthy fat around my tired and jagged nerves.

He also paid me a retainer until I was fit to resume work, an act of kindness not to be forgotten.

Under Helen's gentle guidance and nursing, I made my return to the theatre, appropriately enough, in *The Gay Invalid* at the

Garrick, an adaptation of Molière's comedy *Le Malade imaginaire*, with Elisabeth Bergner and AE Matthews, but it was soon withdrawn.

Matty, as the latter was affectionately known, was quite a character and getting on a bit in years, professing that he read the obituary column in his newspaper each day to make sure he was still alive. He had a habit of relaxing before the show by taking a kip, lying flat on his back on the floor of his dressing room. At one stage of our short run, a new call boy had been engaged. Receiving no response to his knock on calling the half hour, he opened the door to see if Matty was in, and saw the recumbent figure.

Seized with panic, he fled to the stage manager and blurted out, 'Mr Matthews is dead!'

When this disaster was proved untrue, Matty summoned the reporter of his supposed demise and reprimanded him severely. '*Never* say Mr Matthews is dead. It will only spread unnecessary alarm and despondency. In future, just go calmly to someone in authority and say, "I *think* Mr Matthews is dead."'

1951 saw the Festival of Britain, organised to underline Britain's confidence in her own power and future, and to help lift the depressive gloom which had set in following the end of those terrible years of war. Sir Laurence, continuing his managerial role, gave a Festival Season in May, featuring Vivien Leigh in the two Cleopatra plays, Shakespeare's *Antony and Cleopatra* and Shaw's *Caesar and Cleopatra*. I played Bel Affris in the prologue of the latter, and when Wilfrid Hyde-White left to honour a previous commitment, I took over his part of that ancient Briton, Britannus, which Helen thought splendid casting, because she claimed I was so British anyway that if I cut myself I bled woad.

In September these productions were taken to America, but Wilfrid was recalled to play the role over there, so, for me, it was 'back to the drawing board' again.

Helen's father had passed on during this troubled year, and the poor darling was desolate with grief, but she bore her sorrow, like everything else she suffered, with courage and dignity, giving no trouble to others.

Discussing the future with her, I wondered if I should go back into rep, but she wouldn't entertain such a retrograde step. Instead, she bought a copy of the *Radio Times* and from it made a list of all the television producers. She then wrote letters to them, which were typed for me to sign. I wasn't very sanguine about this, thinking they would not have heard of me.

'Peter,' she said, 'you are unaware of your own value, and what your name means to people. They will be only too glad to have you work for them – you'll see.'

She was right. By return post, Harold Clayton sent me a script, asking if I would consider playing the leading character, Charles Appleby, a somewhat alcoholic actor, in JB Priestley's *Eden End*, with Helen Shingler, Rachel Gurney, Julien Mitchell and Jack Allen.

Helen smiled. 'I'm so glad for you, Peter dear, because I'm sure this will be the key to things you deserve. Being what you are, you have been unaware of jealousy in high places, but I've heard and seen things going on behind your back which made me so angry. You received an ovation every time you played Lomov, and practically stopped the show as Britannus. That is why you were not asked to repeat your performance on Broadway. Larry was not the instigator of this injustice—we have good reason to be grateful to him – but there are others at court whose influence is very strong. Wilfrid is excellent, of course, but he is older than you and well established. You are a 'new boy' and represent a threat. They cannot stand that sort of competition. You must become independent. You have all the qualities for true leadership, and are loved and admired by those who count – your audience.'

She gave me a kiss and said, 'Now, while you digest all that, I'll go and make you a cup of tea!'

There was only one television channel in those days, the BBC, and all programmes were transmitted live from Alexandra Palace,

Muswell Hill, and later from the Lime Grove Studios in Shepherd's Bush.

On 2 December 1951, after three weeks rehearsal, I was standing in the studio, awaiting my first entrance into television, feeling like a criminal about to be executed.

Decorating the wall was a large silent clock, the second hand speeding inexorably towards the fatal hour. When it arrived, a sign above flashed 'VISION ON'. My head went numb, as if it had suddenly come into sharp contact with a plank of wood, and my voice seemed to be coming from somewhere else, far, far away – like the view seen through the wrong end of a pair of binoculars.

I proceeded with my performance like an automaton, paralysed with nerves, and when it was all over I said to myself, 'Right, that's it. I'll never be wanted again, so I might as well pack the game up altogether.' In this frame of mind, I couldn't face anyone, so I disappeared unseen from the building and made my way home, still wearing my orange make-up.

On the tube, a considerate passenger leant across, and asked if I was feeling alright.

'Just a little sick,' I managed to inform him. He nodded sympathetically.

'Jaundice, if you ask me,' (which I hadn't), 'there's a lot of it about. Nasty complaint,' Job's comforter commiserated mournfully, before retreating, mercifully, behind his *Evening News.*

As we didn't have a set, Helen had gone to watch the play with some friends and hadn't returned when I reached our flat.

Sitting despondently in the firelight, longing for her comforting presence, I heard her tripping merrily along the tiled floor of the hallway, and my heart lifted as it always did at her approach. There seemed to be something extra reassuring about the spring in her step tonight, and I went to greet her at the door. She looked radiant.

Giving me the thumbs up sign, and a big kiss, she exclaimed, 'You were superb! That was one of the finest performances you have ever given, dearest – I believe you're a secret drinker, from the way you handled that scene when you were sozzled!'

Over a pot of tea and scrambled eggs, we talked until the early hours, and I was more than reassured when we finally went to bed.

The 'phone woke me later in the morning. It was Harold Clayton, wanting to know why I had disappeared last night, and to convey his congratulations. I put the receiver down after our chat, and the bell rang again as I did so. Fred O'Donovan was on the other end of the line, asking me to play the juvenile lead in yet another Priestley comedy, *When We Are Married*, rehearsals starting in a week's time.

I received 60 guineas, minus the usual deductions, for the two months' work required to prepare *Eden End* and *When We Are Married*, and after these forays into this new medium, there came another of those lulls which haunt all actors' lives.

Helen had ruptured herself badly, through heaving heavy furniture about when helping to redecorate her mother's flat, causing a hernia with complications, and had to go into St George's Hospital for operative treatment. I visited her every day, and aware of my concern, she made a joke of her condition. Laughing, she said her stomach was beginning to look like an aerial view of a railway terminus.

The doctor recommended that she should get some sea air into her lungs and a neighbour kindly said we could use her cottage in Polzeath, Cornwall, at a peppercorn rent for as long as we needed it.

Our finances had dwindled, and seeing no alternative, but much against my will, I was forced to ask my father for assistance, and went down to see him.

'Sit down, my boy, I want a word with you. Why don't you get some other job to do when you are disengaged, like your grandfather? You could become a front of house manager, for instance – I can lend you my evening clothes.' Handing me a cheque, he continued, 'You are nearly 40, and a failure.'

This was just a statement of fact, and not meant unkindly, his criterion for success being based entirely upon how much was in the bank. On that basis, he was dead right, but it hurt deeply, and I went back to Helen feeling lower than a snake's belly. She asked me how I'd got on, and I noticed her lips tighten when I told her, but she made no comment.

Gratefully accepting our neighbour's offer, we left Paddington Station bound for the Cornish Riviera. Father's words still smarting painfully, I had packed my watercolours, thinking I might be able to earn some sort of living by painting, and had told no one of our departure, not even my agent. Unknown to me, however, Helen had mentioned it to a dear friend, Irene Sutcliffe.

Many weeks later, attending a theatrical party, Irene heard Robert Helpmann say he'd been trying to get in touch with me for days, because he wanted me for a play he was going to direct, but nobody seemed to know of my whereabouts. She contacted us straight away, and we returned to London.

That chance remark overheard above the clink of cocktail glasses brought me back into circulation once more, and started a chain of events in my chequered career which finally resulted in Helen's prophecy regarding my future coming true.

*   *   *

I had been Robert Helpmann's understudy when we were both in the company at the St James's Theatre, and The Wedding Ring, by Kieran Tunney and Simon Wardell, was his first play as a director. There was to be a fairly lengthy prior to London tour, starting at Manchester.

Wanting Helen to rest as much as possible, I didn't fancy her enduring the fatigue of endless packing and unpacking in dingy digs, and the strain of all those tiring Sunday slow train calls, forever changing at Crewe. This, coupled with the ever present need to economise, made me decide, unhappily, that she should stay at home on this occasion.

Gladys Henson, Adrianne Allen, Irene Browne, Irene Handl and Shelagh Fraser joined me on the excursion to Manchester. I tried to concentrate on the game of canasta they wanted to play as we chugged steadily northwards, but my thoughts were elsewhere, and I spent more time looking out of the window than at my cards, thinking of dear Helen, and watching the beautiful and varied countryside glide by, bathed in August sunshine.

When we reached that commercial capital of Lancashire the sun disappeared, and those lovely blue distances I'd seen on the journey had now turned to grey, and rain. Rain that seeped down the back of my neck, however tightly I buttoned the collar of my mackintosh. But I pressed on to Ackers Street, No 18 painted uncertainly in black on a mustard-yellow door, with sad-looking shrubs in wooden tubs making the tiny front garden seem even smaller than it was.

I was met by Mrs Edmondson, a large landlady, shaped like a biscuit barrel, in an apron and no stockings, with hair that looked like an inverted bird nest made of gun cotton, crimped with resident curlers.

'Oi wus born in Oirland,' she announced by way of greeting. 'Follow me.'

Obeying her instruction, I entered a rather dingy hall, which smelt strongly of fried fish and cheap lino, then up a narrow flight of squeaky stairs, passing stained prints of 'Bubbles' and 'The Monarch of the Glen' on the way, before reaching my room. It was small and clean, but it was not home.

Dumping my baggage, I set off for the Opera House to prepare for a dress rehearsal. As I was leaving, Mrs Edmondson asked if I'd care for some 'troipe an' honions' when I got back. Shuddering at the thought, I declined her thoughtful offer.

The setting for the play looked charming, but problems had arisen over some lighting effects, which would delay the actors going into action for an hour or more, so I went in search of something to fortify myself for what was obviously going to be a long night.

The rain was really determined as I turned into Albert Square, but I headed into it valiantly, wading along deserted streets, the shops and warehouses grim and silent over their Sunday rest, every eating establishment looking as if it had never been open. Ah! wait a minute – there was a neon sign ahead, flickering in scarlet tubing 'Kahdomah Kafé', and the lights were on inside. Thinking how nice it would be to get somewhere dry, I hurried forward and grasped the handle of the door. It was locked. Cupping my hands over my eyes as I peered through the window streaming with condensation, I saw three men in white overalls with white faces, painting the walls white, and 'Closed until further notice' scrawled on a piece of cardboard.

Bracing my shoulders, I traipsed on once again down more endless grey streets, all reeking of stale fish and chips and breweries.

In the meagre shelter provided by the portico of Kendal Milnes emporium stood a 'bobby', but this one was hardly a 'stout arm of the law'. He was tall and tapering, with a tiny head which seemed inadequate to support his enormous helmet.

'Could you please tell me, officer, where I can find a café open on Sundays?'

A pair of eyes, so palely blue that it occurred to me all this rain must have got into them and washed their colour away, looked down upon me from a great height with compassion and hopelessness, as if saddened that anyone could possibly expect such a thing during August Bank Holiday in Manchester. He didn't look well, I thought – but then nobody does up here.

A flicker of triumph lit those pale liquid orbs for a moment. 'You know Maarket Street?' I nodded.

'Take first turn on't' left past traffic row bows, and you'll coom to Continental Cinema, restaurong in t' baysment. T'only won open oop 'ere of a Sonday – you can't miss it'.

I could, and what's more, I did.

With a brave smile and a cheerful 'Thanks so much' I sallied forth, my mac no longer making any pretence of keeping me dry. I was practically out on the moors by now, starvation staring me in the face, and never a sight of the policeman's promised paradise. I must have lost my bearings, or perhaps old blue eyes had been too damp to direct me properly. It was nearing the time when I should have been back at the theatre, so I began beating my retreat from this barren outpost of a sodden Mancunian Moscow.

Turning a corner – wonder of wonders! 'Ping Hong' Chinese Restaurant, open 11.30 am until 12 midnight, Sundays included. Clever, these Chinese, I reflected – trust the artful orientals to make hay while the rain falls.

In dry dock at last, I studied the menu. There was Chop Suey, Foo Lung, Pong Ling Kon, Pee Wee Lung, Pong Pong, and even something that read suspiciously like Ping Pong to my waterlogged eyes. Not fancying any of Mr Hong's specialities, I settled for a delicious cauliflower au gratin instead, followed by some tinned fruit salad, with a dash of Ideal Milk.

Comfortably fortified, the swim to the Opera House was achieved in record time, and the meal sustained me through the evening's work.

There were the usual notes when we finished, and encourage-ment from Robert: 'Well done, everybody! Splendid, darlings! Just remember – speed, speed, speed – and jolly good luck. Ready at 9.30 sharp in the morning, please. Sleep tight!'

From the top deck of the last No 42 bus, I saw another eating place, 'The Hollywood Inn' – closed, of course. Sleepily, I somehow couldn't quite imagine Rita Hayworth ever dining there…

And so ended another day in an actor's life. I rang up the dearest one in all the world to say 'Goodnight, God Bless' and went to bed, knowing the sun would shine again tomorrow, because it always does, even when we don't actually see it.

*   *   *

It would have been nice if our return to London had bespoken a triumphant success, but I'm afraid *The Wedding Ring* needed something more subtle than mere speed to attract the customers, and it failed to capture their hearts. Unhappy and fretful when away from Helen, I wasn't upset when the notice appeared on the callboard, even though it meant I'd be 'resting' once more.

At least, that is what I thought...

Standing in the centre of Helen's homemade table was a glinting Waterford cut-glass vase, filled with a beautiful bunch of roses.

'Hallo, hallo!' I exclaimed. 'Who's your other admirer?'

'Pop,' she said – her nickname for my father. 'It arrived yesterday – better than the old jam jar, isn't it! The flowers are from his garden.'

Knowing how upset I'd been after my last visit, all her thoughts ever for me and my welfare, she'd gone to see him whilst I was on tour. I asked what had transpired.

'I told him that in you he has a son bordering on genius, being endowed with so many gifts, and the burden of those talents is not easy to bear. Your work gives pleasure to thousands, and will be remembered long after we are gone and forgotten. It is up to us lesser mortals to help and support you in whatever way we can, and not crush your spirit as he had done.' Her eyes twinkled mischievously. 'I'm not going to tell you any more – you might get a swollen head! But Pop's a dear when you get to know him, and we parted the best of friends.'

And so they remained in mutual affection and respect, and I felt more relaxed in his company than I had ever been before.

7

'THERE'S A DIVINITY THAT SHAPES OUR ENDS...'

'I say! I say! I say! Do you know what television is?'
'No! I don't know what television is. What is television?'
'Peter Cushing with knobs on!'

That smatter of repartee between a couple of stand-up comics, heard on the wireless during the early fifties, related to my almost non-stop appearance on the 'box' in the ensuing decade.

For three years in succession my work received awards, fulfilling Helen's prediction and her faith in my abilities. They should have been given to her, not me. Whatever success I may have achieved was due entirely to Helen.

Before reaching that enviable stage, we had to contend with my nervous agonies which continued to plague me. Although Helen had convinced me beyond doubt that I could tackle the medium, they were still rampant, and she was fully aware of this complex condition.

When a mistake is made in filming, the director 'cuts' and the scene is shot again until you get it right, and in the theatre you can usually cover up anything that goes wrong. But not on television. In that confinement there was no escape, those cameras with lenses like probing microscopes picked up everything that happened as it happened, as if you were a goldfish in a glass bowl. Added to this terror was the fact that the audience was the largest you would ever play to, and at the same time the smallest, consisting mainly of family groups in their sitting rooms.

'That's enough to daunt the stoutest heart,' Helen agreed. 'But try falling in love with the cameras, and keep only one lucky person in mind before you go on. I leave the choice to you!' Of course, I thought of her alone and it helped to a degree, but my wretched nerves still got the better of me.

Sunday nights were reserved for Drama, and since there were no such things as tapes or videos for recording in that era, the play was repeated live the following Thursday. That waiting period was a form of refined torture. If the show had been well received, it was difficult to recapture the initial impetus four days later, and if the reverse, it was an embarrassment, imagining how bored the viewers would be.

In a further bid to combat this neurosis, Helen went to our doctor and asked his advice. He prescribed some pills which had just come on the market. After my next appearance, he rang to ask if they had helped.

'Not really,' Helen replied.

'How many did he take?'

'Five.'

She heard him gulp. 'Is he still alive?' he asked, obviously shaken.

They were 'purple hearts', one being considered potent enough to stun a fully grown elephant for 24 hours, apart from the danger of turning me into a raving drug addict.

We finally hit upon the only real solution to my problem. I asked if Helen could be present in the studio during transmission. The producers agreed to my request, allowing her to sit with them in the control room. Her proximity gave me the courage I needed, and did me more good than all the pills ever invented.

Soon after my father retired, my mother suffered a stroke and spent the last ten years of her life bedridden but uncomplaining, outliving him by five years. I was glad to have reached some sort of recognition and acclaim before this happened – it gave Mother such joy to see me so frequently on the television set at the foot of her bed, and Father was filled with pride. When my name first appeared on the hoarding outside a London cinema, he took a photograph of it and had prints made for all his office staff.

Whatever the medium, I always like to know my lines well in advance, so that the entire rehearsal period can be used to the best advantage, unencumbered with the 'book'. I would set off in the early morning on long country walks, which were routed by 'Fieldfare' once a week in *The Evening News*, returning in the late afternoon to soak in a bath, whilst Helen sat on the stool reading the cues to me and hearing what I had learnt. I played such a variety of characters that the press referred to me as the BBC's 'maid of all work', and I had many experiences which showed how television personalities become the property of the public, who really take them into their hearts.

Travelling up to Newcastle by train, Helen and I were enjoying a quiet afternoon tea in the restaurant car, when what appeared to be the majority of the British Army, just paid and on leave, came marching down the corridor in single file. Their leader spotted me and barked "ALT!' Springing smartly to attention, he produced a £1 note and asked if I would autograph it for him. I complied with his request, and then proceeded to do the same for his entire retinue. Scrumptious toasted tea cakes and lovely pot of char stone cold by now, my aching palm scrawling my signature on crinkled bank notes as the train swayed and thundered northwards, I asked what must have been about the fiftieth recipient, 'What do you *do* with them?'

The khaki-clad lad closed one eye and grinned knowingly. 'We flog 'em for £1.50!' he replied. Honest, at least – and nice to know my valuation!

Another time, I was knocked flying off my bicycle by a mini motor caravan. My nose and hands having taken the brunt of my fall, I was bleeding profusely and utterly dazed. The concerned driver picked me up, and put me and my buckled bike into the back of his vehicle, and drove me home. His lady companion kept stealing glances in my direction, and at last made the usual observation, 'You are Peter Cushing, aren't you?' I nodded – painfully.

'Coo!' she twittered ecstatically. 'I thought you was! – can't wait to tell our friends who we bumped into on our holiday! Can I have your autograph please?'

Wondering if she had spoken literally regarding the nature of our chance encounter, or if it was merely an unfortunate turn of phrase to use in the circumstances, all I could think to say was, 'Would you like it in blood?'

Rehearsals were often conducted in drill halls, which stank of plimsolls, stale perspiration and attar of cats. One was in North London, and every time I passed on my way to work there, the stall holders plying their trade along the busy road greeted me cheerfully. When presented with my first award, I was deeply touched to receive a greetings telegram which read: 'Congratulations and thanks from all the barrow boys in the Caledonian Road.'

Visiting the City one day to call on my solicitor, I stood opposite the Bank, at the intersection where all those thoroughfares meet at the foot of that famous institution, as if paying homage to the Old Lady of Threadneedle Street, awaiting a chance to nip across the wide expanse of tarmac. Emulating *In Town Tonight*, a constable on point duty stopped the mighty roar of London's traffic from all directions, and beckoned me gravely to his side.

When I reached it, he winked. 'Can't have you run over, Mr Cushing – the wife'll never forgive me if she don't see what happens in the final episode of your serial.'

Looking at me through his mirror, a cab driver startled me by saying, 'Your face worries me.'

'It worries me too, sometimes,' I countered.

'Nah, nah – I don't mean that – but I've seen you before somewhere, 'aven't I?'

'On TV, perhaps.'

'Cor, stone the crows! Yus, that's it! Wait 'til I tell 'em at 'ome 'oo was in me cab terday!'

He refused to take my fare. "Ave this one on me, Pete,' he said – 'you're a bloomin' knockaht on the telly. Tarra!'

Helen had impressed upon me the importance of keeping up my public image. 'Always maintain that aura of fascination and mystery associated with your profession. You are so well known, and should avoid travel by public transport whenever possible. Your fans like to think of you being driven about in a Rolls-Royce and dining at the Ritz every night. You must never disillusion them, because that is the way they like to think all actors live, and they would be very disappointed if they knew the truth.'

I suppose it was because of my past insecurity in so many areas that, even now, I still went through phases of doubts and deep depression. One of the greatest compliments to an actor is to hear people say, 'It all looks so easy.' I have never found it so, and the more I do, the more difficult it becomes, reaching for some sort of perfection 'in an imperfect world'. As ever, Helen knew.

One morning, I had to leave for work at five o'clock, and didn't disturb her at that hour. On my breakfast tray, which she had left prepared for me, was a letter. I quote from it to give some idea of how she bolstered and recharged my flagging spirits, and the light in which she held me:

...There is nothing that can defeat a man – except his own acceptance of defeat. And of all men and women I have ever known – you have the greatest courage, integrity, honour, spiritual love (which glows from you), mental and physical beauty – a keen wit – a quicksilver brain, and the tenacity of a terrier! Your name is held in honour and love by all ... Reflect on your victories over the many seemingly insurmountable obstacles – ill health, poverty, persecution of the jealous and base. All these you defeated and rose and triumphed to win the heart of the nation. Mark that! Think on it, and realise that you still have their hearts – and will never lose them...

Don't use up so much energy worrying about other people! I know when you see the mail on your desk in the morning you will be smitten with a fresh anxiety – about the work it entails for me! Darling Peter – I never get a neurosis about the work you do! And I might well do so! For of all the arduous, exhausting, nerve racking, responsible, difficult and exacting work – yours – in the way you do it – is staggering to a normal person. I couldn't carry your load, to start with. And even if I could, I would never be as charming and thoughtful and attentive towards others! Because I would need all my strength (and a lot more) to concentrate and fulfil the enormous responsibility you bear.

Now – let's get this straight – mine is an enviable and perfect existence. Whatever I do – being for you – it is also for me. We work together. I cannot do what you do (and I stand still in wonder and admiration at what you do, and the way you do it!) ... Please do not undermine the energy, concentration and enjoyment of the great work you can and do give to the world. Once before, it exhausted and depleted you to the extent of a long illness ... All the gratefulness you put into somebody bringing you a cup of tea – or even doing a job for which they are paid! Doing their job, while you do yours. And you, with your great kind heart, overwhelm them with appreciation! Spare yourself my dearest. A sincere 'thank you' and a beautiful smile is all they need, and are fully repaid. All we ask is to serve you – so that you can give of your abundant talent and beauty. Let us do this and spare yourself...

This was just one of many, in similar vein, that Helen wrote when those moods weighed me down. How could I fail, with such incredible love and support – which passeth all understanding? Her words still inspire and steer me on the course I know she wishes me to take...

The studios at Alexandra Palace were extremely limited, and the six-part serial of Jane Austen's novel *Pride and Prejudice* required

Above: The birthday card painted by Peter for Helen, 1949.

Right: With his extensive collection of William Britain toy figures (1950s).

Below: Outdoor painting and indoor cricket – Airlie Gardens, Kensington (1950s).

Clockwise from above: Leading ladies in 1954. Ann Todd in *Tovarich*, Deborah Kerr in *The End of the Affair*, Daphne Slater in *Beau Brummell* and Yvonne Mitchell in *Nineteen Eighty-Four*.

Below: As the dastardly Sir Palamides in *The Black Knight*, 1953.

Above: With Jeanette Sterke in the BBC play *Richard of Bordeaux*, 1955.

Right: With Helen, comparing costume designs for the feature film *Alexander the Great*, 1955.

Two more BBC plays.

Above: With Stanley Baker in *The Creature*, 1955. (Filmed two years later as *The Abominable Snowman*.)

Left: With Helen Shingler in the 1956 production of RC Sherriff's *Home at Seven*.

Above: Brought to book by Mervyn Johns (with Keith Grieve and James Donally) in *Gaslight*, 1957.

Above: Preparing for further surgery on Christopher Lee in *The Curse of Frankenstein*, 1956.

Left: On the cover of *TV Mirror* in July 1957.

Above: Advertising Nescafé, also July 1957.

Left: As the unorthodox Roman Catholic priest in *Violent Playground*, 1957.

Above: In the title role of *Uncle Harry* with Mary Morris, 1958.

Below: As the determined Dr Van Helsing in *Dracula*, 1957.

Above: A light-hearted moment on the set of *Suspect*, 1959.

Below: As the Sheriff of Nottingham in *Sword of Sherwood Forest*, 1960.

Above: Horse-play with Robert Stack while filming *John Paul Jones*, 1958.

Below: Dispatching Martita Hunt in *The Brides of Dracula*, 1960.

Above: The 'Cushing finger', as seen in *The Naked Edge*, 1960.

Above right: In the BBC *Comedy Playhouse* presentation *The Plan*, 1963.

Right: Candid shots of Helen and Peter, mid-1960s.

Below: The daily swim – in Whitstable, 1968.

Above: Bringing Doctor Who to the big screen in *Daleks' Invasion Earth 2150 A.D.*, 1966.

Right: On location on Dartmoor for the BBC version of *The Hound of the Baskervilles*, 1968.

Below: Displaying a selection of his self-crafted model theatres in May 1966.

many settings, every available space being used. The scenery and costumes were quite beautiful, recapturing the graceful days of the Regency period to perfection.

There was a snag, however. Each set was constructed in a different sound stage, and to get from one to the other meant using the connecting corridors of the building itself.

I played the aloof and elegantly dressed Mr Darcy, and having just enacted a tranquil scene in Mr and Mrs Bennet's drawing room at Longbourne, I had to dash like a mad thing, completely out of character, avoiding collisions with turbaned tea trolley ladies peddling their wares – 'Catching a train, luv?' – to the drawing room of Lady Catherine de Bourgh's home at Rosing's Park, trusting it was odds on that I'd make my entrance on cue, after tugging open the massive soundproof door, and enter the correct set, trying to look cool, calm and collected … It took a great deal of concentration, and energy.

'TORTURES ON TV HORRIFY WHOLE NATION'
'TORTURES ON TV START BIGGEST PROTEST STORM'

Those are samples from the front page banner headlines which greeted the nation in December 1954, the morning after the first performance of George Orwell's *Nineteen Eighty-Four,* and many MPs backed a motion in the House of Commons to ban the repeat.

It is a sad reflection upon the times we live in that, when another excellent presentation of this play with a splendid cast was given in 1965, it caused not a ripple, so immune have we become to violence and terrorism.

Orwell's story was a grim warning not to let what he described with such shattering effect in fiction become fact. But the scene which created the biggest brouhaha in Rudolph Cartier's stunning production concerned some rodents. Insidiously uncovering the Achilles heel of anyone who had the temerity to make a stand against Big Brother's ruthless regime, the State used this knowledge to brainwash and completely annihilate the will of such heroic individuals. Winston Smith's weakness was a fear of rats. A rat catcher's services were petitioned, and he procured two dirty grey, scraggy-looking specimens in time for the final rehearsal, and left them on the set. Snug in their bed of straw, they basked in the warmth from the arc lamps, ate bits of cheese which sympathetic members of the unit kept dropping through the bars of their cage, to their surprise, and they certainly enjoyed an unexpected break from the dank sewers of London.

So great was their comfort that when the moment came for them to leap at my throat, yellow teeth bared and snarling, there they were, snuggled together, content with this new existence, satiated with food, and fast asleep. They were sacked on the spot, and a minion dispatched post haste to the nearest pet shop to purchase a couple of tame ones, which were white, and had to be dyed dark brown by the make-up department. Strict instructions were issued not to feed them under any circumstances, in the hope they would be so ravenous when the time came to use them that they would react in the way the script demanded.

This achieved the desired effect, but just before we were due on the air, hunger got the better of them, and like the Pied Piper of Hamelin's hypnotised followers, they began 'drowning our speaking with shrieking and squeaking in 50 different sharps and flats.' They had to be removed into a separate studio, with a camera and microphone all to themselves. When their great moment arrived, morsels of nourishment were dangled tantalisingly above their heads, out of shot, making them leap up and down as if on invisible pogo sticks, snapping viciously.

At a given signal from the floor manager, I reacted to their attack without even seeing it. For this piece of emoting by remote control, playing one of the greatest heroes in literature, I became known as 'The Horror Man of the BBC' – long before my connection with the type of film which carried that certificate. Poetic justice gone a little awry, perhaps…?

Taping had just been introduced, and the second performance was recorded for posterity, but it lacked the spontaneity and inspiration of the first, suffering from the furore provoked during those three intervening days.

I had left Al Parker's Agency, and a few days after I'd played a comparatively small but effective part of a myopic, disillusioned scientist in *Number Three* by Charles Irving, I received a congratulatory letter from John Redway. In my 'thank you' acknowledgement, I asked if he would take me under his wing, and I've been cosseted there since that day in 1953.

He and his charming partner, David Booth, have guided my career and given me their enduring friendship, which I hold in great esteem.

Under John's banner, I started my long and happy association with Hammer Film Productions.

During this period of the film industry's turbulent history, a certain animosity existed towards anyone connected with television, because cinema attendance was dwindling, as audiences found that they could get all the entertainment they wanted in their own homes, just by the flick of a switch.

But one company had other ideas. James (later Sir James) Carreras was the driving force behind that venturesome organisation, and reasoned sagaciously that if someone well known and popular on the rival medium was starred in a film, that name could lure people back to those empty seats. He had been in constant touch with John, inviting me to work for them, but my commitments elsewhere prevented my accepting until 1957.

Way back in the Thirties, after the tremendous stage success of *Journey's End*, which James Whale had produced in London with Colin Clive as Stanhope, they went to Hollywood to make the film version, which led to their collaborating on *Frankenstein*, with Mr Clive in the name part and Boris Karloff as his creation.

I had seen that fantasy, and thought it was splendid, so when I heard that Hammer were going into production with a coloured remake, I asked John if he would suggest me for the part of the Baron. He did, and I was chosen.

Re-entitled *The Curse of Frankenstein*, it caused quite a sensation, and the returns at box-offices all over the world were phenomenal. This snowball of success started an avalanche which rolled on to gigantic proportions, making Hammer a multi-million pound concern, presented with the Queen's Award to Industry in 1968.

James Carreras and his cohorts launched themselves full tilt into this genre. I appeared as Baron Frankenstein in five more such films, interspersed with five as Professor Van Helsing in their Dracula epics, in which my very dear friend Christopher Lee was quite superb as the sinister Count, chilling to the marrow all those who saw his remarkable performance; and, indeed, his 'Monster' in the initial *Frankenstein* film made the same impact, but he also managed to imbue that part with a certain pathos.

The very first time we met he was wearing the grotesque make-up conceived by Phil Leakey, and a story was put about by the Publicity Department that when it was removed at the end of the day's work, he and I came face to face in the corridor, and *then* I screamed! He is a man of so many attributes, among them a most marvellous sense of humour plus the ability to laugh at himself, and uncanny skill as an impersonator, which helped to lighten the darkness hanging over Count Dracula's entombed habitat when we were not shooting.

Terence Fisher, another old and delightful companion, directed these pictures, and the professional team spirit was an inspiration to every one of us.

'The impossible will take a few minutes: miracles a little longer.' This slogan may be heard often within the walls of film studios, when something is needed urgently, usually following the question and answer:

'When do you want it?'

'Yesterday.'

Such was the case during the making of the first *Dracula*, the script demanding Van Helsing to carry so many crucifixes, it read as if he was a travelling salesman in these relics, and could have been risible. At the denouement of the film he forces the Count into a shaft of sunlight by confronting him with one, and so causes his disintegration. Rather than take yet another from my pocket, I asked Terry if there could be some candlesticks on the long refectory table, which I could grab and clash together in the form of a cross. He thought it an excellent idea, and went through the dialogue as described above. But the 'props' department came up trumps, as they invariably do, and by the time the scene was ready to be shot, there were the two perfect candlesticks adorning each end of the table, and dramatic use was made of them.

Whatever a script may call upon an actor to do, it gives him more confidence if he knows he's doing it in the correct way. If trouble is not taken to find out, it would also be an affront to some members of his audience who might happen to be experts on any given subject.

How useful it would have been, for instance, if I'd known how to handle a horse before going to Hollywood!

Since then, I've had to perform so many operations, and wishing to be as convincing as possible, always sought advice from my local doctor, Denis Horan. Each time I rang him he sighed with relief, saying 'So glad it's you – you're not *ill* – you just want to know how to remove a brain or a heart or something, is that it? Get the sherry out – I'll be round after surgery and give you a few tips.'

I may have been the first to transplant a human organ in recent years, but Dr Christian Barnard was to do it with far greater success in 1967!

Today's statistics reveal that these pictures, produced over 25 years ago, are shown on television or in cinemas somewhere in the world every day or every night of every year, seen by a new generation – not born when they were made – who imagine they are watching recent productions.

This time gap is brought home during my travels, when complete strangers look at me curiously and say, 'Excuse me – but are you Peter Cushing's Dad?'

Helen was concerned about my becoming typecast, knowing that other presenters would think of me only in this light if I continued in so-called horror films. We had long discussions about this dilemma, because I knew her to be right. But there had been so many lean years and, much as I disliked going against her wishes, I was desperately anxious to make provision for our old age together, and to ensure she lacked for nothing in the meantime. Throughout all the years I'd known her, she had never once asked for anything for herself, and it was such joy to be in a position, at last, to give her a few luxuries, and above all, more extensive medical care and attention.

Her cough was worse than ever, and her breathing so painfully difficult that she had resorted to using oxygen to assist her lungs, on the advice of Dr Horan. Alarmed by her plight, I arranged for her to see a Polish physician, Dr Galeskwi, who specialised in pulmonary complaints, and he gave her a thorough examination.

'You have left it too late – you should have come to me ten years ago. I can at least get rid of your cough, but I cannot perform miracles.'

I was so pleased that her exhausting cough could be overcome that the significance of his last remark went over my head.

He arranged for Helen to have three weeks' treatment in France at Le Mont-Doré in the Auvergne. It was a thermal town, wonderfully equipped to deal with many ills, using waters and vapours arising out of natural boiling springs, the legacy of erupting volcanoes aeons ago.

We now had a car, so we drove there. Helen's life had been a riches to rags story, and I wanted to restore some sort of riches again, after all she'd been through. Our spanking new pale blue Mark IX Jaguar had been bought with this in mind, and she did appreciate its comfort on the long drive south.

Her treatment followed a strict pattern, beginning early in the mornings, and between each session in the baths, she had to sleep for two hours.

When she was resting, I went for walks on the quiet, sparsely inhabited hillsides. I wore a rather shapeless anorak, with its hood over my head for protection against the chill wind, and as I had started to grow a moustache for my next role, there was a suspicion of soft down upon my top lip.

Meeting a solitary goatherd, clad in wooden clogs and black beret, I thought I'd promote the Entente Cordiale by passing the time of day. Adopting my best Lieutenant Colbert accent, I greeted him with a conventional 'Bonjour, M'sieur.'

He stared at me before asking, 'Est-ce que vous êtes Américain?'

Feeling a twinge of disappointment in this mistaken identity, and manfully standing my ground against the blast of vapourised garlic which smote me smack in the face, I pulled myself up to my full height and proudly announced, 'Non – je suis Anglaise.'

He looked startled and backed away from me, muttering 'Mon Dieu!' as he rejoined his straying flock.

Puzzled by this reaction, I recounted the incident to Helen, and, when she stopped laughing, she translated for me. Apparently I'd told him I was an English woman.

The therapeutic result of inhaling Nature's gases proved more beneficial than my wildest dreams would have thought possible. Helen's cough disappeared entirely, and she was never troubled by it again. She was revitalised, and restored to better health in general. A pair of grateful and elated people returned to England after those three well-spent weeks. To our way of thinking, the doctor from Poland *had* performed a miracle...

* * *

The lease on our flat having expired, we bought a house in Hillsleigh Road, off Campden Hill Square, and since Dr Galeskwi said it was imperative that Helen should breathe as much clean, fresh air as possible, we acquired a terraced cottage in the quaint little fishing town of Whitstable, Kent, which we adored.

Sir William Russell Flint, RA, and his son Francis were near neighbours in Kensington, and we got to know them very well, attending many enjoyable tea parties in the studio at Peel Cottage. There was a pixie-like quality about Willie's personality, partly because he always carried his head a little to one side, as blackbirds do when listening for worms on a lawn, a smile lurking at the corners of his mouth. With an impish wink, and in his delightful Edinburgh brogue, he introduced us to his most beautiful model – 'She's *hid*-jus really – she's just glamor-*ised* for the occasion!'

They came to see me when I was at the Duchess Theatre in *The Silver Whistle* by Robert McEnroe, with Joyce Barbour, Olga Lindo, Ernest Thesiger and Robin Bailey.

'I'm a wee bitty deaf, but I could hear every word that was said. Being a Scot, I do like to get my baw-*bees* worth! I enjoyed it tremendously.'

When it came off after only a few weeks, he was so upset on our account, he presented Helen and me with a lovely sanguine of 'Cecilia', his 'hideous' model, dedicated to us in gratitude for a 'grand evening's entertainment'.

Over the years I have admired the work of Edward Seago, one of the greatest British painters, and we corresponded regularly. When Helen and I went for a short holiday in Norfolk, I rang him up on the spur of the moment, asking if we could meet. He invited us to dinner that evening, so we drove from Cromer, where we were staying, to the Dutch House, Ludham, about 20 miles across the Broads. It was a night of sheer enchantment, and three o'clock in the morning chimed before we could tear ourselves away. As we were leaving, Peter Seymour, his secretary, said, 'I have a sneaking feeling you'll be on our Christmas guest list!' Sure enough, we were, and stayed with them often during the years which followed.

Alas! What inward tumult confounds the truly great. Ted was one of the most cheerful yet saddest men we ever knew. He would often telephone, in an almost suicidal state of despair over his work, begging us to go up and bolster his flagging spirits.

Field Marshal Sir Claude Auchinleck was a frequent visitor, a most charming, sensitive person with a remote air of loneliness about him, as well as a bubbling sense of fun. He loved playing a game called 'Have you anything to declare?' in which he always took the part of a Customs Officer, wearing one of Ted's white yachting caps for the purpose. All the other players drew slips of paper out of a hat, on which were written the various items people bring back from trips abroad, and some left blank. He would then question them, before asking for the 'bags' to be opened. He was invariably right in his suspicions, and I asked him what system he used. 'I nearly always let the men off, but not the distaff side,' he said, and, quoting Sherlock Holmes: 'Women are never to be entirely trusted – not the best of them', smiling benignly at all those present.

Ted had been commissioned to paint a portrait of HM The Queen in full dress uniform as Colonel in Chief of the Coldstream Guards, and was working on it during one of our stays.

3 January 1956 proved an historic day for us. Peter came into the studio to tell Ted he was wanted on the telephone. It was one of Her Majesty's aides, saying she and her mother would like to come over from Sandringham to see how the picture was progressing. Ted suggested to him that they came to lunch, and Helen and I thought it would be diplomatic if we made ourselves scarce until they had gone. He wouldn't hear of this, and explained the etiquette for such a meeting.

During the short formalities, the Queen subjected us to a severe, searching scrutiny, but as soon as they were finished, that radiant smile broke and lit up her whole face, and it was like sitting down to table with old established friends, so easy did they make us feel. It was an absolutely informal affair, no hovering detectives or bodyguards, just a chauffeur taking his meal in the kitchen.

We talked of horses and courses and corgis, of shoes and ships and sealing wax, and the Queen Mother told me I was a great favourite at 'Buck House', and how sorry they'd been to miss me on television in *Richard of Bordeaux* the previous week, but they had had another engagement that particular evening!

Cockleshell Heroes had been given a Royal première recently, and before the film commenced I had appeared as Vice-Admiral Lord Nelson in a staged montage of the nation's famous historical figures. HRH The Duke of Edinburgh had been in attendance, and Helen and I had been presented to him, so this new honour made up a trio of royal encounters for us to remember for ever, with pride and with pleasure.

As we left the dining room after lunch, my eye had caught sight of something familiar, and when Their Majesties withdrew to inspect the portrait I slipped out to investigate, and there in the hallway recess, draped over the back of a chair, were two silken head scarves, one of them bearing the design I had submitted to the enterprising Mr X so long ago... I raised the faintly perfumed hems to my lips and, with reverence, gently kissed them.

Always deeply interested in painting, I had studied during my late teens at the Croydon School of Art, under Percy Rendell. In 1958 I was interviewed on a BBC television programme when a few of my watercolours were shown. The following day I received a call from the Fine Art Society in New Bond Street, asking if they could hold an exhibition of my work.

I was completely bowled over, feeling I never reached anything like the standard I strived for. But Helen said, 'You see? I told you so! Others like your work even if you don't!'

The display was entitled 'Here and There', Willie and Ted being amongst the first to view it, leaving in their wake a couple of those cockle-warming red discs which must gladden all artists' hearts. (A fellow feeling makes one wond'rous kind...)

*   *   *

The slogan 'Join the Navy and see the World' could be applied with equal justification to the business of filmmaking, which often calls for location work in 'foreign parts'. As an itinerant actor, donning the guise of arch villain Sir Palamides, I jousted with Alan Ladd in

The Black Knight within the massive castle walls of Manzanares el
Real, Castilla la Nueva, Central Spain, and plotted against him in
the forbidding granite palace of El Escorial; went to my death in
battle as the Athenian General Memnon, against Richard Burton's
Alexander the Great, on the parched plains of Andalucia; sailed the
mighty Mediterranean Sea off Denia, in the square-rigged frigate
Serapis, as Captain Pearson, to be sunk by Robert Stack as *John
Paul Jones;* from the heat in that country, as Dr Rollason in search
of *The Abominable Snowman,* I climbed up to the frozen, snowy
height of 13,000-odd feet on the Jungfraujoch in the Bernese
Oberland, Switzerland, where the equipment had been tested for
Sir Edmund Hillary's successful assault upon Mount Everest in
1953.

Then it was back to the dehydrating torridity of that barren
wilderness, the Negev Desert, Israel, as Ludwig Horace Holly,
riding a stinking and obstinate camel, traversing the route, against
seemingly impossible odds, demanded by Rider Haggard's Ayesha,
'She who must be obeyed', played by the statuesque Ursula Andress,
where we were all in danger of being caught between the crossfire
of Israeli and Jordanian forces, who were at it hammer and tongs;
another time to the heavy Gothic and Baroque architecture of
Munich, capital of Bavaria, as Otto Wesendonk in *Magic Fire,* to be
cuckolded by Alan Badel's Wagner.

The dewy softness and misty rain of County Wicklow in the
Republic of Ireland was more to my liking, where I played the
beastly Sheriff of Nottingham, outwitted by Richard Greene's
Robin Hood in *Sword of Sherwood Forest.*

But best of all were home locations, in the quiet dignity and
orderly flower beds of Regent's Park, for example, as Deborah Kerr's
civil servant husband, Henry Miles, even though I was cuckolded
again, this time by Van Johnson (as Maurice Bendrix) in Graham
Greene's *The End of the Affair.*

Helen always went with me on 'safari', and I looked forward so
very much to her greeting when I returned in the evenings from

those various hinterlands, and to a refreshing bath and cosy chats over our meal.

I was in Hamley's Toy Shop, Regent Street, one day, and with great sadness saw an actor I'd worked with in Nottingham Rep, demonstrating toy boomerangs. I tried to avoid him, in case of causing embarrassment, but he caught sight of me and, with a show of brave assurance, like Mr Micawber, said it was only temporary work, and his agent knew where he was 'in case anything turned up'. Reflecting upon my own good fortune, I thought, 'There but for the grace of God' … and Helen …

We'd joined the Blackheath Rugby Football Club and enjoyed many Saturday afternoons at the Rectory Field, having tea with the teams after the game, and keenly anticipated the international matches.

On one of those great sporting occasions, England was playing Scotland at Twickenham, in their annual clash for the Calcutta Cup. As I was rehearsing for a television play in the morning, I arranged to meet Helen in our West Stand seats. Surprised and somewhat anxious to find hers empty when I arrived there about 15 minutes before kick off, I went to the elevated entrance to see if I could catch sight of her in the milling throng below. There she was, delicate as a piece of Dresden china, standing in a shuffling queue of enormous men, heading straight for the gentlemen's lavatory, thinking it led to the stand. I went to her rescue, and we sat down just as the whistle blew.

I did a great deal of sound broadcasting for the BBC Home Service over the years, and in 1956 felt flattered when invited to choose my own part in their series 'The Stars and their Choices'. My first choice, of course, was Stanhope *in Jouney's End*, but as this had already been broadcast fairly recently, I was asked to think again, and selected the cockney Able Seaman Badger in *Seagulls Over Sorrento* by Hugh Hastings, a play about naval ratings engaged in hazardous torpedo-testing on a lonely Scottish island. Ronald Shiner created this character in the theatre production, running for nigh on four years at the Apollo, in which Peter Gray brought great authenticity to the role of Lt Com Redmond, DSO, DSC, RN, drawing on his personal wartime experience in that branch of the armed forces.

My fan mail was now being delivered in elastic-banded bundles, and it was a marvellous trip for my ego when the address on an envelope from America simply read 'PETER CUSHING, ENGLAND' – full marks to the Postal Authorities, too! But it became impossible to deal with them by hand, and book-keeping for our accountant was beyond my mathematical powers, so we decided the time had come to engage a secretary.

They came and went in bewildering succession, all to have babies (not guilty, m'lud). In September 1959, Mrs Joyce Buten arrived and promptly announced that she also wanted to start a family. In desperation, I told her it didn't matter how many children she had, so long as she didn't leave us. I'm glad to say she is still with me, happily re-married to Mr Bernard Broughton, with two charming daughters, a dog, two Siamese cats, masses of laundry – mine included – a telephone that never seems to stop ringing and a typewriter. Their kindness, support and loyalty over 25 years has often amazed me, and I cherish their devotion.

On 26 May, after Joyce had been with us for quite some time, I received a card from her, the picture on the front showing a rather bashful if somewhat smug-looking dog, with the engraved words: 'You're dynamic, good-looking, brilliant, intelligent, friendly, forceful, commanding, generous, thoughtful...' As I read those complimentary observations, my expression began to assume that of the hound, until I opened the card flap and saw – 'and a *YEAR OLDER!* HAPPY BIRTHDAY.'

The cheek of some people's kids! – I gave her 50 years' notice, so she only has another 30 to get through!

On the subject of age, I was paid another most endearing compliment by some very young friends of ours who lived next door but one. Helen said I was always surrounded by dogs and children, and these were twins, William and Geoffrey Stanley Hughes, as alike as two peas in a pod, the only discernible difference being that one – I was never sure which – had an enchanting lisp.

We often swam together, and Helen provided scrumptious teas for us to have in the garden, during which they would chatter most engagingly and intelligently. I asked them what they wanted to be when they grew up. One said he'd like to be a sailor, the other a clergyman. 'And I like flying, because it takes me nearer to where God lives,' he added with great gravity. Then – in unison – the question was put to me, 'Now what do you want to be when *you* grow up?' I was 54 at the time of asking, and they were about ten. It made me feel I was on a par with them, and accepted into their Peter Pan realm!

We had bought a house in Kensington so that I could be near the theatres and studios when working, intending to use the cottage at weekends and during 'resting' periods. But we were becoming disenchanted with the changing face of London, and more and more attracted to life by the seaside, where the ozone did Helen so much good, and she appeared to be in better health recently. Therefore I was not surprised, although somewhat alarmed by the suddenness of her appeal and disquieting attitude, when I returned from filming one evening to find her sitting in the hall waiting for me, asking if she could go to Whitstable there and then. Since her mother's passing, she had hidden her emotions, but I knew it had affected her deeply, and thought perhaps depression had precipitated the desire to get away from that association of ideas quickly and permanently.

We sold No 9 Hillsleigh Road, which meant I had to be away from her from time to time, staying at Brown's in Mayfair, or an hotel near the studios, as part of my contracts.

She seemed well again after a few weeks, but occasionally her respiration became very laboured. She took a correspondence course with William Knowles called 'New Life Through Breathing', and many months of conscientious and admirable effort reaped some benefit, but it wasn't enough to allow her to lead a normal existence.

I did all I could to help with the chores, and this distressed her. 'That is my job,' she said. 'You do yours superbly, and I must do mine.'

But it was all too obvious that she just could not cope, so I made enquiries about domestic help. Helen had always loved 'tending our nest', as she called it, which is why we had not had anyone before.

A neighbour had such a 'treasure', and suggested that her sister, Mrs Maisie Olive, should come and 'do' for us.

Maisie, a dear motherly soul, but possessing a highly nervous disposition, was thrown into panic when the proposition was put to her, exclaiming, 'Oh dear! I might meet Peter Cushing!'

Her sister, a much more down-to-earth character, retorted logically, 'I wouldn't be surprised if you do. He lives there.'

I'm delighted to report that Maisie withstood the shock of meeting the man who had scared the wits out of her on television, and she is yet another loyal and faithful friend who, after 16 years, still comes to look after me and my daily needs.

*   *   *

I was kept busy for the next nine months, making a television series of 15 Sherlock Holmes adventures, with the excellent and humorous Nigel Stock playing Dr Watson. It proved a popular programme, but I was most displeased with my performances. Helen's condition was a constant worry, diverting my concentration, and of course I missed her presence in the control box, which gave me the self-confidence I lacked. She was also my sternest critic, and I felt lost without her guidance.

Adding to my anxieties, the BBC's schedule went a little haywire. The original plan had been ten days' rehearsal, plus recording, for each instalment, including location shooting. Unfortunately, our

British climate had not been taken into account, and rain often 'stopped play', losing us valuable hours while we waited for it to stop and leaving little time for the interiors. The series began transmission before we'd completed the full complement, so we were pressurised into getting them ready to keep up with the weekly demand. I can never give my best under such conditions and, to my mind, it was apparent on the screen.

True to the 'gypsies warning' in my early days on the stage – when I had to smoke that church warden – pipes always make me feel violently sick. I rather envy those who do not turn a pale shade of bilious green, but puff away with such sweet content and serenity. Holmes being an inveterate smoker of the things, I had to endure this nausea on top of everything else, and the irony of it was that I became Pipeman of the Year, awarded by the Briar Pipe Trade Association, who presented me with a miniature model poised on a little black plinth, my name engraved alongside notables who had won it previously, such as Harold Wilson, Warren Mitchell and Andrew Cruickshank.

It was my privilege to be the first 'straight' actor invited to appear on *The Morecambe and Wise Show*, in one of 'the plays wot I rote', as those efforts of Ernie's were always prefixed. They were simply wonderful to work with, and I did at least five more, in which a 'running gag' was employed, implying that I had not received the fee for my initial engagement. Each time I demanded or pleaded for payment without success, until my final bow with them about six years ago when, at last, I collected my dues.

Shortly after his first heart attack, someone asked Eric Morecambe if he ever paid me. Giving his horn rims a characteristic swivel, he said, 'Yes – and look what happened to me!'

My next film engagement was based upon Robert Louis Stevenson's classic thriller *Dr Jekyll and Mr Hyde*, with Christopher Lee playing the dual roles. I didn't want to be away from Helen, and rather than risk delays on the long drive to and from the studios each day, I caught the milk train, getting home in the evenings about ten o'clock. Joyce lived in Welling, and journeyed down to keep Helen company every morning or afternoon, and I had asked David Claughton, a staunch ally and local electrical wizard, to install a stairlift, as Helen could no longer walk up the flight to our bedroom.

Her dedicated breathing exercises were helping her, and she strove so valiantly to master the advised techniques, refusing to accept defeat, until she was told by a locum-tenens that what she was doing was a waste of time. It was pitiful to see her spirit crumble, and although it wouldn't have made any difference to the inevitable outcome, that slap in the face took the heart out of her and speeded her decline. Her weight went down to six stone – I had lost three myself – and we were both physically and mentally spent.

Early in January 1971, I started a film for Hammer at Elstree. At the end of the first day, Joyce rang to say Helen had been taken to Canterbury Hospital for a check-up, where she would be kept for a few days.

She looked tired when I got there in the evening, but comfortable enough. As I wasn't on call the next day, I promised I'd bring a little picnic lunch for us to have, as a change from hospital fare. She smiled, and said that would be lovely.

Arriving with the small wicker hamper, containing smoked salmon and avocado salad, I went straight to her private ward, and stopped dead in my tracks. Hanging over the glass peephole of the door was a notice: 'No visitors under any circumstances'. Numbed with consternation, I sought the sister at once, who took me to the doctor attending Helen. He told me she'd had a relapse during the night, her chest and heart were very weak, and she had emphysema.

My mind switched to Dr Galeskwi – this was the terminal illness he could not work miracles to cure…

Something inside me still refused to believe what must have been obvious to everyone else. I knew her invincible will and courage, and had seen her overcome bouts of sickness that would have laid low far more robust individuals.

I begged the doctor to let her come home. He agreed to this, pointing out that she would need constant nursing.

Whilst she was being prepared for the journey, I arranged for a day and night nurse, and then rang John Redway, asking him to cancel my participation in the film.

I joined Helen in the ambulance, for what was to be our last drive together in this world.

There were many times when I had been human and erred: Helen was divine, and forgave, but I could never forgive myself. I spoke about this.

'Peter dearest, I told you, before we were married, I didn't want you to feel possessed. Those things are so unimportant, they don't matter. As far as I'm concerned, they didn't even happen.' She took my hand in hers, as soft and delicate as gossamer, and with immutable love, whispered tenderly, 'You've been wonderful. No one else would have done for me what you have done. I cannot thank you now, because I cannot talk, but I will when I'm better.'

For a little while she improved, amid familiar surroundings and loving care, but it was only temporary, like an electric light bulb that sometimes seems to glow brighter for a few seconds just before the filament burns itself out, and is extinguished for ever...

8

'GOODNIGHT, MY BELOVÈD PETER...'

I HAD GONE into the garden to collect some coal from the bunker to put on the fire, and upon my return found Helen sitting hunched on the divan. A dreadful foreboding overcame me, but I tried to conceal my fears.

'I can't help you any more, Peter dear,' she said.

'You help me just by being here,' I replied truthfully.

'But suppose I'm not here tomorrow...'

I forced myself to say lightly – 'Why? You're not going anywhere, are you?'

'No.' She fell silent for a moment, and then looked at me. 'I shall *always* be with you – everywhere, at all time.' With a little smile, she lay back and closed her eyes. I wrapped a blanket around her, made up the fire, and then went into the conservatory, where I broke down and wept.

Maisie had been witness to this, and kindly brought me a cup of tea. 'Don't give way, sir,' she said, 'she'll be alright.'

I heard myself say, 'Thank you, Maisie – yes, she will be alright.'

I lit a cigarette, inhaled deeply, and drank the tea.

*   *   *

The night nurse arrived promptly at nine o'clock and helped Helen upstairs and into bed. I soon followed. I kissed her, and she whispered, 'Goodnight, my belovèd Peter. You will save me. God bless you.'

These were the last words she ever said.

At about 3.00 am some instinct woke me, and I reached out my hand. I felt her flesh: it was as cold as stone, and had an unnatural clammy dampness about it. I switched on the bedside lamp and the electric blanket. She opened her eyes a little, and I saw that her pupils were just minute black dots.

'Would you like a cup of tea, dearest?' She nodded slowly. I helped her to sit up, and tucked a pillow behind her back. Then, putting on my dressing gown, I went down to the kitchen. The nurse was there, and I asked her if she would go and sit with Helen whilst I made the tea.

When I took it up, Helen was lying down again, her eyes open and glazed, her breathing spasmodic and painful to hear. I put the cup on the side table, sat down by the bed, and rested my hand gently on her hip. I looked at the nurse, who returned my gaze and slowly shook her head. We sat on either side of the bed in silence for what seemed an eternity.

'Is there *nothing* we can do?' I asked at last. The nurse shook her head again.

I had read many times of the 'death rattle', and when it came it was almost with relief that I heard it. To suffer as she had done for so long was too much to bear, and now the end was near. The nurse must have seen my stricken face, for she warned me, 'Don't do anything that might upset her – she is still very conscious of everything that's going on.'

Helen raised both her arms very, very slowly – as if in supplication, and to welcome someone into them. She remained like that for a long time, then – just as slowly – lowered them. Her eyes closed, and her breathing ceased. The nurse leant over her: a few moments passed, and then she said quietly, 'She's gone.'

I glanced at the clock – the hands showed it was nearly nine. I looked down at my darling's face, and as if by some miracle, all the pain and suffering of the past years had been wiped away. She looked serenely at peace, and quite beautiful. I kissed her forehead, and murmured, 'My dear Helen.' That was all. Drained of all emotion, I felt nothing – just empty – my mind as though anaesthetised. The shock was to come later – much later, with devastating effect. But at that moment all I could think of was that if I were playing this scene in a film, I wouldn't be reacting like this at all.

'You'd better get dressed now, Mr Cushing.' The nurse's gentle voice roused me from my reverie. I nodded, and did as she bid.

Later that morning the undertaker arrived. He was a kindly gentleman, tall and thin, with sleek hair as black as his clothes, and wearing a professionally permanent smile of sympathetic understanding. After a few preliminaries, he opened a brochure, displaying a variety of monumental masonry for me to choose from. Some of them reminded me vaguely of the pictures I'd seen years ago of elaborate jelly moulds in Mother's copy of Mrs Beeton's recipes. With his palm uppermost, he pointed delicately with the nail of his little finger to one of the illustrations – an open book – and said, 'This headstone is very popular in the trade.'

Trade! What an extraordinary word to use, I thought – but then I suppose it is a trade, and a brisk one at that. I accepted his choice, and asked for a space to be left by the side of Helen's name, to allow for mine when that joyous day dawns. Again, with that absurd theatricality at such a time, I said to myself, 'You have first billing, dear one.'

Underneath, I requested some lines to be engraved, that I had written for her on our Silver Wedding Anniversary in 1968:

A quarter of a century no less
Oh My! But how time flies
It only seems but yesterday…
But you who have so much to give
Gives all – and having given

Wonders in all humility
What is left to give.
But Helen dear
The Present stands on what the Past has taken
And the Future holds but good
When in such loving hands and care as yours.
I thank God and You for – Oh, so much!
Denied to those less lucky ones than I
Because I know that but for you
This world would be a sad and lonely place
And I as nothing in it.

I went out onto the deserted beach. It was blowing almost gale force, the seagulls were wheeling and mewing above me, the waves pounding the shingle with a deafening roar. I looked up to Heaven, and began humming the tune 'Happy Birthday to you'. I think I'd gone a little mad. A gust of wind blew a sheet of newspaper towards me, which wrapped itself around my legs. I removed it and, by force of habit, thrust it into my jacket, not wishing to litter the shore.

I found myself indoors again, wandering aimlessly about the house, then suddenly started rushing up and down the stairs as fast as I could, in the vain hope of inducing a heart attack. When this subsided, I reached in my pocket for a cigarette, and pulled out the paper I'd put there. I looked at it idly. It was a page from *The Daily Telegraph*, and at the top of the Personal Column my eye caught the following tract:

Ye now therefore have sorrow: but I will see you again, and your
heart shall rejoice, and your joy no man taketh from you.
JOHN XVI, 22

This 'windfall' was surely something more than sheer coincidence.
It was then that I found the letter Helen had left for me: '...Let the sun shine in your heart. Do not pine for me, my belovèd Peter,

because that will cause unrest. Do not be hasty to leave this world, because you will not go until you have lived the life you have been given. AND REMEMBER we will meet again when the time is right … This is my promise…'

I have been doubtful many times about many things during my life, but of this I have no doubt – no doubt whatsoever.

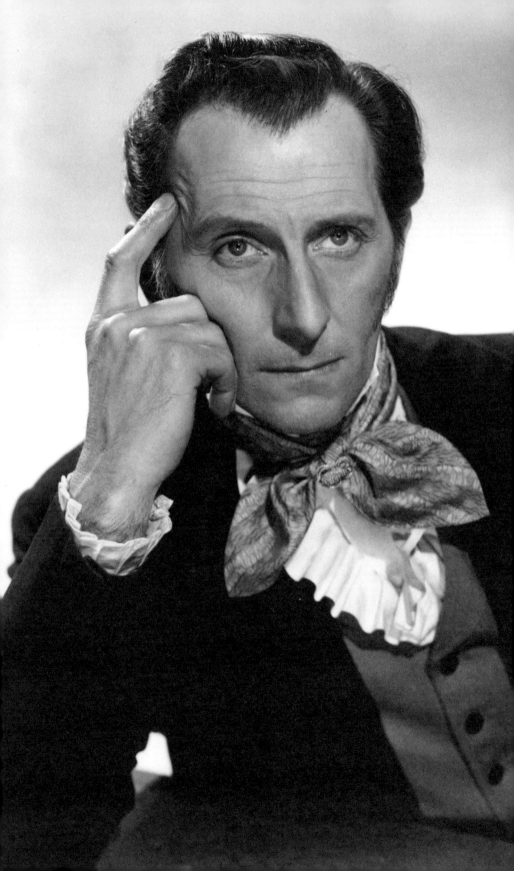

PETER CUSHING

'PAST FORGETTING'

Memoirs of the Hammer Years

Again for my belovèd Helen,
who will always shine in my
heart like a good deed in a
naughty world.

Time may lie heavy between
But what has been
Is past forgetting

(Noël Coward's 'I'll See You Again'
from *Bitter Sweet*)

A FOREWORD BY
PETER GRAY

WHY A FOREWORD? And why by me? The answer to both questions, dear reader, lies in my old friend Peter Cushing's steely will. He would accept no pleas as to my unsuitability for the part. So how could I refuse, owing him so much? At least what follows may throw a little light...

We first met just half a century ago at Euston, on a train bound for Nottingham. I was travelling (it was a Sunday) to take up an engagement with Harry Hanson's Court Players for a long season of weekly, twice-nightly repertory at the Theatre Royal. Having settled myself gratefully into a corner seat in an empty compartment (in those pre-BR days one rarely travelled, as one does now, packed into compartments like sardines into a tin), I was hoping to remain undisturbed. Like Garbo, I 'wanted to be alone' to suffer 'the pangs of despised love'. I had just been jilted. Deeply stricken, I saw myself as the personification of the Tragic Muse: '...'tis not alone my inky cloak, good Mother, Nor customary suits of solemn black, Nor windy suspiration of forced breath,' etc etc. 'That can denote me truly...' I fancied myself no end as Hamlet and dreamed of playing him one day.

Suddenly... rumble, *crash!* The door was flung back, and a substantial hunk of masculine brawn and muscle that would have graced an international rugby team beamed happily at me. 'Mind if I join you?' (With hindsight, how characteristic of Peter to be so considerate as to ask, regardless of his absolute right to any of the unoccupied seats about me!) I felt like saying 'Of course I mind, *Fathead,* can't you *see* I'm on the rack of unrequited love?' But how could I? Flinging an enormous suitcase, as if it were a newspaper, onto the rack over his head, he sat himself opposite me and set about being social. I was defenceless: I had no book, and the 'dejected haviour of my visage' had obviously failed to register! It transpired that he, too, was joining the Court Players, having just finished his first full season of rep at Southampton. Sandwiches were swopped and one of us (plutocrat!) had a Guinness which we shared.

My resistance began to crumble, eroded by the torrent of bonhomie from my companion and his disarming candour. By the time we got to Nottingham I had agreed (though still not without some shreds of reluctance) to join him in a search for digs. We clewed up, at about teatime, at 6 Hampden Street, ten minutes' walk from the theatre. A bird-like little lady answered the door, listened to our needs, and after a shrewd but utterly unsuspicious appraisal showed us up to two spotless 'bedsitters' (on the first and second floors.) 'Terms: Full board' – breakfast, lunch, tea and a 'cooked supper after the show at night', with fires in our rooms – '30 shillings a week'. Her name (with what affection I record it!) was Mrs Robinson. She was a theatrical landlady of the old school – a species, I understand, now sadly extinct. There should be a memorial to such as she in the newly opened Theatre Museum in Covent Garden. Always there, always cheerful, ever providing, she made it a 'home from home', a fact to which her visitors' book bore oft-repeated and grateful testimony.

Those digs were the nursery (horticulturally speaking) in which our lifelong friendship put down roots and became established. I can't resist trying to recapture the magic of those fast-dwindling pre-war days. 'Bliss was it in that dawn to be alive, but to be young was very heaven.' (Alas, in our case, it was not dawn but sunset on the world in which we were fortunate enough to grow up.) Each of us had achieved his heart's desire, after false starts and years of frustration – years, however, remembered by both of us with more affection than bitterness, for the sake of their human contacts and who shall say what wealth of material upon which to draw, once our dreams became reality.

Sixpence was a substantial tip, then, and bought the same quality and quantity at Woolworths year after year. We had to supply our own clothes for the weekly plays, but a made to measure dinner jacket (of superlative cloth and pure silk facings) cost only £3.10s at Montague Burtons! ('Tails' were £7.) On my £7 a week salary I was affluent. But *then* advertising hadn't bludgeoned the gullible into equating happiness with material possessions.

The theatre was a temple of romance, comedy, tragedy and thrills. Goodies and Baddies were, on the whole, clearly defined. There was no glorification, as now, of the anti-hero. It was a world in which there was still (so at any rate it seems with hindsight) some innocence left, some sense of wonder. And the accursed flail hadn't been invented to annihilate the natural glory of England's country lanes and hedgerows.

We worked – rehearsing, playing (two performances nightly), and learning our parts for the following week – almost non-stop from ten in the morning 'til well past midnight, six days a week. And we played to packed houses in which the best seats were half a crown!

We not only shared digs but a dressing room at the theatre as well. (We came to be known as the Two Peters.) 'An actor in his time plays many parts' – especially if in his early years he is lucky enough to acquire experience in weekly rep. Our contracts were 'to play as cast', and although we mostly appeared as dashing juveniles – in those unsophisticated days all eyes and teeth, with lines like 'Who's for tennis?' and bouncing about on sofas with our adorably pretty young female counterparts – 'character' parts sometimes came our way, requiring a veritable mask of greasepaint to conceal the familiar and youthful features beneath! Creating these alien physiognomies was always hilarious. We certainly didn't err on the side of restraint: a broken nose might be deemed a nifty touch for a 'tough guy'. On one such occasion Peter, using subtle shading and highlights, transformed his aquiline schnozzle into something resembling a zigzag path! (He had, even then, a fastidious regard for the minutest detail of make-up, costume and props.)

He has already described our adventures on the Trent, on the cricket field, and how – on the last night at Nottingham (autumn 1938), after a farewell ovation from an audience who had come to see the company in 38 plays in as many weeks – we were standing, after supper, at Mrs R's top window looking out over the rooftops, wondering (in our heightened emotional state) what the future held for us. Had we, I wonder, even the faintest presentiment that (in the haunting words of Cyril Connolly) it was almost 'closing time in the gardens of the West'? I think not; but if we had, it was the merest shadow, rapidly dispelled in the sunlight of our youthful confidence.

Peter confided to me his idea of having a bash at Hollywood. My wits reeled! Hollywood, in those days, was a – how can one describe the glamour it held? – a glittering world of film stars and entertainment, as remote from weekly rep as sky from earth! I think I must have *exuded* doubts (even if I didn't voice them) about his chances – he had no contacts over there, had never even been inside a film studio, was relatively inexperienced and virtually penniless. How wrong I was! (And not for the first, or last, time.) Peter had had a vision. Hollywood and its films had been to him more – much more – than mere entertainment; they had transported him from suburbia and a surveyor's office into a world infinitely more glamorous, more adventurous, more romantic – and yet, because of his addiction to make-believe, infinitely more real – than reality!

Moreover, during the season just finished, he had actually *met* his boyhood hero Tom Mix, and had canoodled (innocently enough!), if not with the girl of his dreams, Loretta Young, in person, at least with her spitting image, her Hollywood 'double'. Given his indomitable will, it wasn't an irresponsible decision. And soon I was receiving snaps of him looking utterly at home with stars in Hollywood who were to me as gods on Olympus. Nothing venture, nothing win, indeed!

Thus our ways diverged and when next we met (a hilarious occasion in 1943 while I was on leave) severe illnesses abroad and during the rigours of wartime touring in ENSA had taken some toll of his powerful physique; there was already a hint of the prominent cheekbones and sunken cheeks so strikingly effective in the roles which later brought him fame. We acted together, alas, only once more – in *The Rivals* at Windsor's Theatre Royal, where I had my first job after demobilisation in 1946, in what was then the permanent repertory company. Peter was 'imported' to play Faulkland, in which role he had recently appeared with great distinction and characteristic panache at the Criterion Theatre with Edith Evans. During rehearsal he gently suggested incorporating a bit of stage business he'd used 'when we did it in London'. The ensuing send up (fully anticipated) from his fellow thespians must have rocked the castle foundations opposite!

I called at Airlie Gardens often during the lean years. Peter would be painting scarves or making his marvellous models and stage 'sets'. Helen would be in the kitchen cooking and contriving, or warming a Guinness on the hearth for her man. They were invariably welcoming, and always cheerful; and I had no idea, then, just *how* lean the times were – and couldn't have done much about it had I known. The tide turned for him with the irreversible advance of television. And his experience of filming in Hollywood – he was ever a quick learner! – must have been invaluable, for he adapted to this new medium with the shrewdest appreciation of its exacting technique (a technique in most respects poles apart from that of the theatre) and with exceptional skill; moreover his particular gifts were tailor made for it; his meticulous regard for detail, infinite capacity for taking pains (one definition of genius) and his dissatisfaction with anything short of perfection could brave the microscopic eye of the TV camera with impunity.

Nevertheless, as he has described in the first volume of his autobiography, he suffered agonies of nerves – and no wonder, for in those early days transmissions were 'live' and error was ineradicable. Helen wonderfully laid that ghost with 'Try falling in love with the camera'. Inspired counsel! He did just that – and the camera reciprocated! It was the beginning of a lasting romance which, in play after play (until his name almost became synonymous with television), brought him countless fans, first of all at home, and subsequently, through his films, all over the world.

What is the secret of his particular and unique appeal? I think it lies partly in the fact that in every good actor there is an element of Peter Pan, the boy who wouldn't grow up – a fixation in that period of childhood when total suspension of disbelief in a fairy tale is possible and even natural. It will be remembered by readers of his first book that Peter fell in love with Peter Pan the first time he saw him in the theatre and wished to be like him. Make-believe, that childhood propensity, had more attraction for him than reality, and it was this total suspension of disbelief in the far-fetched phantasies of his horror films that enabled him to make, for his audiences, 'the incredible credible', to quote from one of his thousands of fan letters.

After all he's been through, it isn't to be wondered at that he has never become blasé about success or its perquisites. Indeed, his attitude to both is endearingly consistent with that of the 'boy who wouldn't grow up'. The adulation, the awards, instant recognition wherever he goes, fan letters from all over the world, being presented to royalty at film premières, travel, accommodation arranged for him in luxury hotels, the acquisition of a brand new Jaguar (a joy in which his beloved Helen was able to share), all these things thrilled him – I fancy it was almost as if he had to keep pinching himself to make sure he wasn't dreaming! He told me about them because he knew they'd thrill me as much as they did him, but they left him more humble (if possible) than before.

He is grateful for critical praise (what artist isn't?) but mainly because (being essentially diffident) it reassures him. Then he forgets it, and only wishes he had done better. He always hopes to do better next time. And although, for obvious reasons, he couldn't fail to be aware of his stature as an actor, he has never thought he knows it all, he is always eager for direction, and receptive to advice or suggestion about his work.

Even the success of his autobiography (what a thing to undertake, at 70 plus, when you've not previously written a line!) delighted him mostly, I think, because of the many movingly grateful letters it brought him from readers who had found inspiration, hope, and solace in its closing pages.

A few months ago the book was selected by the RNIB to be a 'Talking Book for the Blind'. Peter was overjoyed, and asked me to make the recording. Few things in my life have given me greater satisfaction. When it was done, I stayed a few days with the author at his home in Whitstable. What a reunion! Fifty years had passed since we stood at Mrs R's top window contemplating the future. 'Two old men' now, 'two shadows wandering in the light of day'; yet, wonderful to relate, the years had left our true selves untouched. What a uniquely precious thing is friendship. The quotation opposite the title page of Peter's first book says much about it, but not all: there is the mutual enrichment of two natures in harmony, the total relaxation of complete openness, the shared laughter, the memories…

Walking on the foreshore, the morning I left, I happened upon a pebble wondrously stained by mineral salts and marine lichens – a mini Turner, a sunset in miniature! Returning to the house, I presented it to my old friend, who pondered it intently – and marvelled. Then he added it, ceremoniously, to a shelf already laden with a varied collection of his own objets trouvés. He has retained the capacity for wonder. A mossy stone, 'a piece of glass abraded by the beach', a gull paddling in the shallows opposite his studio window, a dew-laden cobweb, model trains (of the steam age), a cut-out figure on a packet of Cornflakes, all these – and many, many more that most people regard not though they see them – in varying degrees delight him. A Peter Pan attribute!

In an indefinable way, I believe that this freshness of vision, this seeing of the commonplace as if for the first time always, adds an extra dimension – a touch of the marvellous – to everything he does as a player, and accounts in part for his worldwide appeal. For most of us 'Heaven lies about us in our infancy! Shades of the prison house begin to close upon the growing boy, But he beholds the light, and whence it flows, He sees it in his joy ... at length the man perceives it die away, And fade into the light of common day;' but not Peter (Pan) Cushing – he 'still is nature's priest, and by the vision splendid is on his way attended'.

Blessed be he! Of such 'children' is the Kingdom of Heaven.

Peter Gray
Devonshire, 1987

CURTAIN UP

PROLOGUE

WHAT *ARE* THEY called? I'd seen them so often in my natural history books ... ah, yes! – it came to me in a flash: AMANITA PHALLOIDES.

Always interested in nature, I suddenly remembered the scientific name for that most deadly of poisonous fungi, the Death Cap, and set off on my bicycle to search for it in the countryside of Kent, where I live. I found some. As the Latin implies, they looked just like grotesque phallic symbols, their sickly white egg-shaped caps shining in a most repugnant way. I left them where they grew, and then considered climbing a nearby pylon to electrocute myself. Deep down I knew I would never take such a step, but because of the numbing agony of those early days following the passing of my dear wife Helen, it was inevitable that I should contemplate suicide. Instead, I sat down under an oak tree and lit a cigarette.

It wouldn't be fair, I thought; someone would have to clear up the grisly mess; it is not allowed by God; it wouldn't get me what I wanted, anyway – to be reunited immediately with Helen – and, in any case, I hadn't the necessary courage. Over-riding all these considerations, there was that message Helen had left me in her last letter:

> *Let the sun shine in your heart. Do not pine for me, my belovèd Peter, because that will cause unrest.* Do not be hasty to leave this world, *because you will not go until*

you have lived the life you have been given.
And remember, we will meet again when the time is right
… this is my promise…

In all our 30 years together she never once broke a promise, and I have always heeded her advice.

The year was 1971, a few weeks after the events described at the end of my first volume of autobiography. Encouraged by public response to that initial attempt, I now venture to fill in some of the gaps…

ACT ONE SCENE 1

WHEN ONE IS lucky enough to attain success, it is very difficult to write about it entertainingly. In my case, that satisfying achievement merely brought hard work in its wake, which, in itself, makes for dull reading – it would from my pen, at any rate.

Many readers were disappointed that in my earlier memoir I did not dwell more upon those years I spent so happily under the banner of Hammer Films. Ay, there's the rub! A quite erroneous conception of life in film studios has somehow embedded itself in the public mind, with the result that people envisage all sorts of outrageous goings on 'behind the scenes'. They imagine film stars to be drink-besotted actors rolling up any old time of a morning, bleary-eyed from a night's binge, drinking a bottle of gin for breakfast, and leaping into bed with their leading lady at the first opportunity, and after staggering onto a sound stage, to reel off a few lines from an 'idiot board', we rollick homeward as soon as we can for another bout of carousing 'til the early hours.

Let me explode the myth, at once. The reality goes something like this: rise at 5.00 am to get to the 'factory' by 7.15, where you are met by the second assistant, forever looking worriedly at his watch, who greets you by saying 'Right, get your toupée nailed on, you're wanted on the set in five minutes, we're working 'til midnight, the dialogue's been altered, and all your best lines have been given to the producer's girlfriend.'

Well, it may not be quite like that, but it is nearer the mark than the above 'grand' illusion!

'What fun it must be, making films!' exclaim the innocent. No. Not 'fun'. That word conjures up the joys of sky-larking in a fairground. Most actors enjoy the challenge of their work, but there is too much at stake, and too little time, to have 'fun' in the true sense of the word.

Nerves, of course, are just one of an actor's worst enemies and nowhere was the pressure greater than performing in a play on live television. I must stress the word 'live' because nowadays almost everything is pre-recorded.

During my early years with the BBC, I appeared with that splendid light comedy player, Frank Allenby. His nervous system was undermined to such an extent that his doctor advised him never to undertake that kind of work again, or he'd risk having a heart attack. The sad outcome of events gave an ironic twist to the play's title, *If This Be Error*, by Rachel Grieve, produced in November 1952. Six months later, Mr Allenby passed away.

At rehearsals for a play to be televised, the assistant floor manager, usually a girl, followed the action with great concentration, making a special note of pauses in the dialogue, so that when the play was being transmitted, she would be instantly aware that an actor had 'dried'. If any untoward 'Macready'* (to use the old pro's expression for forgetting one's lines) occurred she would press a button, which cut off all sound from the viewers' sets, quickly prompt the unfortunate victim, release the button, and, with any luck, the action would continue as rehearsed. It was up to the actor Not to Panic – just to stand where he was, looking completely unruffled and at peace with the world. Those quite ghastly breaks in continuity took but a few seconds, but they seemed like eternity to the paralysed performer. In all the 30-odd plays I did, before pre-recording came to the rescue, it only happened to me twice, in Peter Ustinov's *The Moment of Truth* (how apt!) and *Bird in Hand* by John Drinkwater.

Herbert Lomas was playing the innkeeper, a role he had originated on the stage in *Bird in Hand*, when my moment of

* William Macready, the great mid-19th century actor, had a habit of pausing inordinately during a speech to produce some dramatic effect!

amnesia stunned me. Like an obedient dog I stood there transfixed, a sickly grin on my physog, waiting for the coup de grâce. Herbert's face went ashen: he jabbed me in the ribs with his elbow, with such force that he nearly knocked me out of the shot, and in the loudest aside I'd ever heard, hissed in my ear 'IT'S YOUR TURN!', which didn't help me one little bit. I felt like saying 'I pass,' but perhaps it's just as well I didn't.

There is a story concerning Wilfrid Lawson that deserves remembering. He was a superb actor, and a darling man, but unfortunately addicted to the bottle. He had suffered a terrible injury in 1918, when he was a pilot in the RAF (formerly the Royal Flying Corps). He crash landed in No Man's Land between the British and German trenches, and it was hours before the stretcher bearers could reach him. In an effort to deaden the pain, he drank himself silly from his flask of whisky, and for the rest of his life he could not break the habit. Although he never let the side down, the dear old thing did have great trouble remembering his lines.

Wilfrid and I were in *The Road,* a play by Jean-Jacques Bernard, in which Bryan Forbes was excellent playing my son. The scene was set in the living room of a little house in Burgundy on Nationale 6, one of the main roads in France.

I had a very lengthy 'soliloquy' soon after my entrance, extolling the delights of country living, fresh vegetables from the garden, home-cured bacon, eggs straight from the chickens, etc, etc, and how pleasant it was to listen to the farmyard noises as we ate, which were supplied most realistically by the sound engineers. On the third day of rehearsal, I had a stab at this piece of prose without the script and got through it word perfect. From out of the dim recesses of the pungent drill hall where we were working came the sound of Wilfrid's fruity voice: 'Swankpot!'

When the time came for the play to be transmitted – and I emphasise that this was 'live' TV – I came to the end of this same speech. With impeccable timing, just after a cow had mooed, there was an almighty crash, which sounded as if J Arthur Rank's gong-basher had suddenly gone berserk somewhere off screen. Without turning a hair, Wilfrid ad-libbed 'Mice?'

*   *   *

The actor's nightmare came to my aid once, in a backhanded way. I had been invited to introduce Marlene Dietrich at the Café de Paris in London, where she was the star cabaret attraction during 1955. Helen had helped me prepare a carefully worded eulogy, which I learnt by heart. Dressed in my best bib and tucker for this great occasion, I rose from my table to address the glittering gathering. A pink spotlight suddenly stabbed across the room to pick me out. It was quite unexpected and I was momentarily blinded. I could not remember a word of my speech.

The chatter and clatter of cutlery slowly died away, and there was a breathless hush. I looked at Helen, always my inspiration, and she mouthed the opening gambit. That got me going, and I delivered my 'spiel' without further faltering, although badly shaken. Later in the evening, Sam Wanamaker, the American actor-producer, who was one of the guests, came over to me and said, 'That was masterly! The way you just stood there, waiting for silence before you began, had us all riveted to our seats!'

(Sheila Sim and I had worked with Sam Wanamaker in 1954, when he produced Ian Stuart Black's light comedy *The Soldier and the Lady*. By way of relaxation he indulged in acrobatics, directing the play as he performed handstands on a flimsy cane chair placed right on the edge of the stage, which seemed to us a most dangerous practice.)

Miss Dietrich was utterly charming, and she adored Michael Wilding. 'He really does need someone to *mother* him,' she declared, and that was precisely what she did. They enjoyed great comfort and happiness in each other's company.

*   *   *

German television staged an Exposition in 1953 at Düsseldorf, and the BBC was asked if they would make a British contribution. PN Walker-Taylor's comedy thriller *Portrait by Peko* was chosen, which starred Ursula Howells, Patrick Barr and me. The audience could watch the performance on monitors, or from catwalks erected around the sets.

A revolver was essential for one particular scene, and after a rapid change of clothes I held out my hand to take the weapon from the man in charge of props. Instead, he shook it and with a beaming smile murmured a greeting in his native tongue. Alarmed, I indicated what was required but couldn't make him understand. The floor manager, John Jacobs, turned to give me my entrance cue and, seeing my predicament, mouthed 'Don't worry' (a silent command I found difficult to obey). I made my entrance, wondering what on earth I could improvise when the moment came to threaten Patrick Barr at gunpoint. To my relief I caught sight of Mr Jacobs making his way towards me on his knees, dragging a monitor behind him with one hand, holding his script and the revolver in the other. Carefully watching the screen, he chose a moment when I was in close-up to hand over the weapon, just in the nick of time.

My relief was short-lived, however, because I sensed another catastrophe. Something was burning, and out of the corner of my eye I glimpsed a large bundle of rags in flames, set alight by a Bunsen burner on a workbench which was part of the setting. The thought flashed through my mind: Don't rush – that might give rise to panic stations. So, controlling my already shaken nerves, I picked up a jug of water from the table, assumed a casual air, strolled over to the conflagration and dowsed it, which caused smoke to billow up into the faces of the absorbed viewers above. They were most impressed, gasping 'Wunderbar, wunderbar!' between bouts of choking.

The valve on the Bunsen had jammed and the flame was dangerously high. Continuing my dialogue, I jerked the rubber tube from its socket and was nearly asphyxiated by the sudden escape of gas. Dropping the tube to the floor I put my foot on it to stem the flow until a stagehand, seeing my plight, turned off the tap on the main cylinder. I suppose the audience thought this business was all part of the act – subtle symbolism perhaps? But they must have found it somewhat confusing!

* * *

It took me 11 years to surface publicly after the passing of my wife. The only antidote to that devastation was work, when I could immerse myself in whatever character I was called upon to portray, and thus take refuge from myself. I saw no one socially, hiding myself away whenever I was unemployed which, mercifully, was not often.

Between 1971 and 1982 I made 32 films and appeared on television at least 13 times, in a variety of entertainment, and also recorded half a dozen books for the Talking Book Service for the Blind. Wherever I went, I was treated with the greatest understanding, and met with nothing but kindness, consideration and courtesy. I remain so deeply grateful to all those people who did their best to help me.

My engagements took me to such diverse places as Madrid, Hong Kong, Florida, Aranjuez in Central Spain, Montreal, Munich, Austria, Lusaka in Zambia, Santander on the Bay of Biscay in Northern Spain, West and East Australia, Cannes, Paris, Nice, Hollywood and – to me the best of all – Bristol, and many other favourite spots in my dear mother country!

* * *

I think it was in the month of February 1971 when my friend and agent, John Redway, rang and asked me to come up to town and have lunch with him and a newly recruited client, John Hough, who was to direct a film for the Hammer company entitled *Twins of Evil*, in which I was cast as a Puritan witch hunter, Gustav Weil. The venue for the meal was Brown's Hotel in Mayfair, which, incidentally, has become my home from home whenever duty calls me to London.

As I entered L'Apéritif Restaurant, a hovering waiter, of Latin origin, very nearly dropped the tray he was carrying, his eyes popping out of their sockets. 'Ah!' he screamed. 'It's-ah da-Petah da-Coosh! He afrighten my wife! She *love* eet!' – and, kissing me resoundingly on both cheeks, hurried off to the kitchen quarters to spread the glad tidings, with delighted cries of 'Buono buono! il attore magnifico!' as he weaved his way between tables and chairs occupied by the quiet dignified clientele. With typical British reserve and politeness, they ignored this charming enthusiasm, although I did overhear a bemonocled gentleman murmur to his lady companion 'Excitable lot, these foreigners.'

In *Twins of Evil*, I had a spectacular death scene, and to answer the many who write asking how many times and in what manner I have met my doom in films, I will now endeavour to satisfy their curiosity with the macabre details, as far as I can recollect them.

Are you sitting comfortably? Then I'll begin: battered to pulp by Alan Ladd in *The Black Knight*, who used a jumbo size mace for the purpose (how's that for starters?).

As the Athenian General Memnon, in *Alexander the Great*, having taken a fond farewell of my wife, played by Claire Bloom, I rode a horse, bareback, to be slaughtered in the battle of Granicus, by Richard Burton's legions.

Stabbed in the back by Oliver Reed, when I played the Sheriff of Nottingham in *Sword of Sherwood Forest*; shot in the chest by Bernard Lee in *Fury at Smugglers' Bay*; impaled by a harpoon hurled at me by a mulatto as *Captain Clegg* in the film of that name, to die in the arms of my trusty servant, played by Michael Ripper (soft music); turned to stone by looking at *The Gorgon* in that film (as I had to stagger down a staircase at the same time, this was not an easy way to cash in my chips); killed in a no holds barred fight with Jack Palance in *Torture Garden*; a hatchet buried in my back causing me to hurtle over the edge of a balcony, plunging to the stone-flagged floor 30-odd feet below (do I hear someone say 'a stunt man did that?' – if so, ten out of ten whoever you are, but I did top and tail that happy landing myself – just the free fall bit in the middle was left to some other brave body) – the film was *Twins of Evil*; committed suicide by hanging myself as Mr Grimsdyke in *Tales from the Crypt*, but I had my revenge, rising from my grave to make sure my tormentors got their comeuppance.

In *Dracula A.D. 1972* I played my own father – or was it grandfather? – in a flashback sequence but, whoever I was, I conked out after a ferocious encounter with Christopher Lee's stupendous Dracula, which started on the top of a swaying coach and finished up in the mud when the coach overturned. One of the wheels had broken in half.

(Re-reading this list, I'm wondering if there might have been easier ways to earn a living … but hey-ho, on with the motley.)

I'm sure something nasty happened to me in *Asylum*, but I can't for the death of me think what it was. I dimly remember Barry Morse taking a swipe at me with his handbag, but that couldn't have done much harm. Perhaps I stayed in the establishment and went bonkers myself?

My antagonist in *The Revenge of Dr Death** was my greatly loved, incredibly funny friend, Vincent Price. What a dear man he is! I came to grief in this bit of skulduggery by falling into a glass tank full of poisonous spiders, following a titanic ding-dong with the old rascal. With lovely wit, he wrote in a magazine article about this '…totally preposterous scene. Yesterday, Peter had to fall into a tank of spiders. It's very difficult to fall into a tank of spiders and be Brando…'

---

* Working title of *Madhouse*.

In *The Ghoul* I took the easy way out, and simply shot myself in the temple. The next merry little prank took place on Miami's Palm Beach, Florida, in a film called *Death Corps*, when some rather unpleasant gentleman drowned me by holding my head under the stagnant waters of the Everglades and left me there as crocodile bait. I was playing a Nazi officer, so I deserved all I was forced to swallow.

Trial by Combat had the cosy idea of my being used as a sandbag by a group of narrow-minded knights in armour, who took it into their heads to charge at me full tilt and en masse, plunging their lances in my midriff, by and large an unpleasant experience. Last of all (SO FAR) came The Big Bang: playing Grand Moff Tarkin (I've always wondered what a 'Grand Moff' is, or in view of what happened to him, perhaps I should say was) in *Star Wars*, I was blown to smithereens by those two intrepid young lads, Harrison Ford and Mark Hamill, who managed to blow up my little pied-à-terre, a modest DIY affair about twice the size of Jupiter called, appropriately enough, 'Death Star'. (I would have preferred 'Mon Repos' or 'Dunroamin' but I wasn't consulted.) A pity this happened to me really, because it meant I couldn't very well take part in any of those subsequent outer space adventures, and actors do have to eat.

So that's yer lot. Ah, no! but wait a minute – I've forgotten one. I suppose the 'ham' in me wanted to make my ultimate exit in the Grand Manner – 'Make it big for Bath' as the saying goes. So it's a bit of a let down to my ego when I humbly report that my final demise was less explosive.

I was set upon by a mob of mangey moggies in *The Uncanny*, who leapt at me from out of the darkened back streets of Montreal, tripping me up, so that I tumbled headlong down a narrow flight of stone steps, breaking my neck in the process. Charming, what?

There we are, then – a sum total of 16 'When you gotta go, you gotta go's', warts and all, plus one 'Don't know'. I wonder what they'll cook up for me next?

Happy now, dear children? Pleasant dreams.

ACT ONE SCENE 2

NOWADAYS, VIOLENCE AND corruption in one form or another are taken for granted, and man seems bent upon his own destruction, morally and physically. It is therefore most rewarding, and gives me grounds for hope in the future of mankind, when I receive letters from all age groups, particularly the present generation, giving their views on the old so-called 'horror' films. One and all prefer them to their modern counterparts, especially the vintage Hammer and Amicus productions.

According to those who write to me, they feel that the producers of today's epics in this genre rely too much upon brutal savagery, explicit sex scenes, nudity, obscene language, special effects, and little or no characterisation. They find all this repellent and are sickened by the general decadence offered to them in the name of entertainment, so different from that of yesteryear. Those older classics hold for them the delights of a joy ride in the ghost train at a funfair, when boyfriends put their arms protectively around their sweethearts' shoulders, and although there may be some gasps and screams, they all know they'll come out safely into the sunlight again at the end of the journey, after a healthy 'scare', and enjoy a good giggle together. They love the unbelievable being made believable, and, above all, the fact that good always prevails over evil.

To me, this aspect is the most reassuring of their reactions, and augurs well for the eventual salvation of the world, because theirs is the future, and it's up to them to make it as they want it to be. Hope springs eternal … Subtract an 'o' from 'Good' and add a 'd' to 'evil', and you have the two greatest antagonists the world has ever known, or ever will know.

I've always regarded Baron Frankenstein as a forerunner to Dr Christian Barnard, the South African surgeon who was the first man to transplant the human heart, which he did in 1967. (One of his early patients, Philip Blaiberg, survived for 20 months after this operation.) I did my first similar experiment with that particular organ (and lots of other bits and bobs as well) in the Hammer Films production of *The Curse of Frankenstein* in 1957. It was my first appearance as that enterprising individual, the action taking place during the early part of the 19th century. It proved to be an enormous box-office success, and six more of this anti-hero's adventures were made by the same company over a period of 15 years.

In 1959, I played Dr Robert Knox, the famous anatomist of Edinburgh, in *The Flesh and the Fiends*. His left eye was atrophied, and he closed his only good one to the way Burke and Hare procured the cadavers he required, so that he could carry out his examinations of the human body to find out how it works. All for the eventual well being of mankind, so don't be too hard on him.

Now, it seemed to me that Knox and Frankenstein had a lot in common. The minds of these exceptional men were driven by a single desire: to enquire into the unknown. Ahead of their time, like most great scientists, their work and motives were misunderstood.

Knox shocked the medical world by his practices, and was hounded out of his home town by those in authority. The same sort of thing happened to poor old Frankenstein, persecuted by ignorant and frightened officials and indignant villagers, who didn't like him meddling with THINGS BEST LEFT ALONE.

This view of the characters I played helped me a great deal in getting to grips with Mary Shelley's creation. In order to give some sort of credibility to Victor Frankenstein's nefarious deeds, which became more and more bizarre, and he more and more ruthless, as the script writers burnt the midnight oil in their efforts to ring the changes, I needed to hold on to his basic motivation. The script writers did their best with variations on the same theme, but

Miss Shelley's original conception reigns supreme. Her finished masterpiece must have given her quite a turn when she re-read it, for, in her own preface to a revised edition of her novel, she questioned 'How I, then a young girl, came to think of, and to dilate upon, so very hideous an idea?'

John Bell and Croyden, the analytical chemists in Wigmore Street, London, were most helpful to me and the props department at the studios. They allowed us access to their museum of old surgical instruments, and replicas were fashioned by skilled craftsmen employed by the producers of the films.

But, my word, how glad I am that I wasn't around when the originals were in general use, with a noggin of rum and a swift uppercut being the only means of anaesthetising the patients!

Dracula. Now that was a part my old chum Christopher Lee could really get his teeth into, and, by gum, he *did*! – several times. I think he showed great courage when he weighed anchor and sought different characters to play in Hollywood, where he spent about ten years before returning home to Britain. He intuited that when the demand for so-called 'horror' films waned, he might wane with them, and he wanted to cast off the mantle of the Count that shackled him. When asked by the press why he didn't want to play Dracula any more, he replied, with typical humour, 'Because I'm getting too long in the tooth.'

We were on location down in the West Country in 1972 making *Nothing But the Night*, a film for his own company, Charlemagne Productions. He is a first class golfer, and on days off I volunteered to caddy for him on the course at Thurlestone near Dartmouth, suggesting that he made impossible strokes, such as 'Now I want your ball to hit that tree on the left of the fairway, bounce onto the green and hole in one.' To my astonishment, he succeeded nearly every time! I think *he* was quite surprised, too – and I asked him why he didn't play like that when participating in the Pro Celebrity matches on television. 'Oh, that's for real,' he replied, 'and I wouldn't have the nerve!'

I took him out to dinner once, and offered him a steak … (glad to say we're still on speaking terms).

Whilst on that subject, that is – the *other* kind of 'steak' – you would not believe how difficult I found it to strike a stake smartly on top of its head, as I was so often called upon to do as Professor Van Helsing, Dracula's arch enemy. The Professor carried his whole caboodle of vampire extermination kit in a small Gladstone bag, so out of necessity the essential mallet couldn't be very big. I would have liked one similar to those wielded by sturdy young locals anxious to impress their lasses by walloping the 'TEST YOUR STRENGTH – HIT THE GONG!' contraption at country fairs, but, as sure as 'eggs is eggs', that would have got laughs in quite the wrong places. Even now the knuckles of my left hand, which held the wooden spike in place, still bear the scars of many a miss.

Harking back for a moment to the list I made some pages ago of how I 'shuffled off this mortal coil' on celluloid, there's another little gem I'd forgotten. I did the Roman version of the ceremonial Japanese 'way out' by indulging in hara-kiri ('ripping the belly' as my copy of Chambers puts it so delicately). That was as Cassius in *Julius Caesar* on the plains of Philippi, when he was fed up with fighting and feuding. Paul Eddington was absolutely splendid as Brutus, and a cast of all-round excellence included Keith Michell (Antony), Barry Jones (Caesar), David Williams (Octavius Caesar) and Jane Wenham (Portia).

Come to think of it, I carried out a neat job or two myself, to send others packing into that far, far better land that awaits us all if we're good: like lopping off Ingrid Pitt's head, f'rinstance, in *The Vampire Lovers* (1970), a kindly act, actually, because she was suffering from some vampirish syndrome at the time, and apparently this was the only way to cure her of her nasty little habits.

As for that old blood sucker Dracula … whatever I did to get rid of him, he would keep turning up again, like a bad penny.

There was no stopping the fellow – a glutton for punishment as well as gore.

A dear little old lady had been engaged to 'double' for one of his victims who, at this stage of the proceedings, had to look extremely ancient. The shot called for a close-up of her face as she lay in a deep lidless coffin. That was all the old darling had to do – just lie there, no dialogue, no action. The scene took some time to set up and light, and just when everything was in apple pie order, ready for shooting, a break for lunch was called and we all trooped off to the canteen.

An hour later, when we reassembled, the double was missing. A frantic search ensued, but to no avail. Terence Fisher, the director, had just decided to get on with another scene to save wasting any more precious time, when a gentle snore came from the interior of the casket. There she was, cosy and warm under the huge arc lamps, an angelic smile on her face, having nodded off before lunch and remained there ever since.

Terry gently roused her, and with the sweetest imaginable smile she looked up into his eyes and said drowsily, 'I'm quite ready when you are, Mr Fisher.'

Alan Ladd played the name part in *The Black Knight*, a film made in 1954 at Pinewood with locations in Spain. I was cast as the villainous Sir Palamides, and I wore a large jewelled ring on my finger. Whilst haranguing my servant, I had to deliver a vicious backhander across the poor fellow's face. It worried me that he might be scarred for life, so as a precaution I asked the first assistant if he would kneel beside me, out of shot, remove the ring before the blow was struck and replace it when I let my hand fall back to my side. This succeeded, but it was strange to play such a scene with someone fiddling about with my digit, as if we were becoming engaged on the sly.

Having no car, I took the tube train from Kensington (where Helen and I lived) to Uxbridge, and then walked some three or four miles across fields and along country lanes to the studios.

Returning home one evening, a sleek limousine pulled up beside me. Alan leaned out of the window and asked if he could give me a lift. I accepted gratefully, and asked to be dropped off at the station, but he insisted on driving me all the way to my doorstep before going on to the Savoy Hotel where he was staying. 'Any time, Peter,' he said, 'otherwise you'll be worn out before we've finished the movie.'

He was a shy, reserved person and this gesture was typical of his kind thoughts for others. At the end of shooting, I presented him with a tiny replica of the Black Knight as a souvenir, which I'd had made by a modeller who specialised in miniatures. Some months later, Alan wrote from Hollywood saying how grateful he was: 'I've never had any hobbies until now, thanks to you, I've started collecting figurines and have already filled a large cabinet, representing uniforms throughout the ages ... Thanks a million...'

*   *   *

It is a truth universally acknowledged that all filmmakers are ruthless, hard-bitten, cold-hearted swine.

I take the liberty of pinching (and adapting) that titbit from the opening lines of Miss Jane Austen's delectable novel *Pride and Prejudice*, before proving how untrue these assumptions can be. 'Lies and Muck!' to quote Ben Travers of treasured memory. There may be a few who could qualify as ogres, but I've been lucky enough never to come across one in all my 51 years as an actor. Here are some examples of the sort of treatment I have enjoyed at the hands of this much maligned breed.

The denouement of Hammer's first Dracula picture depicted his disintegration before your very eyes, the camera lingering on a ring worn by the bloodthirsty Count lying amongst his ashes. The company had not anticipated the resounding success the film made when it was released, so they had to devise ways and means to resuscitate that character for sequels. In 1966 Tony Hinds produced *Dracula Prince of Darkness*, in which I could not appear due to other commitments. He rang to ask if I would mind them using that final sequence as a prologue for this new production, the ring playing an important part in bringing Dracula back to life, so I gave my consent.

Helen and I had recently purchased in London a house which needed extensive repairs to the roof – a very costly affair. Some weeks after the work was completed, I found a receipt from the builders on the doormat, although I hadn't paid them because I'd not received their invoice. Upon enquiring, I discovered that the bill had been settled by the Hammer company in lieu of a fee for the use of Dracula's (temporary) death scene, for which – in the earlier film – I'd already been paid: an unsolicited and most generous gesture.

The indefatigable and extraordinarily talented Sammy Davis Jnr asked me if I'd 'do him a favour' by appearing for a few seconds in his 1969 production of *One More Time*, which would only involve a morning's work. He had already shown such kindness and hospitality to Helen and me – first night tickets for his shows at the Palladium, dinner afterwards at the White Elephant Club and endless appreciation for the enjoyment my performances had given him. I happily agreed and he took us both out to lunch when my stint was finished. A fortnight later 12 bottles of the finest champagne and a colour television set were delivered to our house in Whitstable, with a note of thanks from Sammy and his director Jerry Lewis. Moreover, when Helen was so ill he sent her a large bouquet of flowers with a little message 'Get well soon – Love Sammy'.

In 1974 I made my first film for Tyburn Productions at Pinewood Studios. That company is run most successfully by the dynamic young entrepreneur, Kevin Francis, and I had been enlisted to take part in his production of *The Ghoul*. For many months prior to this engagement, my late stand-in cum chauffeur, George Holdcroft (a

very dear friend), had driven me to Shepperton Studios, where I
had been constantly employed. When leaving London, Shepperton
and Pinewood lie in different directions. George picked me up
from Brown's Hotel in the early hours of the morning, and we
set off as usual through the maze of one-way streets to reach the
motorway.

I was deeply engrossed in my script for most of the journey,
but after about half an hour, I glanced out of the window and
saw unfamiliar surroundings – unfamiliar, that is, on the route to
Pinewood.

'Are we going a new way?' I asked.

'What new way?' asked George, sleepily.

'To Pinewood.'

'We're going to Shepperton.'

'That's interesting,' I said, 'because we're not working there this
time.'

Dear old George did a slow double take followed by a quick
double turn, and we eventually arrived at our correct destination
about four hours late, the rush-hour traffic having built up to an
alarming degree.

I hadn't worked for Kevin previously, and had only met him
once (when he was a boy), so he wasn't aware of how punctual I
like to be, always allowing myself plenty of time to get ready for
the day's enjoyable toil.

I expected to find him waiting at the gate, looking like the
wrath of God. Instead, a polite message was handed to me by the
attendant on duty, requesting me to go to Mr Francis's office as
soon as I could.

Instead of bawling me out, as he had every right to do, he offered
me a cup of tea. As I gratefully sipped it, he said how relieved
he was to know we hadn't been involved in an accident, his only
concern had been for our safety on the high road, and that we
had not held up the production for very long, because he'd simply
reorganised the schedule, shooting a scene I was not in.

'Relax, old son, and take your time,' he said, refilling my cup.

What a wonderful way to start a new friendship, and there were more kindnesses to follow.

The character I played was mourning the passing of his adored wife. As I was in the same boat (I still am, for that matter) I had no difficulty in identifying myself with his emotions and state of mind. A photograph of the man's wife had a prominent position on the mantlepiece of his living room. Kevin's father, Freddie Francis, directed the picture, and I asked them both if we could use a picture of my Helen for this purpose. They thought it a lovely idea, and Freddie made sure there was a close shot of her dear face on the screen in the final cut.

Soon after shooting was completed, I received a package from Aspreys and a note which read 'You were smashing, mate! With love and thanks – Kev.'

Inside was that same photograph in a silver frame.

On my 74th birthday, Kevin and his associate Miss Gillian Garrow paid a surprise visit to Whitstable, bearing gifts: a splendid shooting stick (not that I shoot anything, but so useful to rest my weary limbs whenever I toddle about!) and two scrumptious cakes made by Wolfgang, the head patisserie chef at Pinewood Studios. One of these splendid creations was a Hollywood Oscar replica, the base inscribed with sugar 'Retep Gnihsuc Yppah Yadhtrib' (try that backwards!) 'Worst Actor Award', and the other a remarkably realistic deerstalker hat complete with marzipan bees (a reference to Sherlock Holmes's retirement studies), captioned 'Happy Birthday Peter. We'll make you eat your hat including the bees in your bonnet.' Both are far too beautiful to be eaten – they'll be preserved in the deep freeze! You never know, they might become exhibits at the recently inaugurated Theatre Museum in Covent Garden!

Freddie Francis had won an Academy Award for his cinematography of *Sons and Lovers*, and I shall always remember the tranquil beauty of a scene in the countryside covered with virgin snow, and the fine quality of Wendy Hiller's and Trevor Howard's performances in that superb film.

To return to our filming of *The Ghoul*: Gwen Watford played the ayah who nursed my tragic son (sympathetically portrayed by the excellent Don Henderson, whom I met again when we were both in *Star Wars*). It was a great pleasure for me to work with Gwen, such a charming person and an actress of the highest order. We'd been together before, in 1958, on BBC Television in Terence Rattigan's play *The Winslow Boy*, in which Nora Swinburne and John Robinson were also outstandingly good.

Another film I worked on at this time was *Tales from the Crypt*, an Amicus film, produced by Milton Subotsky. The script had been sent to me in 1971, soon after the passing of my belovèd wife. It embodied several short stories, linked by the crypt keeper, played by Sir Ralph Richardson. I didn't care for the part offered me, which was eventually played by Richard Greene. Instead, I asked if I could take the role of Mr Grimsdyke and be allowed to make a few suggestions to improve this cameo. As originally written, all his lines were spoken to himself, as he'd been a recluse since the death of his wife, with only a faithful dog for company. A lonely, sad figure, but somehow the situation didn't ring true to me.

I drew inspiration from personal experience, as I was in similar circumstances, except for the dog. I found I could address some of the dialogue to this pet, as one so often does in real life, but, for the major portion, I needed something else.

At home, a lifelike photograph of Helen hangs on the wall above my writing desk, and during those dark days I often found myself looking at it and speaking to her. I thought this would be the answer to my problem with Grimsdyke, and Freddie Francis, who was to direct, entirely agreed. We didn't use Helen's picture this time, because it would have been wrong 'casting', but a suitable face was found and put in a cheap wooden frame, upon which the old boy whom I was to play could gaze lovingly as he mused.

Happily, this worked and towards the end of the sequence, when Grimsdyke hangs himself, Freddie panned the camera down from my gently swinging body to the floor, disclosing a little withered nosegay lying like a pathetic wreath amongst the shattered glass of the loved one's portrait, both having fallen from the suicide's hands as he died.

I'm proud to say that this combined effort won me the Licorne d'Or Award for the best actor of 1973, when it was shown at a Film Festival in France.

ENTR'ACTE

THOSE WHO HAVE read the first volume of my autobiography will have learnt a little about my oldest and dearest friend, Peter Gray, who has so kindly contributed the foreword to this present work.

We've spent such happy times in each other's company over the years, and laughter is never very far away when we are together.

I can still recall

> *the thrilling-sweet and rotten*
> *Unforgettable, unforgotten*
> *River-smell, and hear the breeze*
> *Sobbing in the little trees*

when he taught me how to scull on the River Trent in Nottingham, where we were in rep in 1938, and hear the exhortations he made to his land lubberly pupil, who was an expert at catching crabs; 'In – OUT! (wait till the cows come home) In – OUT!' as we slid along the smooth, silvery surface of the waterway. He was a first class oarsman, having learnt that skill in Oxford, where he was employed by Basil Blackwell, the bookseller, before he became an actor.

In wintertime, when our summer reach wore a thin coating of ice, we cracked it, threw off all our clobber and stood on the bank, shivering and shouting 'Last one in's a cissy!' (er . . . that was (ahem ahem) always the *other* Peter!).

My dear mother, who had my welfare very near to her heart, adored him, and said to me, 'It's so nice for you to have a real *chum*, a real *pal* and *friend*.' We've addressed each other as 'My dear old P and F' ever since that declaration.

In 1987, as I was unable to undertake the task, he offered his services to the Talking Book Service for the Blind, and travelled up to London from Devonshire, where he lives, to record the first volume of my autobiography on my behalf.

It was a most generous and courageous gesture, because he suffers from a severe handicap. He joined the 'senior service' during the last war, in which he served as an able-bodied seaman, rising to the rank of First Lieutenant. He was rendered totally deaf soon after the cease fire, as a result of the incessant barrage of explosions inflicted upon his eardrums from his own ship's guns.

When I sailed for home in 1942, after my sojourn in America (which I recounted at some length in my previous book), he was on the same Atlantic run, and upon referring to the diary he kept during those years at sea, he discovered that he missed escorting me and the convoy I was with back to Blighty only by seven days! How closely our lives have been linked since we first met so long ago. He is also bravely facing up to life since the passing of his deeply loved wife in January 1986.

I wanted to send him something as a greeting when he arrived home from recording, hoping it would cheer him up after a long car journey back to an empty house. I got an idea of what to write from a chance remark of his in a recently received letter, in which he had written 'Thank you for your two telecoms ('and a partridge in a pear tree! ...')' Those bracketed words end each verse of that seasonal song 'The 12 Days of Christmas', which irritates me intensely with its constant repetitions. So I set about doing my own version, and as Peter enjoyed it ('It's good enough for *Punch*,' he chortled), I reproduce it here, in the hope that you may also be diverted by this taradiddle.

ON THE FIRST DAY OF CHRISTMAS

My own true love,
What a delightfully unique present you sent to me – a partridge in a pear tree. I've planted it in the greenhouse, and the dear little game bird seems so happy and at home in its branches. Thank you, *thank* you so very much for such a sweet thought.
With all my love – ME

ON THE SECOND DAY OF CHRISTMAS

My own true love,
Well! Well! A second gift has arrived! Two adorable turtle doves plus another pear tree with a partridge in it! You really are too generous, my sweet, but I do appreciate your thoughts. I've put the doves in a cote in the greenhouse, and Percy (as I've christened the first partridge) seems very contented to have a playmate.
With all my love – ME

ON THE THIRD DAY OF CHRISTMAS

My own true love,
I wonder if there's some mistake? Today I received yet *another* pear tree with a partridge in it, two more turtle doves, *and* three French hens! I've built a coop for them, and put it in the greenhouse amongst all the other livestock, and planted the two extra pear trees. But perhaps you meant these prezzies for someone else, and put my address through force of habit? Do let me know, dear, if this is the case: things are getting a little overcrowded, and Percy has turned nasty over the new arrivals.
With all my love – ME

ON THE FOURTH DAY OF CHRISTMAS

Luv – Aren't you overdoing it a bit, or have you won the pools?!!!? Carter Paterson has just delivered four singing blackbirds, two *more* turtle doves, three more French hens *and*

another pear tree with – would you believe it – a partridge in it!
In haste – affec. yrs – ME
P.S. I'm having to extend the greenhouse.

ON THE FIFTH DAY OF CHRISTMAS
Look, this is getting too much of a good thing. It's costing
me a small fortune in bird seed and glass for the greenhouse.
Today I not only received *five* more of *everything* which came
yesterday, but five gold rings to boot, which I've had to pawn
to help pay for above. And I'm getting sick of the sight of
partridges in pear trees. If you *must* keep sending me things,
please don't keep repeating them.
Yours – ME

ON THE SIXTH DAY OF CHRISTMAS
What are you trying to do to me, you old bat? Mother's up
to her waist in bird droppings, and is threatening to leave
home, when there arrives, by special delivery, one pear tree,
one partridge, two turtle doves, three French hens, four singing
blackbirds, five gold rings (*those* I was *glad* to get) and a
cartload of *six oversexed geese* laying eggs all over the place.
ME

ON THE SEVENTH DAY OF CHRISTMAS
YOU HAVE GONE TOO FAR THIS TIME. I've had to get
planning permission to build a farmyard and dig a pond to
accommodate the seven swimming swans which arrived today,
along with all the other pests. I've been kept awake by all those
damn doves cooing at each other all night, the neighbours
are beginning to complain about the noise, and I'm driven
balmy by colly birds twittering all day, French hens clucking,
partridges fighting and the thud of dropping eggs. Stop it, d'you
hear? – *STOP IT.* I'm losing patience, as well as all my friends.
ME

ON THE EIGHTH, NINTH, TENTH, ELEVENTH AND
TWELFTH DAYS OF CHRISTMAS

> Tweedle, Dum and Dee,
> Solicitors,
> Carey Street,
> LONDON E.C.

Dear Madam
Before our client left the country for an indefinite
period (desnation unknown) he instructed us to get
in touch with you regarding the following items, as
to what you'd like done with them. (He did make a
suggestion, but in the interests of common decency, we
have decided not to pass it on.)

12 Partridges (extremely aggressive) in a like number
   of Pear Trees
22 Turtle Doves
30 French Hens
36 Blackbirds (singing)
40 Gold Rings (pawn tickets)
42 Laying Geese
42 Swimming Swans
40 Milkmaids
36 Drummers
30 Pipers
22 Dancing Ladies
12 Leaping Lords

A total of 364 gifts, plus innumerable goose eggs.

We would appreciate the favour of an early reply,
owing to the fact that there are no cows available to

keep the maids occupied, and hostilities have broken out between the drummers, the pipers and the leaping lords, all seeking the attentions of the aforementioned maidens and ladies.

The behaviour of the fauna is equally disgusting.

We regret to inform you that our client went berserk when offered roast partridge stuffed with pears for dinner, and that the goose eggs have addled.

We are, Madam, your obedient servants.
HY AM DUM
(Signed for and on behalf of Tweedle, Dum and Dee)

ACT TWO SCENE 1

I LOVE THE theatre, either side of the tabs. It was a great disappointment for me that I never had the opportunity to play Stanhope or Osborne in my favourite play, RC Sherriff's *Journey's End*, a moving drama of life in the trenches during the 1914-18 war, but I was lucky enough to play in another of my favourites.

In 1975 I watched with ever-increasing enjoyment a beautifully produced serial on television, dealing with the life and times of King Edward VII.

Miss Helen Ryan took the part of Queen Alexandra and played that royal personage as if she had lived and breathed and had her being during that period of our island's history. I was deeply impressed by this remarkable recreation and wrote her a fan letter.

She was married to Mr Guy Slater, and a few weeks after I'd written I read an article in the *TV Times* which stated they were going to run the Horseshoe Theatre in Basingstoke, their local town.

I had not been on the stage for ten years – way back in 1965 at the Garrick, when I played Sir Hector Benbow, Bart, MFH, in *Thark*, that glorious farce by Ben Travers (which I shall refer to later), and was anxious to try myself out again 'on the boards', after such a long gap and so many films. So I wrote once more, this time to Miss Ryan's husband, asking if it would be possible to open their season with *The Heiress*, a play by Ruth and Augustus Goetz, based on the novel *Washington Square* by Henry James, with myself in the rôle of Dr Austin Sloper.

Helen and Guy were generous enough to applaud the idea, and those few weeks I spent in that lovely part of Hampshire were the happiest I had experienced since 1971. Guy proved to be a super director, and Helen was simply stunning as Catherine, Dr Sloper's maltreated daughter.

I always pay strict attention to correct detail, and in researching the period of the piece, which was set in 1850, I discovered that it was de rigueur for members of the medical profession to sport beards. Because of a skin allergy, I cannot apply any form of gum to my shaving area, and always sprout homegrown whiskers when needs be, if warned beforehand. Due to the time element, I was unable to become hirsute for this characterisation, which bothered me a great deal, but I hope this was only a minor defect from the audience's point of view.

Guy rounded up a splendid cast, which included Joan Miller, Julia Schofield and Jonathan Newth, and we played to full houses for the allotted run of two weeks.

Thark, my previous venture on stage, was directed by the clever Ray Cooney, and Alec McCowen played Ronald Gamble, the part originated by Ralph Lynn in 1927. Mine, that of Sir Hector Benbow, had first been played by Tom Walls. Before coming into London, it was tried out at the Yvonne Arnaud Theatre, so delightfully situated upon the banks of the River Wey in Guildford, Surrey, where swans swam majestically by amongst the weeping willow trees growing beneath the dressing room windows.

At one point in that uproarious romp, Sir Hector and Ronnie are sharing an enormous four poster, engaging in squabbles and struggles over the sheets and blankets, which gives rise to one of the funniest lines from an exasperated Ronnie: 'Oh, you *are* awful in bed!' Ours was on castors, and the rake on that particular stage is exceptionally steep.

Ray Cooney's inspired inventiveness involved us in tremendous exertions, and on the first night we suddenly realised the bed was edging closer and closer to the footlights, and we were in danger of 'going over the top'. After a rapid consultation under the counterpane during a roar of laughter from the audience, we both popped out from either side of our oversized cot, ran round to its end and shouldered it back into place, like a two-man rugger scrum. This went down very well with those in front, adding to the general mirth, and they joined in the fun by encouraging us with cries of 'Heave – heave!', like the crowds at Twickenham when an international rugby match is in progress.

Ray was all for leaving this bit of business in the show, but when we transferred to the Garrick Theatre the slope was less severe, and our tussles could no longer take place on the move. But we enjoyed a long stay in London's West End, with Kathleen Harrison and Ambrosine Phillpotts doing wonders with the parts of Mrs Frush and Lady Benbow respectively.

I do not recommend making a film and at the same time appearing in a play. I did it once, and lived and learned never to do so again.

It was in August 1959. William Fairchild had written *The Sound of Murder*, staged at the Aldwych Theatre in London, in which I played the lead, Charles Norbury, opposite Elizabeth Sellars as his wife. The drama commenced with Norbury alone in the living room of their cottage somewhere in Surrey, and it is an unwritten law in the theatre that all members of the cast should arrive there at least half an hour before curtain up.

Although it was not all that long ago, in those days you could still park your car outside the stage door, with no fear of it being pinched, or towed away by vigilant coppers, and, unlike the modern travel-wearied commuters who face delays practically every time they venture forth, the roads were comparatively empty. Even so, there was always the danger of the unexpected, and time and time again I'd arrive late and in a state of nervous exhaustion, after a long day in the studios, to find the stage manager and my understudy waiting anxiously on the pavement. This was unfair to all concerned, and after three months I took advantage of a get out clause in my contract and Charles Norbury was taken over by Michael Goodliffe for the remainder of the run.

Going back even further, to 1943, I became involved in an epic that would have seemed ambitious in peace time let alone during a world war.

There is a rumour that Tom Arnold mounted Tolstoy's mammoth spectacle *War and Peace* in the hope that it would flop, so that a legitimate loss could be shown on his returns when the tax man cameth. True or false I know not, but if that was what Tom wanted, it sure was what he got!

I was summoned to an interview, and Peter Gray, on leave from the navy, came with me, just to savour once again that magical theatre atmosphere which he missed so much. To this day, he assures me that I accepted the engagement whilst munching my way stolidly through great chunks of chocolate cake, a rare luxury in wartime, thoughtfully provided by the management.

The overhead costs for this curate's egg of a show were enormous. It was not quite in the 'A-CAST-OF-THOUSANDS-TOOK-TWO-YEARS-TO-MAKE' category, as boasted in the advertisements for Hollywood film epics, but the cast was huge nonetheless. It was presented at the Phoenix Theatre, London, where it just scraped through for three weeks, forcing everyone concerned to beat a hasty retreat from the Charing Cross Road after having done the same sort of thing nightly from Moscow.

The story was adapted by Robert Lucas, based on the translation from the Russian by Constance Garnett, produced by Julius Gellner, decor and costumes by Hein Heckroth.

A gifted cast was gathered together, which included Paulette Preney, Yvonne Marling, Dorothy Hammond, Chattie Salaman, Marjory Clark, Georgina Cookson, Barry Morse, Julian Somers, Henry Oscar, Ronald (now Sir Ronald) Millar, Frederick Lloyd, Frederick Valk, Deering Wells, Charles Doran, David Dawson, Percy Walsh, Peter Bennett, Peter Illing, Old Uncle Tom Cobbleigh and – er – Peter Cushing.

I played two parts, Alexander I, Emperor of Russia, and Captain Ramballe, a French army officer. (Rather diplomatic casting, that –

having a foot in both camps, as 'twere.) Other performers doubled, trebled and even quadrupled their bewildered way through a maze of scenery, and at times were not absolutely certain who they were supposed to be impersonating.

The situation was not improved by the use of magic lantern slides projected onto a huge screen up stage, because, true to form (as witnessed in many a church hall), some of the views were presented upside down, causing one waggish fellow to suggest we should play our parts standing on our heads whenever this embarrassing situation arose.

There were three acts, comprising 32 scenes, ranging from 'An anti-aircraft battery Moscow, 1941' to 'Moscow, 1812', where the Russian emperor was giving a ball. This involved a varied repertoire of dances – polonaise, mazurka, etc – to the music of such masters as Tchaikowsky, Glinka, Mozart and Rameau. After cavorting around and about Moscow, we were transported swiftly to Borodino, where a mighty battle ensued. As World War II was being waged at the same time, this proved slightly confusing to those on both sides of the curtain, as it became increasingly difficult to differentiate between our improvised gun bangs and the real ones popping off outside. The wailing of air raid sirens didn't help much, either.

Peter Illing, who was magnificent as Napoleon, saved his voice during rehearsals, causing the producer to call out repeatedly: 'I cannot hear you, Mr Illink.'

'You will, Mr Gellner, you will,' Peter assured him, and how well he kept that promise when the time came, whipping himself up into a frenzy on the outskirts of Moscow, ranting and roaring like that latterday maniac Adolph Hitler (of whom an aunt of mine once observed, 'What a *fidget* the man is').

Then came the famous retreat, and we finished up where we'd started, in the anti-aircraft battery, 1941. Background music was especially composed by Clifton Parker, and recorded by the London Symphony Orchestra conducted by Muir Matheson.

During a matinée which was attended by a few out of work actors ('resting') who got in on free passes, and theatre cleaning ladies (snoozing) in the stalls, something went wrong with the effects, which were supposed to depict the entire city of Moscow being burnt to a cinder. Instead, there was a deafening explosion and we were plunged into a blackout, except for one pathetic 100-watt amber bulb, which did its best to create the required illusion by blinking feebly but regularly, like a Belisha beacon at a zebra crossing.

Out of the stygian gloom the voice of an anguished actress, playing a Russian peasant, rose gallantly to the occasion with her line 'See! the flames are spreading!' (but they weren't, you know).

The Empire period is considered by many to be the loveliest in the history of fashion, and Hein Heckroth had designed exquisite gowns for the ladies in the ballroom scene. There were some 20-odd costumes, varying in shades of yellow from the palest delicate primrose to the deepest chrome.

In the traditional shambles of a dress rehearsal, when jagged nerves are soothed by the optimistic reassurance that 'It'll be alright on the night', Mr Gellner asked to see the creation worn by Miss Paulette Preney as Natasha. Poor harassed Monty Berman, whose firm supplied the clothes, was up to his neck dealing with the many importunate demands upon his time and patience. Adjusting a bejewelled tiara on the bewigged head of a lady-in-waiting, he proffered this bauble for the approval of Mr Gellner, who, with a hint of exasperation, bellowed 'Nein-nein! I vish to be seeink zee yell-ow cowstume.'

Monty rounded on him in desperation, and with equal asperity yelled back, 'But they're all yeller, Mr Gellner – they're ALL yeller!'

The men's wardrobe was also splendid, and one veritable giant amongst us had to wear a pair of figure-fitting buckskin breeches. At the dress parade Mr Heckroth, standing in the stalls whilst admiring his handiwork, was constrained to lean upon the orchestra pit rail, and beckon the warrior to come nearer the floats.

Then, lowering his voice so as not to offend any feminine ears, he hissed loudly (through cupped hands used as a megaphone), 'I vood suggest ze wearink of zer jokestrap.'

'I *am* wearing one, Mr Heckroth,' quoth the proud thespian, loudly.

The astonished Mr Heckroth smote his own cheeks with open palms, just like SZ (Cuddles) Sakall, and, with ill-concealed admiration tinged with envy, was heard to say 'Oi-*vay! Vot* a *man!'*

Each performance lasted over four hours, with some moments of glory, but the war put paid to our endeavour to take people's minds off it for a spell.

Even as I write, I hear that yet another old comrade in arms, Esmond Knight, has died in harness. (How lonely this life becomes; but no matter, we can always look forward to the next, when we'll meet again all those we wish to.) We were members of Laurence Olivier's company at the St James's Theatre in King Street (alas, no more – the site was taken over and turned into an office block, I believe). Laurence staged the two Cleopatra plays – Shaw's *Caesar and Cleopatra* and Shakespeare's *Antony and Cleopatra*, as part of the Festival of Britain, 1951.

Teddy (as Esmond was affectionately called) was another victim of the Second World War. Like Peter Gray, he had joined the navy in 1940, and whilst serving in HMS Prince of Wales was blinded in action against the Bismarck, and only partially regained the sight of one eye.

Since the settings of both dramas switched back and forth, from Egypt to Rome and all points north, south, east and west, a revolving stage was employed to facilitate the ever-changing scenery. These changes were undertaken in darkness, and Teddy was the only one of us who could step on and off the merry go round with complete confidence – a very slight compensation.

He made so light of his appalling affliction. We shared a dressing room and one evening, as we chatted whilst putting on our make-up, he told me he was going to do some sound broadcasts for the BBC, which normally involves visual cues. I wondered how he was going to cope with that situation, so I asked him.

'I'm only blind,' he expostulated, 'not bloody deaf as well!'

The courage of the man.

I do admire the phlegmatic British mastery of understatement, so often used in times of stress and great personal danger, exemplified by the classic example made on the famous postcard sent home from a 'Tommy' serving in the Far East, which read: 'Dear Mum, this war's a bastard. Tell Auntie. Love Joe.' (Says it all, really, doesn't it? – without any fuss.)

Oliver Messel, whose ethereal designs and décor enhanced many theatrical presentations, one of which I was fortunate enough to appear in (*The Rivals* by Richard Brinsley Sheridan) also contributed to our heritage of bons mots. He was in the army, and upon his return with the British Expeditionary Force after the horrendous events and eventual evacuation from the beach of Dunkirk in 1940, someone enquired what it was like.

'My *dear*,' he sighed, 'the *noise* – and the *people*!'

Brevity is indeed the soul of wit, and this inherent ability to rise above things can never countenance defeat. I am filled with joyous pride in the knowledge that I belong to such a nation of unsung heroes.

Actors are very lucky people, in more ways than one, learning – perforce – other arts and crafts in the line of duty and the course of their careers.

The Silver Whistle, written by Robert McEnroe, was presented at the Duchess Theatre in 1956, the production in the hands of Lee Marvin's brother Mark, after its great success in New York City. I took the part of Oliver Erwenter, a tramp, originally played by José Ferrer. Erwenter was a similar character to the one so superbly portrayed by the late Robert Preston in the film *The Music Man*, a con merchant who wheedles his way into a home for elderly people and offers to pay for his keep by entertaining the inmates with conjuring tricks, eventually redeeming himself by bringing a little ray of sunshine into their otherwise bleak and empty lives.

By no stretch of the imagination am I a Paul Daniels, so I had to learn a few tricks of his trade, being assisted in this difficult task by a clever conjuror at that lovely toy shop, Hamley's in Regent Street. I can still do – *very* badly – a disappearing card trick, but it amuses my local children chums at Christmas time.

A splendid cast included Olga Lindo, Joyce Barbour, Mary Merrall, Una Venning, Jennifer Wright, Ernest Thesiger, Robin Bailey, Bartlett Mullins, Alfie Bass, Peter Vaughan and a gorgeous pet cockerel, called Omar, which I adored, carrying him around wherever I went, in a large parrot cage. The director was Martin Landau. When *The Silver Whistle*'s run was over we were all shocked to hear the news that Mark Marvin had taken his own life shortly after returning to America.

Other things I have learnt how to do in the line of duty include snooker for *The Skull*, my Steve Davis contestant being Christopher Lee, who came to a sticky end on the green baize amongst an assortment of coloured balls. I'd turned rather beastly and hit him over the head with something hard. The reason for this caddish trick eludes me, but I don't think it was because I was losing the frame.

In Rider Haggard's *She* I had to ride a camel. Now that is a mode of transport I do *not* recommend to the uninitiated, especially when that capricious quadruped takes it into its mulish head to sit down and/or get up, which was all too often in my experience. (If you are ever in contact with one, be warned – get nowhere near its breath… !)

That was not an achievement which has proved handy in later life, as I cannot quite see myself perched perilously on top of a hump, jogging down Whitstable High Street to the Tudor Tea Rooms for an afternoon snack, shopping bag clenched between my teeth. Anyway, where would I park the brute?

Cone of Silence dealt with civil aviation, and I had to learn how to control an aeroplane (simulated, of course). I rather liked the collective noun used by my instructor when operating the hand accelerators: there were four of these bunched together, which could be manipulated independently or en masse. When the latter procedure was required, he ordered me to 'take a fistful of throttles', to which I sang rather fatuously, à la Julie Andrews, 'to help the aircraft go down'.

'Or up,' he said, stonily. ('We were not amused.')

My co-pilots in this entertaining picture were Bernard Lee and Michael Craig, with George Sanders contributing his immaculate style as a smooth executive of the airline. We were directed by Charles Frend, but woe is me – I never got my 'wings', so today's passengers need have no fear that I might be in the cockpit, transporting them to the far-flung corners of the world.

As for operations on the human body – well! – having performed so many since Hammer Films lured me into those specialised practices, I think I could lay claim, with some justification, to being the English equivalent of that great American neurological surgeon, Harvey Cushing (pure coincidence, no relation!), who pioneered brain surgery, to say nothing of my 'affiliation' with Dr Christian Barnard!

This muster of 'all in a day's work' would be incomplete without some reference to horsemanship, or lack of: I cannot say with any conviction that my debut was an outstanding success, since my evil-minded mount showed some spirited horse sense by chucking me over its back without so much as a 'do you mind?' when I was filming *The Man in the Iron Mask*, way off in Hollywood at the outbreak of the Second World War.

However, Helen was a first class equestrian, and it was she who taught me the fundamental principles, enabling me at least to *look* as if I knew what I was doing.

I've driven a coach and pair a time or two with average aplomb, it being much safer *in* something than on top of anything. Professor Van Helsing and Baron Frankenstein often drove about their environments inside those cosy vehicles, and in *Tender Dracula* I even had the temerity to steer a hearse drawn by four magnificent black geldings with matching feather plumes adorning their tossing heads.

I rode at my peril in many films, among them being *The Black Knight, Alexander the Great* (bareback!), *Sword of Sherwood Forest, Twins of Evil, The Creeping Flesh, Battleflag* and *Fury at Smugglers' Bay.*

I adore Westerns, and always wish I could have been in one. (Gary Cooper was an especial favourite of mine, and it was a great pleasure to work with him and Deborah Kerr in *The Naked Edge.*) I suppose the nearest I ever got to realising that ambition was *Fury at Smugglers' Bay*, it being a sort of English 'cowboy' picture set in the 19th century.

The scenario contained all the traditional ingredients: lots of shootin', the inevitable brawl in a saloon, a *High Noon* confrontation between duellists, using swords instead of six-shooters, and the cavalry charging to the rescue in the nick of time. It was shot on location in Wales, near Fishguard, with stunningly beautiful coastline scenery and a simply spiffing cast. Bernard Lee was the 'baddie', George Coulouris the alien homesteader in trouble, and Miles Malleson the comic hick town governor; Liz Fraser 'set 'em up' behind the bar in the tavern, quenching the thirst of roysting pirates, John Fraser and William Franklyn played the James Stewart and Richard Widmark parts, Michele Mercier the heroine. I had the grumpy-old-dad-who-turns-up-trumps-in-the-end Lee J Cobb part, with a beautiful daughter, thrown in for good measure, in the shapely form of June Thorburn. It was written and directed by John Gilling.

When it was shown on television recently, my old sparring partner Christopher Lee kindly rang to say how much he'd enjoyed it, adding: 'You rode the horse very well, dear fellow, and the expression on your face when you died was exactly the same as when you were told what your salary for the film was going to be.'

Now we come to swashbuckling, a term sometimes applied to the noble art of self defence with an épée and other such dangerous weapons. I was taught by M'sieur Cavens, when I had to fight with Warren William in *The Man in the Iron Mask*.

If the duel is an affaire d'honneur, you leave your card, in a manner of speaking, challenging your aggravator beforehand by sloshing the poor blighter across the kisser with your glove, which is liable to make the serenest amongst us feel a trifle vexed.

Tovarich, a masterpiece by Jacques Deval, tells the story of a Russian Prince and a Grand Duchess who go, by force of circumstances, into domestic service with a banker's family in Paris.

Ann Todd and I played these two exiles, the Grand Duchess Tatiana Petrovna and Prince Mikail Alexandrovitch Ouratieff, on BBC Television in 1954, with Frances Rowe and Clive Morton as our employers, Monsieur et Madame Charles Dupont. Their son, Georges, was portrayed by Michael Newell.

Eric Fawcett produced, and in the scene where the Prince teaches Georges how to fence, he suggested I did so while taking occasional sips from a glass of wine held in my left hand, which was not easy to accomplish. Michael and I took lessons in the evenings after rehearsals, and it was worthwhile making this extra effort, because Eric's clever idea worked wonderfully well, demonstrating perfectly the nonchalance and expertise of the Prince, causing a journalist to comment in a periodical: 'Russians may be red or white, nice or nasty, but they are seldom predictable.' Plus ça change... ?

Finally, in *The Morecambe and Wise Show* I had to trip the light fantastic for a dance routine with that irresistible pair of comics who brought so much sunshine into so many lives for so many years. They took me through my paces, teaching me that classic song and dance number 'A Couple of Swells', magically originated by Judy Garland and Fred Astaire in *Easter Parade*.

It is perhaps of passing interest to note that Gene Kelly was the original choice, but he had an accident and broke his ankle; as a result, the debonair Astaire was persuaded to come out of early retirement and take over the role, and the film became one of his biggest successes.

Eric Morecambe was a passionate lover of birds, as I am. Both of us are members of the Royal Society for the Protection of Birds. I use the present tense, because his name, linked with that of his dear wife Joan, still does such sterling work in support of this splendid Trust. In 1971 we did a nature programme together for the BBC in the delightful countryside near his home in Hertfordshire.

I wore my RSPB tie, navy blue with silver avocets beautifully embroidered on it. During the recording, I pointed to these lovely birds, saying how rare they are in this country.

'Young man,' he said, twiddling his glasses as only he could, 'how right you are – especially on ties.'

Heaven is the richer for his presence, and we the poorer.

Having deep love and respect for all creatures great and small, I do hope I didn't give the impression earlier that I dislike camels – it's only riding them that I object to! When making *She* I asked the herdsman what I should say or do to make my mount get up, expecting him to use coaxing expressions such as 'Giddy-yup Neddie' or 'C'mon, ole fellah', but to my dismay he simply walloped the poor beast up its backside with his boot. That certainly did the trick, but I could never bring myself to emulate my instructor.

In Western Australia, where I thoroughly enjoyed working with John Izzard of Swan Television on the series *A Land Looking West* in 1977, I had a quite extraordinary experience with an ostrich, a tobacco addict! It stalked me, its beady eyes watching my every move, and each time I lit a cigarette it shot its neck out (like a chameleon's tongue catching some unwary insect) and snatched the fag from my lips. Perhaps Rod Hull encountered that same bird, and got the idea for his act with Emu?

We were based in Perth and covered enormous distances to different locations by small aircraft, which held about a dozen passengers. On our way to Dampier Land up in the North Western region I sat next to the pilot, who, after about half an hour in the air, leant back, closed his eyes and dozed off for a spell. When he awoke he turned to me and said, 'I orlways hev a kip over thet stretch – gets a bit borin' doin' this run every dye and the 'plyne knows the wye.' There's faith for you, I thought.

We journeyed by car as well, and on one occasion our driver also went to sleep – unintentionally. The motorways in the outback run for mile upon mile, as straight as those tracks built by the Romans in Britain, but wherever bends do occur there is always an escape road. We shot up one quite suddenly, executed a perfect parabola (just like Starsky and Hutch) and carried on as if nothing out of the ordinary had happened, bumping over the scrub until rejoining the route.

'Thet heppens orl the tyme, cobber,' our chauffeur assured me, yawning.

'Makes a change,' I said, blanching.

The stars at night may be big and bright deep in the heart of Texas, but none more so than those in the black velvet heaven down under. I could read by their glow, and they seemed close enough for me just to reach up and pluck one from out of the galaxy, like a beautiful shining blossom off a tree.

*   *   *

What endless pleasure toys can bring into our lives! I haunted Hamley's, especially the department which displayed those much sought-after model soldiers and farm figures made by William Britain, giving such lasting joy over so many years to countless thousands, young and old alike.

When we were little, my brother David and I had several sets of tiny Boy Scout signallers with movable arms, their hands holding semaphore flags. We learnt the code from the 50 cigarette cards issued by Wills entitled 'Signalling Series', so that we could leave secret messages for each other on the table in our play room.

In later years I had a large and varied collection, which I greatly treasured. Helen's sister, Rosita (Beck), knew the love I had, and still have, for these things. It delighted her whenever she went shopping for my Christmas or birthday presents, watching the toy counter assistant's expression when, in reply to his question 'How old's the little chap?', she'd say, quite seriously (and, I might add – truthfully), '42!'

Another dear lady who added generously to my farmyard and battalions was Vivien Leigh. I was in Laurence Olivier's Old Vic Company which toured Australasia for a year in 1948, and one day she caught sight of me looking longingly through a shop window, nose pressed against glass, hopelessly captivated by a boxed set of the 11th Hussars, their officer in resplendent uniform and mounted on a prancing horse.

'Would you like that for your birthday?' she asked.

'Oh, so very much,' said I, wistfully.

Several weeks later, when that day dawned, I was a little dismayed not to find it amongst all the other wrapped gifts which arrived at the hotel where Helen and I were staying. But in the evening when we got to the theatre, there it was on my dressing room table, with a card saying *'AH-HAH!* – you thought I'd forgotten, didn't you?! Love – Vivien and Larry. x'

I was deeply touched by this 'secret surprise', as Helen called it, and I'm glad to say that like all old soldiers they never die, or even fade away. They are still with me.

Our house in London had a big studio with a lofty ceiling, so I constructed a scale model aeroplane and suspended it from a high beam. On its wings I laid four seated gunners, two on either side to maintain balance. They were pressed into service from my Royal Horse Artillery set, temporarily transferred for duty with the Parachute Regiment by attaching homemade silken 'chutes to their bodies. The 'plane was hoisted and lowered by an elaborate system of pulleys, using a fishing tackle reel and strong nylon line.

Amongst my 'armoury', I had an air gun which discharged ping pong balls when fired, and all our visiting friends, knowing they had to obey my slightest wish or they wouldn't get any supper, were made to lie prone, face upwards, one-pop-gun-for-the-use-of-in-hand. On my command 'Take aim – FIRE!' they would do that, and it was sheer bliss to see the brave little figures float gently down to earth, surviving each jump with ne'er a breakage, or even so much as a scratch. Oh, happy days! This military exercise was filmed for one of those *Look at Life* magazine features which were shown at cinemas in those days – but, alas, I never saw it.

In his small and quite delightful book *Little Wars*, first published in 1913, HG Wells writes enchantingly upon this subject, and on the title page he gives the following description: 'A Game for Boys, from 12 years of age to 150 and for that more intelligent sort of girls who like boys' games and books … by HG Wells, the Author of *Floor Games* and several minor and inferior works…'

Little Wars is based loosely upon Kriegspiel, the German version (played on a map) to train officers. Wells and his great literary friend, Jerome K Jerome, used to engage each other in this innocent pastime, with forays on the lawn of a garden in Sandgate, Kent, and Mr Wells goes to great lengths to expose the idiocy of the real thing, suggesting that any belligerent-minded leaders of the world should be locked up together in a large room with unlimited supplies of toy soldiers and guns, waging their battles in this fashion, without death and destruction, and so perhaps learn the folly of their ways.

A pity his advice wasn't taken, because a year after he'd given it, the First World War broke out.

That emporium of Boy's Own delights, Hamley's, also supplied table games such as Monopoly, Totopoly (a marvellous horse race, in which you have to train your gee gees before the 'off'), Buccaneer, Careers, and endless other indoor excitements.

Helen and I often entertained our friends by inviting them to games parties. First dinner was served, and when that enjoyable repast had been consumed, the game commenced about 9.00 pm. Rosita, a permanent member of 'we happy few', being a working girl, had to rise at six o'clock in the morning, so she always warned us beforehand that she 'couldn't stay much after three'. At the conclusion of these soirées, it was part of the ritual for me to give a subtle hint about the time, by saying 'Well, I'm home – I wish everyone else was' as I noisily plumped up the cushions and cleaned the ashtrays, before grasping her by the arm and propelling her to the front door to deposit empty milk bottles. My parting shot was 'So sorry you have to go – at LAST. Do come again when you can't stay so long.'

The object of Careers is to collect 60 points, the first to do so being the winner. There are several categories to choose – Big Business, Politics, Hollywood Films, Farming, etc, and each player writes his or her Success Formula on the forms provided, with strict instructions in The Rules – 'BE SURE TO KEEP YOUR FORMULA SECRET'. To reach your goal, you divide your marks under the headings Money, Fame and Happiness. Whichever career Helen chose, it was typical of her sweet and tender, undemanding nature that *her* total was always amassed by Happiness, because that was all she ever asked for or wanted. So we all knew in advance what she'd be aiming for every time that particular game was played, but no one ever took advantage of that knowledge!

Among our many guests on those occasions were my solicitor and his wife, Mr and Mrs Simon Pritchard (Simon dealt so kindly with the harrowing demands made by officialdom which I had to face after the passing of my dear Helen, and they both treated me with such warm, sympathetic understanding); Ellen and Stanley Baker; James Bree; Edward Seago (that superb artist in the great English tradition); Billie Whitelaw and her husband Peter Vaughan; Helen's other sister, Betty Sutherland; Richard Pasco; Ann and Michael Redington; Irene Sutcliffe and her husband George Cooper; Gordon Jackson and his darling wee wife, Rona Anderson.

Helen and I first saw Gordon donkey's years ago (1943) when he was but a stripling, in *Millions Like Us*. Before the film was half over we both agreed that he would 'make it', and by jingo, how right we were! He is always first rate, in whatever he does – and I, for one, could watch *Upstairs Downstairs* all over again – twice, at the very least. Bless him, he still addresses letters to Mr and Mrs Peter Cushing, because he knows she is still with me, and so does Ronnie Millar, a dear friend and fellow survivor from the days – and nights – of the ill-fated *War and Peace*!

ACT TWO SCENE 2

AMONGST THE MANY and varied possessions this country of ours nurtures is an abundance of talent in the arts, with a treasury of outstanding players. I wish I could name them all, but that would be like reading *The Spotlight*.

It was my great pleasure to work with that brilliant writer, actor and raconteur all rolled into one – Peter Ustinov, a man for all seasons if ever there was one. He wrote *The Moment of Truth* for the theatre in 1951, and four years later it was presented on BBC Television, with me playing the Prime Minister. The theme was one of high tragedy, the story of Pétain retold as a variation of Shakespeare's *King Lear*. Peter repeated his performance as the tragic old Marshal, his daughter was played by Jeanette Sterke, and the play produced by Rudolph Cartier, who had been responsible for the shattering success and impact of George Orwell's *Nineteen Eighty-Four* a year before.

An atmosphere of gloom prevailed over the rehearsals, engendered by the play's content, and no doubt it was due to this that the author decided to throw a little light relief into the proceedings. Anyway, for whatever reason, there ensued an impromptu exchange of correspondence between the Marshal and the Prime Minister (Peter U and Peter C, respectively).

It seems only fair that this inspired lunacy from so great a brain should have some sort of posterity, therefore I commit a selection of these documents to print, from the original 'memos' which I have kept all these years with enduring affection and respect for the man who instigated them, as souvenirs of those days spent in his company. No reference was ever made to them verbally, and as you will see, they were just scribbled on odd scraps of notepaper and sheets torn from scripts.

Peter Ustinov had written a wonderfully funny series, called *In All Directions*, which was first broadcast on the wireless in 1952. He and Peter Jones played a couple of Jewish spivs, Morris and Dudley Grosvenor, the particular episodes in the programme featuring those characters starting with 'Can you tell me the way to *Grow*'ven-ner Street?' – the tag line being 'Wrun for rit, Morrie!' after they'd made an awful hash of some diabolical con trick and were being hotly pursued by their outraged victims.

The names of the directors on the 'Account Rendered' from 'Amalgamated and General Electronics' were derived from other members of the cast in *The Moment of Truth*, so to help you to identify them, here they are: Donald Pleasence, Ian Colin, Hugh Griffith and Noel Hood.

The usual venues for TV rehearsals at that time were London drill halls, this particular building being in Harrow Road, with an imposing plaque over the door which bore the title 'Inkerman House'.

One soggy, dismal day, from out of the non-existent blue, I found the following, tucked under my tea-break mug:

AMALGAMATED AND GENERAL ELECTRONICS

DIRECTORS
MORRIS GROSVENOR
DUDLEY GROSVENOR
RUDOLPH CRTR (CZECHOSLOVAK)
DON. E. PLEASANCE (CHANNEL ISLANDS)
E. N. KOLIN (TANGIER)
NOAH EL KHOUD (ALEPPO)
HUGRI FITH (HUNGARIAN)
TELEGRAMMES : ATOMPICCY

M & D GROSVENOR

167-7⁹ INKERMAN BUILDINGS

OMDURMAN WAY

OFF LAHORE GROVE
E. C. 42

ALSO ÷ ﺍﻟﺸﺮﻛﺔ

ﺍﻟﺸﺮﻛﺔ

TANGIER
TELEPHONE ﺍﻟﺸﺮﻛﺔ

INVOICE FOR ÷ Mr. Peter Cushing

To repairing, solidifying and undermining double
baffle indicators   £ 9 / 17 / 6

To counterigizing helical nuts and two
nipples   £ 14 / 4 / 9

To greasing additional nipples   £ 19 / 8 / 7

To maraying two female switches   £ 26 / 9 / 4½

To oxydizing reciprocating groin   £ 29 / 12 / 0

To demoralizing bakelite valve-code £ 84 / 19 / 7¾

To soldering G-Type 98 Superhet
                            orifice   £ 91 / 12 / 7

                        Tax   £ 143 / 9 / 7
                  Cover Charge   £ 82 / 14 / 8
                        Labour   £ 463 / 19 / 7
                                      £ 1,826 / 12 / 4

SECOND AND FINAL APPLICATION
WILL BE POSTED THIS AFTERNOON

— 243 —

I took up the challenge and replied:

> "Til.i.Go"
> Arcacia Ave.,
> Tulsa Hill
> N.11
> Feb. 23 - 1955
>
> Thee Messurs
> M. & D. Grosvenor
>
> Deare Surs
>   i am inn receet of yore a/k
> receved of too daiz dayt and franklea,
> Surs, i am harryfyried - i Never -
> repete. NEVER - had me nipples done
> and me switches arr spinsters tew this
> very dai.
>   Furver moor - yore porysez arr
> for xorbeedant -
>   Reeluck tautlee i am refurring thee
> hole sawdya ayafare too mie solelissiturs -
> Messurs Renfrick, Renfrick, Renfrick and
> Renfrick & Son Sons, Ltd. - whoo no dout
> wil bee gettin inn touch wiv yew same.
>   Moyst unfaythfully yurs.
> P.S. see? i'm enjuiy
>   already   Peter Cushing
>   P.S.

Houltworthy, Riller, Riller, Spragge & Bullion

SOLICITOR · AT · LAW

TELEGRAMS : *LITIGATE*

TELEPHONE : *DICKENS 1275-82*
    OR *ZAHAROFF 9211*

REF : PC/MG/DG/AES/WR

19 FOIE GRAS CHAMBERS

GREAT VICTUALLERS

OLD CROCK YARD

AMBROSE'S INN

THE CITY C.I

Sir,

Being under distraint hereinafter appelleted the rejoinder, our clients Messrs. Dudley Armitage de la Ville Grosvenor and Morris Valvason à Bechet Grosvenor do hereby and hereat call you in lieu to Sunday Courts-at-law in the Citye of London to answer or forevermore remain silent under charges of criminal non-honouring of money or moneys due to said them for works of a mechanical or electrical or electronical or metaphysical or constructive or architectual or any whatever nature do you now we charge you solemnly and under or over duress appear as summoned by the beadle or beadles or yeomen to the stocks at Hungerford Hill there to plead penury before the advocate argent of ye British Isles

Your obedient servant

pp. Houltworthy, etc R Riller etc

After this seamy start, the pursuit of Cushing in his various alibis spread worldwide until we reached (somehow) the point at which I had taken refuge in a banana crate aboard what turned out to be a boat belonging to the abominable Mr Grosvenor. And so it went on:

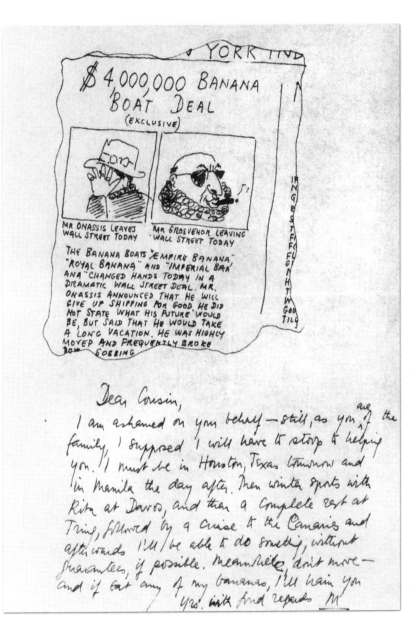

$4,000,000 BANANA BOAT DEAL
(EXCLUSIVE)

MR ONASSIS LEAVES WALL STREET TODAY

MR GROSVENOR LEAVING WALL STREET TODAY

THE BANANA BOATS "EMPIRE BANANA" "ROYAL BANANA" AND "IMPERIAL BANANA" CHANGED HANDS TODAY IN A DRAMATIC WALL STREET DEAL. MR. ONASSIS ANNOUNCED THAT HE WILL GIVE UP SHIPPING FOR GOOD. HE DID NOT STATE WHAT HIS FUTURE WOULD BE, BUT SAID THAT HE WOULD TAKE A LONG VACATION. HE WAS HIGHLY MOVED AND FREQUENTLY BROKE DOWN SOBBING

Dear Cousin,

I am ashamed on your behalf — still, as you are of the family, I suppose I will have to stoop to helping you. I must be in Houston, Texas tomorrow and in Manila the day after. Then winter sports with Rita at Davos, and then a complete rest at Tring, followed by a cruise to the Canaries and afterwards I'll be able to do something, without guarantees, if possible. Meanwhile, don't move — and if eat any of my bananas, I'll have you

Yrs. with fond regards M

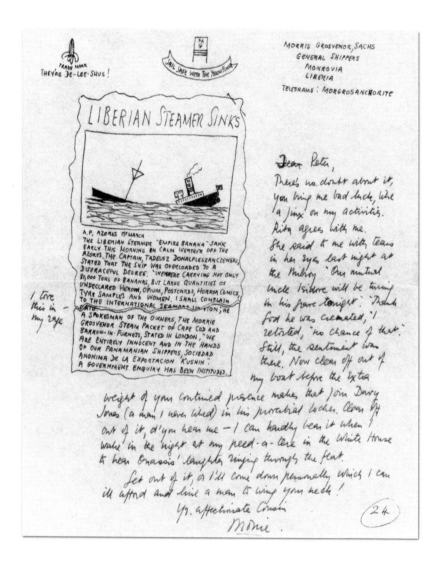

PRESS CUTTINGS AGENCY
WOOLGAR AND ROBERTS
CLACTON GAZETTE. 27.111.55

NEW MILK - BAR
OPENS ON CLACTON
PIER - GLUT OF
BANANAS MAKES
SMALL FORTUNE FOR
ENTERISING PROPRIETOR

PEDRO KOCHINI - in an interview
with our special correspondent
stated that his thriving business
is due to large sales of
Banana Splits and Sundaes.
Mr. Kochini - who says he
hails from Sunny Italy -
anticipates opening a chain
of Milk Bars all over the
country. Reuters.

ESSEX CONSTABULARY - MEMO -
TO M. GROSVENOR. % U.S. IMMIGRATION DEPT. N.Y.C.
N.Y.
CAN YOU IDENTIFY THE ABOVE INDIVIDUAL
AS PETER KUCHIN? - WANTED FOR
VAGRANCY AND LOITERING - AND MANY
OTHER OFFENCES AGAINST THE REALM.
Chief of Police.
ESSEX DIV.

KU-CHIN'S CHOP HOUSE
' LEWISHAM'S OWN XANADU

MENU :—

VEGETARIAN BIRD NEST   9/6
DUNG CRAM BO (HONG KONG STYLE) 11/6
CRAP GAME (GROUSE)   17/6
CHINESE LACQUER TART   8/9
MA'S HOME MADE JONG   15/4
SCUTTLED JUNK ET   9/2
WILLOW PATTIES   2/4 each x
CANTON CANETON   £1/5 for two
STUFFED KITE (LOW FLYING)   7/6
DUM CLUCK (IN SEASON)   15/1
HAN KOW CHIEF   9d each x
PING PONG BALLS GARNIE   9d the dozen
DONT LUCKNOW (CURRIED)   18/7½
DED IZZY (KOSHER)   10/11

SERVICE   20%
COVER CHARGE   10%

ONLY DISHES MARKED X ARE ON

Dear Cousin — Saw you was back, so dropped in. Thanks for nothing. Just had time to scribble to taste your Junk. this note while Rita's vomiting in the Kibs. Not even the Ded Izzy was a delicatesse! Monie

DOG DIES AFTER EATING BANANA

FROM ANGELA BONE, OUR CANINE CORRESPONDENT

CHOP SUEY WARLORD OF ORPINGTON AT CRUFTS THIS YEAR

CHOP SUEY WARLORD OF ORPINGTON, A CHAMPION PAPILLON DOG BELONGING TO MAUD LADY WAYNESCOTE DIED AT BATTERSEA CANINE CLINIC EARLY THIS MORNING AFTER EATING A CONTAMINATED BANANA. A BOAC AIRLINER, CHARTERED BY LADY WAYNESCOTE TO BRING ANTIPROTOBIOBANANINE, THE SWISS SERUM, ARRIVED FROM ZURICH TOO LATE. LADY WAYNESCOTE SAID: THIS A PROFOUND AND TERRIBLE BEREAVEMENT. HE WAS THE LIFE AND SOUL OF EVERY PARTY. HE LOVED BANANAS SO.

THE BANANA WAS PURCHASED FROM THE STALL OF MR. KUCHINO, DESCRIBING HIMSELF AS A MALTESE, AT CLACTON. HE WAS ORDERED BY THE MEDICAL OFFICER OF ESSEX TO DESTROY ALL HIS BANANAS, AS PAW AND DEWLAP PEST IS SUSPECTED

LADY WAYNESCOTE TODAY

P. Thought you might like this for your scrapbook   M

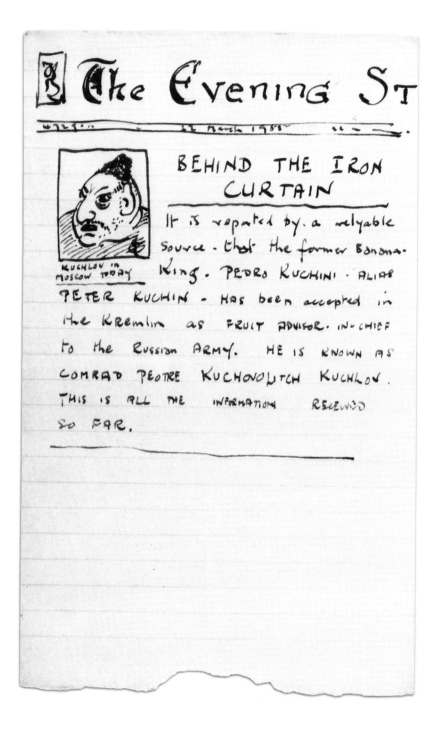

The Evening St

BEHIND THE IRON CURTAIN

It is reported by a relyable source that the former Banana King. PEDRO KUCHINI · ALIAS PETER KUCHIN · HAS been accepted in the Kremlin as FRUIT ADVISOR-IN-CHIEF to the Russian ARMY. HE IS KNOWN AS COMRAD PEOTRE KUCHOVOUTCH KUCHLOV. THIS IS ALL THE INFORMATION RECEIVED SO FAR.

KUCHLOV IN MOSCOW TODAY

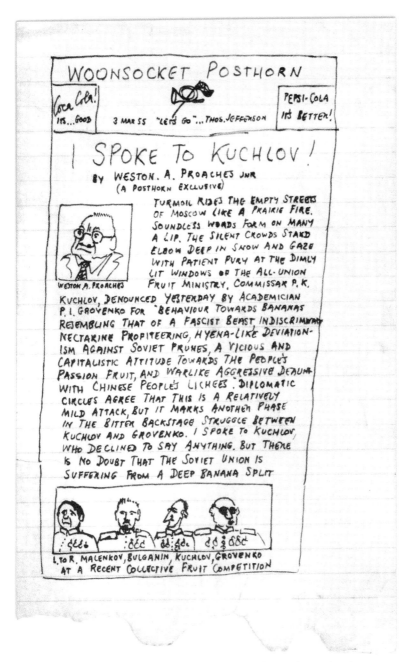

Kuchlov (alias Cushing) eventually ends up in the
Siberian salt mines!

Souvenirs of a different sort, equally cherished, came into my possession when the shooting of *Biggles* was completed. Captain WE Johns wrote 98 stories centred around that schoolboys' hero, a flying ace in the First World War, and his inseparable companions Algy, Ginger and Bertie.

Compact Yellowbill Films made a film about them in 1985, and I was cast as Colonel Raymond, a survivor from the Royal Flying Corps of 1914-18, which became the Royal Air Force during the last year of that conflict.

I have a penchant for silk ties, and asked if I might wear the attractive RFC colours: pale blue with alternating red and dark blue stripes. My request was granted, and it was given to me when I finished working on the picture.

I'd had a nodding acquaintance with a charming gentleman and his wife, who often lunched at my favourite tea rooms in Whitstable, my home town. (I *prefer* to call it a village, because it has that atmosphere which towns lack.) Being so proud of my new acquisition, I risked wearing it locally, thinking no one would recognise it or question what right I had to give the impression I was a bona fide member of that select group of brave men.

Sipping my tea one day, the gentleman just mentioned came over to my table, his eyes twinkling as he said, 'Excuse me, but may I ask what squadron you were with?', handing me a card. I glanced at it and read Wing Commander John E Jacobs, QBE, RAF ret'd.

I confessed all, and we became great friends. He had seen *Biggles*, and declared that I had every right to sport those colours, because he considered the film had been a great tribute to those daring young men in their flying machines. He also commented upon the skill of the helicopter pilots, who executed manoeuvres he could not believe possible in their efforts to capture the exciting action sequences in the sky. I was smitten when I heard he'd died suddenly from a heart attack, having received a present from him only a few days before; two more ties which he considered I deserved – Surrey because I was born in that county, and Kent for obvious reasons. God bless him.

In my role as Colonel Raymond I used a walking stick which took my fancy. I'm fond of those things and have quite a collection, so useful on country walks. This one was made of black ebony with a curved bone handle, girded by a silver ring.

When it was handed to me by the prop man, I immediately asked Miss Pom Oliver, one of the producers, if I could make a purchase. She shook her head, saying, 'Oh, no! You cannot buy it.'

At a small gathering when I said farewell to the crew and cast on my last day, the stick was handed to me as a gift from Miss Oliver. I bore it away with gratitude, and took a closer look at a monogram on the silver circlet. Beautifully engraved in flowing script were the initials HCB. Helen's maiden name was Beck, so I felt this lovely article had found its rightful home at last. What an extraordinary coincidence!

On 22 May 1986, at the Empire Theatre, Leicester Square, *Biggles* had a Royal World Charity Première in the presence of Their Royal Highnesses The Prince and Princess of Wales, to aid the Prince's Trust and the RAF Benevolent Fund. Before the showing, all those responsible for the film's production were presented to the royal couple, and you can imagine how overjoyed I was when Prince Charles concluded our brief chat by saying, 'You're marvellous as Sherlock Holmes.' How nice to give him some small pleasure as a break from his onerous duties.

*　*　*

When I was young and innocent, at which time no one in the land was safe from marauding wolves, I was told by a producer that the part on offer was 'only a supporting role'. In my ignorance, I had visions of myself standing behind some grizzled veteran, my hands tucked firmly under his armpits to prevent him falling flat on his face whilst he spouted Shakespeare. But 'only supporting' is misleadingly dismissive, for how important it is to have good players in minor roles, which are sometimes as difficult to play as the lead, because there's so little time to establish yourself and convince the audience that the character is 'flesh and blood'.

It is thought by some people that actors are a rather insincere lot, as demonstrated by their tendency to use over-familiar endearments even when they first meet. They are mistaken. That is all part and parcel of getting to know each other. Due to the peculiar nature of our work, it *is* expedient to break down all barriers and inhibitions as quickly as possible, but still show genuine respect.

Acting is acting in whatever medium, but each has its own particular requirements. For instance, in the theatre your voice has to be heard in all parts of the house, but the first rows of the stalls mustn't be deafened by an actor endeavouring to let the back row of the Gods have their share, too. So you learn to project your voice, which is something very different from shouting. The volume of sound in all other media is controlled by microphones, which can pick up the merest whisper.

You cannot give a stage performance in front of cameras, because that would look too exaggerated. Consider the size of a close-up in the cinema, a face on average being, what? – say about 18 feet by 12. So the merest flicker of an eyelid will register, whereas in the theatre everything has to be broader to achieve any desired effect.

Before starting a film it is a good idea to know all your lines well in advance, otherwise you're in trouble. For economic reasons scenes are not always done in consecutive order, those taking place in the same setting being shot regardless of continuity. When on location bad weather can create last-minute changes in the original schedule, so – like Boy Scouts – one must 'Be Prepared'!

In 1962, during the shooting of *The Man Who Finally Died*, the unit was on location in Richmond, Surrey, and permission had been given by the local council for the company to create a mock-up cemetery in the lovely park. The setting was necessary

Above: With Veronica Carlson, displaying his Pipeman of the Year award on the set of *Frankenstein Must Be Destroyed*, 1969.

Below: Bloody business in the same film, reluctantly assisted by Simon Ward.

Right: As General Spielsdorf in *The Vampire Lovers*, 1970.

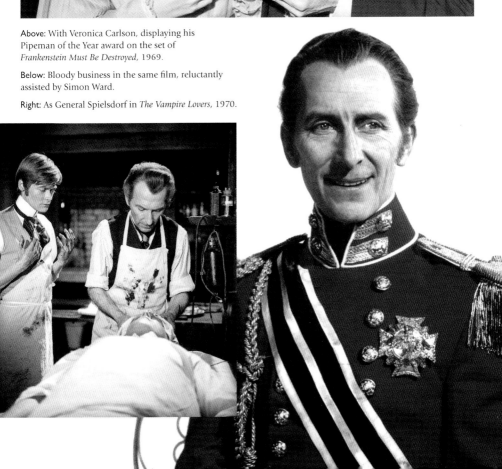

Above: On location for *The House that Dripped Blood* with director Peter Duffell, 1970.

Right: In Madrid for *Pánico en el Transiberiano*, aka *Horror Express*, 1971.

Below: As Arthur Edward Grimsdyke, with 'Jamie', in *Tales from the Crypt*, 1971.

Above: On location in Dartmouth with Christopher Lee for *Nothing But the Night,* 1972.

Above: One last outing as the now insane Baron. With Shane Briant in *Frankenstein and the Monster from Hell,* 1972.

Left: As Dr Pope in *Bride of Fengriffen* (released as
~ ~ *And Now the Screaming Starts!*), 1972.

Above: Final stage performance. With Helen Ryan in
The Heiress, Horseshoe Theatre Basingstoke, 1975.

Below: On location in Hong Kong with David Chiang
for *The Legend of the 7 Golden Vampires*, 1973.

Above: As Grand Moff Tarkin in *Star Wars*, 1976.

Right: Guest starring in the *Silent Scream* episode of *Hammer House of Horror*, 1980.

Below: With costume supervisor Rosemary Burrows on the set of *Arabian Adventure*, 1978.

Above: Relaxing in Paris during the filming of the Hallmark TV movie *A Tale of Two Cities*, 1980.

Right: Cushing's caricature of Joyce Broughton as the 'secretary bird' – and a 1990 'bird-book' compiled by Cushing's old friend Peter Gray.

Below: Breaking protocol with Princess Diana at the royal première of his last film, *Biggles*, on 22 May 1986.

Above: Proud recipient of the Order of the British Empire, 22 March 1989.

Above right: With Joyce Broughton at 'The Great Hip Walk' for the British Orthopaedic Association, 4 June 1989.

Right: Honoured on *This is Your Life*, 21 February 1990 – and debating his long overdue fee with Ernie Wise.

Below: Raising a glass at his 80th birthday party, 26 May 1993.

for a scene where a body was exhumed, and when the ritual was being filmed a very officious bowler-hatted gentleman in pin-striped trousers, black coat and carrying a neatly furled umbrella bore down upon us, crying angrily, 'This is an outrage! Stop it at ONCE! How *dare* you desecrate consecrated ground, just for the sake of some stupid film! I shall report this to my superiors at the Burial Board, and you will be hearing from us. What is the name of your company?'

It was given to him, and, without giving us time to explain, he left in a huff.

The rest was silence. Bureaucracy gone a little haywire...

Incidentally, a clip from *The Man Who Finally Died* was used recently for one of those extremely clever Holsten Pils television advertisements (the easiest job I've ever had! – with excellent comedy playing by Griff Rhys Jones).

My entry into the world of films as a leading man was very fortunate. I had previously been well known for my work on television, and in the 1950s television was keeping people away from cinemas. Any actor connected with that rival medium was frowned upon by film magnates. I'd worked for the BBC practically non-stop between 1951-6, and became known as 'the uncrowned King of Television'.

In 1954 Alan Melville wrote a highly successful comedy, *Simon and Laura*, which was presented by HM Tennent's at the Strand Theatre, later transferring to the Apollo. It concerns an actress/actor partnership who quarrel fiercely in private life but present perfect harmony in public to preserve their image of a happily married couple.

Laura is offered a 12-part television serial, but Simon frowns upon the idea and tries to persuade her not to do this early form of 'soap'. But Laura says: 'Why shouldn't I agree? I don't relish the idea of wearing black in the programme, but David promised it would only be for six weeks.' (With a happy smile) 'Then I was to meet Peter Cushing.'

When the film version appeared my name was cut, replaced by Gilbert Harding's, which illustrates the animosity that prevailed between the two media, happily now a thing of the past.

Mr Harding was not an actor, but a very popular personality, lending great distinction to such shows as *What's My Line?* He was also a sad, kind and generous person, who never failed to ring me up after viewing my performances on the 'box', voicing heart-warming congratulations and encouragement.

I was the mystery guest on that programme once, and nearly fooled the team as to my identity by using a variety of accents, but was pipped at the post by Gilbert, who recognised my involuntary laugh caused by something said by one of the panellists.

Amongst my many hobbies was modelling, in which Gilbert showed keen interest. As earlier readers may recall, Helen's mother was Swedish, and her command of the English language was eccentric, to say the least. She once tried to express her feelings regarding some earrings I'd made for Helen. 'Ah, Petrushka!' she exclaimed. 'Your work! It is – it is like Fabergé's – it is...' She searched for the elusive word, and found it. With exultation she declared: 'It is *worthless!*'

*   *   *

When I made my first film for Hammer (*The Curse of Frankenstein*), at Bray in Berkshire, there was no motorway. The journey took longer but we wound through lovely country lanes and pastoral scenery, which looked so beautiful in the early morning sunlight. Dick Turpin Country I called it, as many of the byways we passed along had been the stamping ground of that notorious highwayman in the early part of the 18th century, when he waylaid the horse-drawn coaches on their way to and from London.

In 1957 Bray Studios consisted of a vast rambling old house, set in sylvan serenity upon the banks of the River Thames, with wide lawns reaching down to the water's edge. In the spacious garden stood a little sound stage, which was turned into the Baron's laboratory for *The Curse of Frankenstein*, all the other interior scenes being shot inside the house and the exteriors in the grounds.

Nigel Kneale, who had adapted *Nineteen Eighty-Four* for the small screen, wrote an original play called *The Creature*, presented by the BBC, about an expedition to the Himalaya Mountains in search of the Yeti. On the evidence given by several climbing parties, who have discovered huge footprints in the snow, it is still believed that this mysterious creature, like the Loch Ness Monster, actually exists.

Stanley Baker played the leader of the party, Tom Friend, and I was cast as Dr John Rollason. Hammer obtained the film rights for this adventure story, calling it *The Abominable Snowman*, in which I repeated Rollason, and Friend was taken over by Forrest Tucker.

Bernard Robinson, the production designer, did wonders with limited financial resources. Under his expert supervision, a most realistic Tibetan village was constructed, tons of salt strewn about to represent snow. Successively, he transformed the studio lot into Transylvania for the Dracula epics: the mythical streets where Baron Victor Frankenstein stalked, the impressive façade of Sir Henry Baskerville's Hall on Dartmoor in Devonshire for *The Hound of the Baskervilles*, India for *The Stranglers of Bombay*.

His magical ingenuity also provided Chinese backgrounds for *The Terror of the Tongs*, a vast courtyard adjoining a house on Romney Marsh, Kent, used in *Captain Clegg*, and Russian exteriors for *Rasputin the Mad Monk*.

All this and Heaven too, in England's green and pleasant land!

Jack Asher's superb photography added a lushness to so many of these productions. It was said of him that he 'painted with light', which was not a bad summing up of his masterly contribution.

Terence Fisher directed *The Mummy*, another Hammer production, and Bernard conjured up some exquisite Egyptian interiors for the prologue, glistening with gold and other luminous colours.

When I saw the posters advertising the film, I noticed that Christopher Lee, who was playing the name part, had a large hole in his diaphragm with a beam of light passing through it, which was never referred to in the script, so I enquired how it got there.

'Oh,' said the publicity man, 'that's just to help sell the picture.' Oh, I thought – that's just not on.

John Banning (my part) was attacked by Kharis, the mummy, so I asked Terry if I could grab a harpoon hanging on the wall of Banning's study and during the struggle for survival, drive it clear through my opponent's body. And that's what I did, thus giving some sort of logic to the illuminated gap depicted on the posters. Christopher was pleased, too – he said it made a nice change from stakes.

Making movies is such a co-operative industry, everyone tossing ideas into the melting pot, which are weighed, considered, accepted or rejected, according to merit.

Roy Ashton, a dear man of gentle disposition and an expert make-up artist, took care of that department when I played Mr Grimsdyke in *Tales from the Crypt*. The moment when that character emerged from his grave, having spent quite a spell underground, was scheduled for shooting immediately after lunch, up to which time I had to look normal. Roy kindly gave up his hour's break in order to get me ready for resurrection.

I possessed an ugly set of false teeth, acquired from the BBC when I was playing Sherlock Holmes (that man of many disguises) in *The Greek Interpreter*. Roy agreed that these would fit the bill perfectly, helping to give me a skull-like visage, but the empty eye sockets presented a bit of a problem. I asked Roy if he could use black gauze which I would be able to see through, instead of Max Factor painted over my eyelids, because that might have made me look like a panda. He could and he did. After matting my hair with real mud, and colouring my face lustreless grey, the effect we were after was achieved in about 45 minutes, giving us time to snatch a sandwich and a glass of milk before we were called onto the set.

My first spell of duty as Sherlock Holmes had actually occurred before the television series, when the Hammer production of *The Hound of the Baskervilles* was made. Tony Hinds, the producer, said how professional I was to have lost weight especially to portray that gaunt detective. I'm afraid I hadn't been as conscientious as all that – 'it was Spain what done it!' – I'd been out there making *John Paul Jones,* and a bout of mild dysentery had fined me down.

Producers of *The Hound of the Baskervilles* always experience tremendous difficulties over making the hound seem realistic and truly frightening. This is what they have to aim for:

> *...I sprang to my feet, my inert hand grasping my pistol, my*
> *mind paralyzed by the dreadful shape which had sprung out upon*
> *us from the shadows of the fog. A hound it was, an enormous*
> *coal-black hound, but not such a hound as mortal eyes have ever seen.*
> *Fire burst from its open mouth, its eyes glowed with a smouldering*
> *glare, its muzzle and hackles and dewlap were outlined in flickering*
> *flame. Never in the delirious dream of a disordered brain could*
> *anything more savage, more appalling, more hellish be conceived*
> *than that dark form and savage face which broke upon us out*
> *of the wall of fog.*

Thus spake Dr Watson, at the end of Chapter 14 in Sir Arthur Conan Doyle's gripping yarn. Such a description is enough to turn those in the special effects department grey overnight, and I don't think that infamous hound has ever been entirely successful in any presentation of *The Hound of the Baskervilles.*

Packs of unlikely canine contenders were auditioned by Terry Fisher, most of them just wanting to roll over and have their tummies tickled. Even Crufts failed us.

Eventually one was chosen and given a good coating of glycerine. The production team, endeavouring to create an illusion of the dog's massive proportions, hit upon the idea of employing three young boys corresponding in relative size to André Morell (Dr

Watson), Christopher Lee (Sir Henry) and myself, dressing them in replicas of our clothes. A miniature set was erected depicting a stretch of Dartmoor, clouds of dry ice pumped in, representing fog. The decision was to take a long shot of this set-up, and when all was ready for the cameras to turn, a prop man flung a meaty morsel into the set, whereupon 'Fido', who'd been starved up until the last moment, pounced upon it ravenously.

On the following day the rushes were viewed and disappoint-ment deflated all concerned. We saw three small boys dressed up as if playing a game of charades, foggy toy scenery with a wet, hungry dog in the middle, contentedly wolfing a bone. The sequence was scrapped.

Hammer Films were slated in some quarters when they were first shown, but are now preserved in the archives of the British Film Institute as classics of their kind.

*   *   *

I mentioned *John Paul Jones* some lines back. This spectacular seafaring epic told the life story of that man, born in the Scottish county of Kirkcudbrightshire and founder of the United States Navy. He was played by Robert Stack and the director was John Farrow, both with naval experience, having served in that branch of the services in the last world war.

Captain Alan Villiers was advisor-in-chief for all the sailing sequences. In 1957 he had sailed Mayflower II, a replica of that original vessel which carried the Pilgrim Fathers to New England in 1620. (It was presented by Great Britain to form part of the National Shrine at Plymouth, Massachussetts.) He combed seaports, and succeeded in finding the hulls of two wooden-wall sailing boats, which were employed hauling salt and fruit between Spain and Marseilles, and had them converted into square-rigged frigates. With different rig-outs, they were made to represent the Serapis, Bonhomme Richard and Providence, the British, French and American ships engaged in the historic battle off the coast of Britain in 1779, during the American War of Independence.

To give the impression of gunshot hitting planks and bulwarks, small charges of gunpowder were placed in strategic positions all over the decks. At given moments they were detonated electrically by the special effects department, but in the fury of mock battle with so much noise and action, plus other things to think about, it was extremely difficult to remember exactly where these explosions occurred, so we had to leave our safety solely in the hands of those splendid experts, and to their credit we all emerged from those dangerous skirmishes unscathed.

King George III was played by Eric Portman, Benjamin Franklin by Charles Coburn, King Louis XVI by Jean Pierre Aumont; Catherine the Great was portrayed by Bette Davis and Marie Antoinette by Susana Canales. Basil Sydney appeared as Sir William Young, Bruce Cabot as Gunner Lowrie, David Farrar as John Wilkes, and I was cast as Captain Pearson.

As always, Helen accompanied me, and the whole unit was stationed in Benidorm, a small isolated town on the East Coast of the Iberian Peninsula, where the enterprising inhabitants had built a desalination plant, thus providing that arid region with a plentiful supply of fresh water. The year was 1959, and I understand the place has grown considerably since then. It was the only spot with any decent accommodation within striking distance of Denia, our location site.

We put to sea each day from this little port, after a good hour and a half's drive along a winding coastal road, with jagged rocks towering up on one side and a sheer drop into a chasm on the other. Those journeys were hair-raising, as Spanish drivers have Evel Knievel tendencies, driving on their brakes, all sounding horn and screeching tyre. If any other motorist dares to approach or overtake them, they remove both hands from the steering wheel, gesticulating furiously whilst screaming lengthy abuse at each other with garlic-ridden breath, not looking where they're going, leaving the vehicle to fend for itself as it hurtles along at what seems like a hundred miles an hour.

Filming at sea presents problems, especially when canvas sails need the wind to blow in the right direction. That element has a will of its own, paying no attention to the whims of impatient filmmakers.

On my final day as Captain Pearson, I had arranged with Helen to pick her up from the hotel in Benidorm as soon as I'd finished work and then catch the midnight flight back to England. The airport lay in the opposite direction, but I didn't want her to travel alone along that twisting route at the mercy of a crazy speed merchant. But Lady Luck was not on my side: we had many difficulties out at sea getting the required scenes, eventually returning to drop anchor in Denia harbour about nine o'clock in the evening. I rang Helen immediately, to be told by the desk clerk that she had already left. Being unable to make contact, she was on her way to join me, having realised the reason for my delay and knowing we'd miss the 'plane if she stayed any longer.

I waited in an agony of suspense, praying with all my might whilst pacing up and down, chain smoking like an expectant father, and almost sobbed with relief when she finally showed up safe and sound.

My fears for her safety were not unfounded. A few days after we reached home, I learnt that our chauffeur in Spain had plunged his car accidentally off that precipitous road and had been killed instantly.

*   *   *

Two members in the cast of *She* and one of the crew were victims of the hazards actors are sometimes heir to, our lives not being all beer and skittles.

Hammer Films remade Haggard's exciting adventure story in 1965, directed by Robert Day, with locations in Southern Israel. The desert region of Negev is potted with deposits of potash, bromide and copper, thus providing just the right settings described in the novel as 'the Mountains of the Moon', traversed by those three brave explorers Major Ludwig Horace Holly, his faithful batman Job, and Leo Vincey in their quest to help Ayesha (She who must be obeyed) regain the soul she forfeited by sinning, or she would be doomed 'to wander in the deep and endless night of Solitude' for all eternity.

Ursula Andress took the name part, I played Holly, Bernard Cribbins Job, and John Richardson was cast as Leo.

During their trek, Leo is overcome by exhaustion and in dire need of water, which he gulps from a goatskin container. Unfortunately, the water was contaminated, and poor John was laid up for several days with a nasty bout of gyppy tummy. Production was held up until he was fit again, and Ursula, a kind lady with deep maternal instincts, nursed him back to health.

In that unexpected break Helen, Bernard and I visited a kibbutz, and also explored the clear waters of Eilat's sea port, where we were staying. Wearing snorkels, and vests to protect our backs from the sun's blistering heat, we floated about the coral pools, looking down into a wonderland of marine life, teeming with tropical fish darting amongst the colourful vegetation.

Bernard was not as lucky as I'd been on the quarter deck of HMS Serapis in *John Paul Jones*. The three characters in *She* were attacked by hostile tribesmen bearing firearms, and gunpowder charges were buried in the ground by the special effects man, spouting up sand most realistically to depict near misses. Several 'takes' were needed to allow the editor enough footage to make the sequence exciting, but our continuous movements caused the explosives to shift. Bernard, lying on his back as he reloaded my revolver, suddenly gave a yell of agony. One of the charges had exploded beneath him, wounding him dangerously near his anus.

He was sent to hospital for treatment, but next day insisted upon returning to work, not wishing to delay filming again, manfully struggling on in considerable pain, yet still managing to keep us all amused with his irrepressible sense of fun.

'It could have been worse,' he philosophised. 'If I'd been t'other way down I might have been blinded.'

He smiled ironically when he read a critique after the film was shown, which commented, 'What a pity Mr Cribbins tried to get laughs by adopting a funny walk...'

The special effects man, furious with himself for inflicting this injury on Bernard, albeit unwittingly, had wrenched the wired contraption away and, in so doing, blew off his own right hand.

John Richardson left the industry to take up photography, concentrating on humming birds and other wild life. How peaceful.

*　　*　　*

The magic of the theatre has always lured me. When I was at school, my form was taken to see *Hamlet* and we sat in the gallery on hard, backless benches. I was mesmerised by those tiny figures far below me, and although I didn't understand one word that was spoken, the drama and the atmosphere seeped into my very bones. I even forgot to eat the sandwiches Mother had made for me to have in the intervals.

Then, as a gawping stage-struck youth, I'd sneak into London playhouses, concealing myself in the upper circle by kneeling on the floor, my nose over the edge of the balustrade like a wartime Chad as I gazed down upon actors rehearsing, with a painful yearning in my heart to be amongst that chosen community.

In 1936, unlawfully ensconced in my hidy hole at the Lyric, I saw *Charles the King* being licked into shape by the author, Maurice Colbourne, who was also producing the play, little dreaming that nearly two decades later we'd meet, become friends and work together, or that by June of that year I would be established as a professional, in as much as I'd be paid to work in that world of make believe.

Barry Jones, in grey flannels and blue blazer, seemed to me every inch a king. I could imagine him in a long, curly wig, bearded and moustached as Charles the First and dressed in the finery of that period, with Gwen Ffrangcon-Davies as his adored adoring wife, Queen Henrietta Maria.

I remember Maurice looking at his watch as he said to one of the players, 'You want to leave now, don't you?' – and thinking to myself 'Fancy *wanting* to leave.' Obviously, the fellow had some previous appointment to keep, but it still bothered me.

So many stories concerning famous actors and actresses have become legends, and are enjoyed by the public as much as by those who have the privilege to recall them from personal experience.

The offices of that renowned production company HM Tennent Ltd were above the Globe Theatre in Shaftesbury Avenue, reached by a minute lift, barely big enough to accommodate one normal size human being.

Mrs W Graham Browne, better known as Marie Tempest, stepped into that unreliable conveyance, finding it occupied by a pretty hefty juvenile lead. They juddered upwards in silence, pressed close together. As they squeezed out upon reaching the top floor, Miss Tempest turned to the embarrassed youth, looking at him severely. 'Young man,' she said, 'there's only one thing for it after that. *Marriage!*'

She was very popular with audiences, who packed the theatres whenever she appeared. Her supporting players were of the highest order, and she was asked by a reporter why she always insisted upon such expensive company, when her name alone was enough to draw the public. With her disarming smile, she replied 'Why surround a rose with weeds?'

Her husband produced and played in *Retreat from Folly* by Amy Kennedy Gould at the Queen's Theatre in 1937, which starred his wife. She was overcome with grief when he died during its run, but insisted upon continuing. There is a therapist for all actors' ills – he's called Dr Theatre. It is a remarkable fact that actors waiting in the wings can feel quite ghastly but as soon as they make their entrance they're as right as rain, almost collapsing again when they exit. A phenomenal cure – yes – even for a broken heart. One of the last things Helen said to our doctor was 'Don't let Peter stop working...' I imagine that is one factor which has kept me going since 1971, and I commiserate with Pagliacci, whose fate illustrates so poignantly the time-honoured adage 'the show must go on' – an inborn instinct to keep going until we drop, no matter how we feel.

Like Marie Tempest, Edith Evans was another formidable doyenne, who also possessed a heart of gold. NC Hunter's *Waters of the Moon* was just one of Edith's many outstanding triumphs. It ran for over two years at the Haymarket Theatre, beginning in 1951. This Chekovian comedy revolves around a group of frustrated guests staying at a remote hotel on the edge of Dartmoor in the middle of winter. Sybil Thorndike was a member of the star-studded cast, playing a disapproving lady, dowdily dressed – in contrast to Edith's stunningly expensive haute couture. A friendly rivalry existed between those two splendid actresses.

After about a year, Edith requested a completely new wardrobe, as she considered all her original clothes were showing signs of wear and tear. Almost as an afterthought, she threw in, 'Oh, and perhaps our dear Sybil should have a new cardigan.'

She lived in chambers at the Albany which – although situated in the heart of bustling Mayfair – enjoyed the quietness of cloisters. Helen and I were often invited to tea, her only companion at that time being a very old dog. 'He's always asleep when I come in,' she said. 'Sometimes he looks at me with mournful eyes when I disturb him, as if to say "Oh, it's only you, Edith. I thought it might be a burglar." I don't think he'd have done much about it if I haaaad been.'

Another (*less* golden-hearted) actress, who shall be nameless, guarded her declining looks and ability jealously. A very attractive and talented ingenue had been engaged, and when the first morning's rehearsal finished, the director was delighted. 'Isn't she marvellous!' he exclaimed, beaming at his leading lady, who glowered back, looking him straight in the eyes as she said meaningfully: 'Yes. What a pity she *won't be here* after lunch.'

In May 1987, that delightful comedienne Athene Seyler celebrated her 98th birthday. Back in the Fifties, her name was put forward by her agent for a part in a film to be directed by a young American, who insisted on an interview.

'Now tell me what you've done,' he demanded aggressively.

Since Miss Seyler's theatrical career stretched back to 1909, she paused briefly before fluttering her eyelashes and enquiring demurely, 'You mean to-*day*?'

She got the part.

Just before the outbreak of the Second World War, she went on tour with a play written by Stephen Haggard entitled *Weep for the Spring*. The advance publicity had not been all it should, and a local paper rang up the management in London for details of the cast and title of the play. The line couldn't have been very good, because when the company arrived in the town advertising their presentation, they were astonished to read the following announcement plastered on a billboard:

ALL THIS WEEK AT THE THEATRE ROYAL
A TEENY SAILOR WILL WEEP FOR SOMETHING

No doubt exaggerated, but that was the story as related by Athene herself to our mutual friend, Edward Seago, who had suggested the title for William Golding's comedy *The Brass Butterfly*, and also designed the setting, staged at the Strand Theatre in 1958. The action takes place in Ancient Greece, and Ted thought he was being economical by using a vast cyclorama to give the impression of distant sky. It proved to be the most expensive item, but the outlay was more than worthwhile. As the curtain rose on each performance, the audience gasped at the breathtaking beauty revealed, and broke into spontaneous applause. Alastair Sim produced as well as taking the leading part, with George Cole playing a dedicated man of science, frustrated by the ignorance of mankind who were unable to visualise how useful his inventions could be, one of them being that type of screw which gave Ted the idea for the play's title.

Due to an ailment when he was a child, Ted was forced to spend hours lying on his back, preferably in the open air. To keep him occupied, his mother bought him a watercolour set and he started making studies of the sky. Mainly self taught, he became one of the greatest painters of our time. In common with nearly all the truly great, Edward suffered tortures over his work, seldom really satisfied with it. He strove for perfection which he alone felt he never achieved, but his countless admirers think otherwise, ranking him with such masters as Constable, Turner, Boudin and all the Impressionists.

However, his depressions and vulnerability did not prevent him from being a most gracious and amusing host, seldom letting any note of melancholy spoil the enjoyment of his company, except on very rare occasions. I encountered one when we were painting together. Sensing his spirit was flagging, I attempted to lift it by asking jocularly and, with hindsight, foolishly, 'Are you happy, Ted dear boy?'

The atmosphere could have been cut with a knife when he replied, 'What a stupid question', and a feeling of ice towards me lasted for almost two hours.

Helen and I spent so many happy Christmas times in his beloved Norfolk countryside mantled with snow, The Dutch House, Ludham lending itself perfectly to that season of the year, the decorations on the traditional tree twinkling in the glow from a crackling log fire as we made toast for tea.

His housekeeper, Miss Annie Thompson, was overawed at first by a new acquisition of Ted's: a television set, very rare in those parts at that time. When she'd become accustomed to it, she brought a friend along and showed it to her with pride. As the set wasn't switched on the friend was unimpressed by the blank screen, whereupon Miss Thompson aired her superior knowledge by explaining 'It doesn't shoine all the toime,' and, with a flick of the wrist, she turned the magic knob and the face of a news presenter sprang into view. The friend was still sceptical. 'There's someone behoined adoin' thart,' she said, shaking her head.

The same friend had a son living in Australia who invited his mother to visit him. Having never ventured outside a radius of about 15 miles of the remote village where she'd been born some 50 years ago, she confided to Miss Thompson, 'It must be a long journey – I 'as to change trains at Norwich.'

The royal family figured largely in Ted's life, amassing a large collection of his masterpieces. In 1956 he was invited to join Prince Philip on the royal yacht Britannia for a trip to Antarctica, and returned with some magnificent canvases of that icebound region. He told us of the Prince's aversion to waste of any description. 'We don't want rows of food on hot plates for breakfast if we're not going to eat it, so please tell your steward exactly what you'd like.'

One of Ted's favourite pastimes was doodling, making caricatures out of friends' signatures, and the late Queen Mary requested one. He was delighted with this royal command, but had to ask Her Majesty if she'd mind leaving out the straight line she always drew under hers, as it was difficult to incorporate in his composition. She obliged, at the same time granting him a full pardon for lèse-majesté.

Lt Gen Harold Alexander was another admirer and friend, also a most talented amateur painter. When he became Commander in Chief of the 15th Army Group in Italy, he asked Ted to join him out there as an unofficial war artist. Ted recalled their experience together in the morning of 9 April 1945, when the final offensive was about to commence.

Helen's signature and mine – transformed by Ted Seago!

At breakfast, Alexander remarked on the lovely weather, suggesting they went up into the surrounding hills where they could do a sketch or two. Ted was amazed, and asked how he could even think of such a thing at such a momentous time.

'I've planned the whole campaign,' replied Alexander. 'Now my generals have got to put it into action. I can't do anything more until their reports come in, and until such time, they'll be much happier with me out of the way.'

After a lunch of grapes, bread and wine, he lay on the grass and had a snooze, returning to the operations HQ in the late afternoon, where he remained awake throughout the night. You have to be a very special sort of person to be able to do something like that, Ted reflected.

In his younger days, he piloted an ancient Tiger Moth biplane, which he described as being made of old shirts and wood held together by bits of string. Aerial views of the landscape proved invaluable in 1944 when he was a major in the newly formed Camouflage Corps, having noticed that even a solitary walker left a very distinct track. A large portion of Southern England concealed troops in wooded areas, awaiting D-day, the code name for the Allied invasion of Europe. Ted advised the defence authorities to confine them to barracks, otherwise their whereabouts would be all too evident to reconnoitring enemy aircraft. This was not very popular with the PBI, as a game of soccer or cricket in the open helped relieve the mounting tension as they awaited the signal to embark.

He possessed a dachshund which he adored, christened Chaucer (because it came from Canterbury and had a long tail). Chaucer often accompanied Ted in the air, and one day they got into a row with a farmer when they made an emergency landing in a turnip field. As Ted explained to the irate gentleman: 'I'm sorry, but my dog needed to spend a penny very urgently.'

He went on many painting trips abroad, and was appalled by the poverty he saw in Hong Kong when there in 1962. Distressed to such a degree, he decided to do something practical to help at least one of the teeming millions by adopting a young man called Chan Nam Tsui as his son. He spoke hardly any English, but using gestures and drawings Ted gradually learnt that Chan had escaped from Communist China by swimming out to sea, where he'd been picked up by a sampan. He was now working in a factory, and sleeping in a room with half a dozen other boys.

He returned to England with Ted, adding his benefactors' Christian name in front of his own. As a welcome to this strange land, Ted took him to that fashionable restaurant in Arlington Street, the Caprice. Edward Junior requested Heinz Tomato Ketchup with his meal, and to the undying credit of the maître d'hôtel, a bottle was brought to their table on a silver salver and not an eyebrow raised. He had no idea when he was born, so Ted suggested he should choose a day in order to ensure a yearly celebration. Edward the younger selected December 25th. Edward the elder pointed out that as that was Christmas, he'd only have one lot of presents to look forward to, so a summer date was drawn out of a hat.

Edward Tsui eventually married a lovely Chinese girl and became an executive with a British firm in the Far East. For a wedding gift, Ted bought them a cottage in Ludham.

He had a studio on the Costa Smeralda in Sardinia, and during a busman's holiday out there he began to feel unwell. Peter Seymour, his secretary and constant companion, said he should see a doctor, but Ted refused, as he was sure the sunshine would soon put him to rights. He always sought Peter's criticism about his paintings, and asked what he thought of his latest effort.

'It'll be splendid when it's finished,' commented Peter.

'It *is* finished,' Ted replied, frowning.

Only the right hand side of the canvas was painted, the other completely blank. Two weeks later Ted collapsed and was taken to hospital, where he underwent an operation for a brain tumour. Peter brought him back to England after his recuperation, but in January 1974 he died. As requested in Ted's will, Peter scattered his ashes over the marshes near their house, under the sky he had loved and painted all his life.

* * *

Actors require tremendous stamina. In the theatre our working day starts in the evening, and when the curtain falls the adrenaline is in full flood. Stimulated and hungry we have a meal and more often than not a long chat about this, that or the other, and dawn is often breaking when we retire to bed, therefore breakfast at noon is not an uncommon feature of our lives.

I cannot think of any other profession in which clothes are changed so often, and it is essential for us to feel 'at home' in anything we wear when performing. If we are at all self-conscious in period attire and strike unnatural poses, it looks as if we're ready for a fancy dress ball and audiences can be embarrassed. Although dressers are most helpful and, indeed, necessary for quick changes, I never ask for their service unless I have to, preferring to dress myself as the character would in ordinary life, putting on his everyday clothes.

Monty Berman (Junior) now runs that famous firm of theatrical costumiers in North London, allied with Nathans. They have a veritable museum, and I love to wander about their vast emporium, admiring the splendid uniforms and costumes worn since Roman times to the present day, and the framed designers' sketches enhancing the walls whichever way you turn. They have looked after my professional and personal needs for over 40 years, and I'm always made to feel so welcome, with the ever-refreshing cup of tea on hand. All the details I desire are given the utmost attention, and they never think of me as 'Oh dear, here comes old fuss pot again!' (although they have every reason so to do!).

Only once did they fail me, and that was due entirely to lack of time. I have enormous feet – wide size 12 – which can present problems, and we met our Waterloo when *Star Wars* was being equipped. I wore what looked like an Edwardian chauffeur's outfit, complete with knee-length boots. Usually these items are made to my measurements, but on this occasion 'Time's wingèd chariot' caught up with us and, perforce, I had to make do with a pair from stock. 'It was agony, Ivy!'

After the first day's work I could bear it no longer, so I approached the director, George Lucas. 'Dear fellow', I said, 'I'm not asking for close-ups, but do you think you could shoot me from the waist up from now on?' He consented kindly, and I was allowed to stomp about looking very cross as Grand Moff Tarkin for the rest of the picture in carpet slippers.

Encouragement is another important factor, because – contrary to general belief – most actors are not all that sure of themselves. Sir Henry Irving was made a knight in 1895, the first in our profession to receive that honour, but his private life was marred by his wife Florence, a woman of jealous nature, who didn't understand the demands made by her husband's vocation.

He enjoyed a tremendous success as Mathias in a melodrama entitled *The Bells*, which had been adapted by Leopold Lewis from Erckmann-Chatrian's *Le Juif polonais*, and presented at the Lyceum Theatre in 1871. On their way home after an exhausting but exhilarating first night, Florence rebelled against the adulation conceded by his vast public.

'Are you going on making a fool of yourself like this all your life?' she asked.

Irving told the driver of his brougham to stop, and without another word he got out, never to return to his home or speak to his wife again.

In the 1920s, Ben Travers became famous for his Aldwych farces, which were always staged at that theatre with the same brilliant team headed by Mary Brough, Winifred Shotter, Tom Walls, Robertson ('Bunny') Hare and Ralph Lynn. I attended a garden fête which was opened by that last-named wonderful farceur, and I remember his indispensible monocle falling from his eye as he heard an ardent fan hiss to her offspring 'Touch 'im! Go on! – *TOUCH* 'im – then you can tell Gran'-ma!'

I took one of our great actor's name in vain on one occasion. Walking along a narrow pavement, I stepped aside to allow a group of middle-aged ladies to pass. They stopped and stared at me, one of them saying accusingly, 'I know you, don't I? On the telly, aren't you? 'oo are you?' For some reason it came into my head to answer 'Sir John Gielgud', whereupon she cried triumphantly, 'Of course! I knew you at once – would have recognised you anywhere!' As I left, I heard her remark to her companions. "e's luvly, in'e?'

What's in a name, I ruminated – or a face, for that matter.

Noël Coward had a similar experience when someone bounded up to him in New York, exclaiming, 'Hi there! Remember me?

I'm Brown!' To which Noël replied, 'I know the name, but the face escapes me.'

Years ago when I was desperately seeking advice as to how to become an actor, I waylaid the late Leslie Henson, that superb comedian with bulging eyes and voice like a corncrake. With a kindly smile he placed his hands on my shoulders, saying 'There's nothing I can do to help you, old son. But if it's meant to be, you will succeed. Have faith in your own ability – good luck and God bless.'

I hope he has looked down on me from time to time with some satisfaction.

*   *   *

Thumbing through some scrapbooks to find a few details I needed, I came across an interview Helen gave in 1955. Here is part of what she said:

> At the coach station I saw a man with an old suitcase listing to
> starboard and a grubby ancient mackintosh, wearing a very old
> hat. Yet … it was Peter. He swept the hat off and greeted me as
> if I were royalty – he seemed unconscious of his appearance.
> I thought: This is the strangest individual I've ever met – but
> the most attractive!

> I soon realised he's a person who can't bear to seem unsociable
> but must be alone quite a lot (talent develops in solitude,
> character in the stream of life) so I used to think up dodges to
> prevent others disturbing him – we were living in hostels, you see
> – during the war on an ENSA tour … What's he like at home?
> Scrupulously clean – has about 27 toothbrushes – and the most
> superb manners. Behaves like a courtier. I might be the most
> wonderful lady in London. Immensely honest. He can't bear
> to owe a shilling for the papers. Punctual? NO! If he had an

*appointment with the Queen he'd still be late, in a
daydream probably.*

*I found out that side of him when we were first married and
decided I'd just got to accept it as part of his personality! About
food? He's as fastidious as a child that's never hungry. You have
to think up things and play tricks to get him interested. He's
painfully tidy – and always knows if I've been to his desk even
if I've put things back exactly where they were. Domestically?
Quite hopeless!*

*I've never known anything like Peter's patience. He'll go on
hours after anyone else would give up over a thing – perhaps
that's one of the reasons why such a hard fight in the theatre
has at last begun to repay him ... one of the reasons. He's never
irritable and loathes gossip...*

*I love the theatre. In fact, if I hadn't met Peter and loved him –
and his talent – better...*

The interviewer ends the article '...her love made Mr Cushing a
star ... they are among the gayest, happiest couples I know. Their
marriage of devoted companionship is the other part of the story
... and I rate it the vital part.'

'To see oursels as others see us!' I would just like to mention
one thing I know has changed over the years since that was written
– I am always punctual now!

An anonymous fan in Belgium sends me a bunch of red roses
equalling the years on each anniversary of my birth. I have received
innumerable tributes and letters of encouragement from those
people all actors strive to please – their public. A volume could
be devoted to those writings, and although it seems invidious
to select just one from so many, I ring down the curtain on this
penultimate scene by quoting the following:

FOR PETER CUSHING – THE ACTOR

In the endless fables of good and evil that we tell and want told to us, you are the teller and the tale, the kind conjuror, the vulnerable miracle worker.

With sleight of mind you can steel your face and eyes to become the glacial fire that would wreck a world. You can leash and unleash the very devils of hell. You are the raised rapier behind which no fiend could reach – the gray grained oak (from remembered childhood) that held the earth and sky in place.

But most of all – you are the long awaited story teller (no one gives life to a legend as you do), the beloved enchanter, enfolding us in the simple power of a gesture, turning each moment like a spinning apple on a stem until it falls into our upturned hands. And the only price we pay is loss of ignorance.

By Mary Ann Rosberg – a fan, 1978.

EPILOGUE

'HOW LONG DO you give him?'

'A year – 18 months at the outside.'

It was in May 1982 when Bernard Broughton, my secretary's husband, rang my doctor, John Ribchester.

For some weeks before the above conversation, I had not been feeling too well, and, without any apparent reason, my left eye became swollen to about three times its normal size.

Some of you may have seen me in the small part I played in a film entitled *Top Secret!* – shot during 1983 – in which the make-up artist had adorned me with such an optic, as though viewed through a powerful magnifying glass. If you did, then that was how I looked, without the make-up. Not a pretty sight, and extremely painful. As this eruption occurred on a public holiday, I didn't want to pester overworked doctors, and thinking it was just an oversized stye, I bathed the offending protuberance with Optrex and lay down on the couch, hoping it would 'go away' after a rest.

It didn't.

The next thing I was conscious of was being rushed by ambulance to the Kent and Canterbury Hospital. Maisie, my housekeeper, had come in to do her daily chores and found me recumbent and speechless on what – bless her – she thought was my deathbed, so she immediately rang the Health Centre. Dr Ribchester was on leave, but having been examined by no less than three of his colleagues, they decided I should be seen by a specialist, at once. ('I 'ad to 'ave a stiff brandy, 'e looked so *hawful*,' Maisie confided later to Joyce, Bernard's wife, in a blow by blow account of the breathless drama she had witnessed. 'You oughterof *seen* 'im – fair turned me stummick.')

With infinite care, Mr Darvill and his colleague Dr Rake of the Cancer Care Unit, having diagnosed a form of that canker in my prostate gland which also affected my eye, nursed me for several days and put me on a permanent course of drugs. They held little hope of my recovery, as recounted at the beginning of this epilogue, although I wasn't made fully aware how serious my condition was until some time later.

To their utter amazement, I confounded science and, with no operative treatment, made an almost complete recovery. I nearly lost my eye but it was saved, leaving me with slight double vision. If you look closely at the photograph on the dust jacket of volume one of my autobiography, you can just detect a little squint.

I am still regarded by the local medical fraternity as 'a walking miracle'. Miracle maybe, thanks to them, but tottering is a better adjective. Anyhow, that's merely old age, and I can still get about on 'me bike', especially when the wind's behind me!

The only reason I have made public this very personal revelation is the fervent wish that it will encourage others in similar straits, and their loved ones, *never* to give up hope. God indeed works in a mysterious way His wonders to perform, and I am convinced that in the not too distant future cures will be found to combat this ravaging disease in all its forms. The means are somewhere, yet to be discovered by Man. Perhaps in space where radium abounds? – who knows? The simplest analogy is the stinging nettle; wherever that weed grows, alongside it nature obligingly provides its own 'medicine', the dock, whose leaves neutralise the sting of the former...

Now I must record how deeply touched I've been, and always will be, by the love and devotion showered upon me by Joyce and Bernard Broughton. They have even gone to the extent of uprooting themselves from Hartley, near Dartford, and moved house and home to be within a hundred yards or so of where I live, in order that they can look after me now, and in my dotage. I am so grateful to them, and so blest.

Twenty-eight years ago, when Joyce first became my secretary, I used to complain rather petulantly about having to cough up for National Insurance stamps, just to collect some paltry pittance in the autumn of my days here on earth. 'Never mind, Sir,' she would say politely, 'I'll push you to the Post Office in a wheelchair so that you can collect it.' Her prophecy is almost coming true!

However, in the five years that have elapsed since that shattering news shook those who hold me dear, I have made four films for the cinema, three for television (plus a commercial), given a vast number of interviews on that medium, written my first volume of autobiography and had it published, which involved many weeks of signing sessions up and down the land in the care of a delightful 'minder', Mrs Rose Joly (née Scott) of Weidenfeld and Nicolson; had the enormous pleasure and privilege of being presented to the future king and queen, Their Royal Highnesses the Prince and Princess of Wales, at the royal premiere of *Biggles*; recorded a promotion video, with a pop group, of that film's theme tunes; had a rose named after Helen through the kindness of Jimmy Savile and the BBC; been honoured by the British Film Institute when I was invited to give a Guardian Lecture at the National Film Theatre, receiving a most heart-warming welcome and reception, and staged *An Evening with Peter Cushing* (in which I was more than ably assisted by Bernard Broughton, who acted as Mr Interlocutor) at St Edmund's Public School, Canterbury, to raise funds for the local Cancer Care Unit.

In September 1987, one of my recent watercolours was accepted by HRH The Prince Edward and auctioned at a charity he had organised in aid of the Duke of Edinburgh Award Scheme, and, just for good measure, I've written this (final?) part of my life story. Like Johnnie Walker, I'm still going strong!

Those accomplishments have not been inserted as mere idle boastfulness – 'see-what-a-clever-boy-I've-been' sort of stuff. Oh, no! They were written simply to beg those who suffer to take heart; many were helped by learning of my utter belief in the life to come, and I hope most earnestly that my close encounter with the Great Leveller will be of equal value to those who need such assurance, and to show what can be done against all odds, with a lot of loving help, a lot of faith (which can move mountains), and a modicum of will power.

'Look at me – I'm dancin'…!'

CURTAIN

Acknowledgements

FOR THOSE WHO may have a copy of *Peter Cushing, An Autobiography*, published in 1986, perhaps you would like to note an amendment.

In my reference to *The High Toby* (page 139), I inadvertently stated that Miss Joyce Redman was in the cast, when I should have said Miss Phyllis Calvert. My sincere apologies and felicitations to both those dear ladies.

It is now my pleasure to thank those who helped with this production, which I do with all my heart: Mr David Roberts of Weidenfeld and Nicolson, my publishers, who stage-managed the show with such kindness and understanding; Mr Graham Payn of the Coward Estate, for permitting me to use 'Past Forgetting' as the title; all those who so generously gave their permission, allowing me to use the photographs which illuminate these scenes; Mr Peter Gray for his beautifully written foreword and constant support; Mr Peter Ustinov for allowing me to use our 'correspondence', and Mr Alan Melville's estate for the quotation from his play *Simon and Laura*. My secretary, Mrs Joyce Broughton, for deciphering my spider's scrawl and typing it, who somehow managed to find time to keep me well supplied with tea in the intervals; her husband Bernard, for his helpful interest and occasional promptings, and both for their encouragement; my audience who requested this encore; and finally, the inspiration of my belovèd wife who was, is, and ever will be, the light of my life.

In gratitude, and may God's blessing be with you always.

In all sincerity

Peter Cushing
Whitstable, 1987

THE PETER CUSHING STORY

Note: The following memoir was prepared for press serialisation in 1954, and revised in 1955. Structurally, it formed the basis of *An Autobiography* some 30 years later, with many of the same stories recounted – though often with interesting variations.

ONE

Before I could start my career as an actor I had to overcome a language difficulty. I wonder if you can guess which language?

Many of you who think of the real-life me in terms of my exotic television roles will probably say French, Spanish or Russian.

In each case you will be wrong. I was born on the outskirts of London – on 26 May 1915* – at Kenley, near Purley, Surrey. Till I was 20 I spoke English carelessly and indistinctly. And that, as you can imagine, just would not do for an actor. It was only after an intensive course in speech training that I was able to speak what is known as the Queen's English. Ironically enough, I was later to judge students of the Central School of Speech and Drama! And despite a career that has taken me to many colourful lands, I still speak no foreign languages.

---

* Cushing tended to 'reduce' his age at this period. 'Try not to mention how old I am, dear boy. I try to make out I'm two or three years younger. You see, I've still got my teeth and hair and I'd like to have a crack at some romantic roles before I settle for character parts.' (Interviewed by Dick Richards in *The Sketch*, 16 January 1957.)

How then, you may ask, am I able to put conviction into those French, Spanish and Russian parts? The credit is due to my ex-actress wife, Helen, who coaches me for foreign roles. Helen speaks French, German, Spanish – and Russian. In fact, she could almost have stepped out of one of my TV plays – *Tovarich*. She was born in St Petersburg (now Leningrad). With the 1917 Revolution, her wealthy parents had to flee. They brought her, then a baby, to England… But more of Helen later on.

I was not the first member of my family to go on the stage. My father's stepbrother, Wilton Herriot, after whom I am named – my full name is Peter Wilton Cushing – was an actor of talent. And my father's sister, Maude Ashton, toured Britain with the celebrated Gertie Millar.

My grandfather – also on the paternal side – was, like my father, a quantity surveyor by profession. But he loved the theatre and must have had considerable acting ability. For, while still a surveyor, he managed to get himself a part playing with that great actor Sir Henry Irving, with whom he toured America.

When I look back on my life I cannot help feeling that I was destined to become an actor. Ever since I can remember, I have seen things in terms of shapes and movement. I have always found it easier to draw, paint or mime something than to describe it in words. That, I think, is what is known as a visual imagination. It is indispensable to an actor.

As a child of five I used to draw my own strip cartoons. My hero was invariably Tom Mix. It was then my ambition to meet the cowboy star. And meet him I did – 18 years later, when I was an actor myself.

My early passion for drawing, allied to a mischievous temperament, frequently got me into trouble. Once, however, I was wrongly accused of poking fun at a master and punished. In protest I ran away from school.

The master wore huge boots that turned up steeply at the toes. They were a constant source of amusement to the pupils. One day a wicked caricature of 'The Boots' appeared on the blackboard. It was the work of another boy whose powers as a cartoonist were as yet unsuspected. But, with my record, it seemed there could only be one culprit. After I ran away, the guilty young artist confessed. The master posted an apology to me and I consented to return to school. I was seven.

It was about that time that I began to take an interest in acting. Characteristically, my first part was as an elf in a pantomime. Unseen by the audience, I could not resist pulling the fairies' wings. I was not the most popular elf in the show!

Despite my family's theatrical background, my parents held conventional views on life and showed little interest in the stage. My elder brother David – three years my senior – always intended to be a farmer. He now owns a poultry farm at Norwood Hill, near Reigate, Surrey.

My father wanted me to take up surveying. When I was nine he decided it was time to start thinking seriously about my education. So I was packed off to Shoreham Grammar School as a boarder. Not even the sea, which I have always loved, prevented me from feeling homesick. I did not return to Shoreham after my first term's holiday.

I then enrolled at Purley Grammar School, where I stayed till I was 18. My father, always an optimist, continued to believe I could become a surveyor. But even today simple arithmetic baffles me. At school I was good at only three things – drawing, rugger and theatricals. By the time I was 16 I was in the first-fifteen rugger team. I stood 6ft and weighed 12st 5lbs.

As a child I had my share of embarrassment. My mother had always wanted a daughter. Which explains why she let my hair – then fair and curly – grow very long. And why she dressed me in Little Lord Fauntleroy clothes, such as velvet trousers with mother-of-pearl buttons and lace-trimmed blouses. It may have been those early blows to my manly pride that later spurred my interest in rugger and 'toughness'. Till I was 16 I insisted on wearing short trousers that showed off my scarred knees. I even refused to have my rugger injuries bandaged.

There was one master at Purley to whom I shall always be grateful. He was our physics master, Mr DJ Davies. Now, Mr Davies needed no gift of insight to conclude that I was no budding Einstein. In fact, if he had not also been the school's play producer, I am sure he would have banned me from his physics class on the grounds that I was mentally deficient in that department.

I like to think of him as the 'talent scout' who discovered me. He cast me for the leads in many of his productions. He also let me paint the scenery. I think it was he more than anyone else who encouraged me to take up acting professionally.

Chaplin and Buster Keaton supplanted Tom Mix and his horse as my idols when I was at Purley. I studied their techniques and tried to evolve a clown-like style of my own. I think I won some kind of recognition, because the masters always referred to me as 'that clown Cushing!'

TWO

I have always found it difficult to absorb knowledge through books. I seem to be one of those people who learn only by experience. One day, when I should have been studying in the form room at Purley Grammar School, I was sitting backwards on my bicycle careering round the quadrangle. I was spotted by a master who was feared for his heavy sarcasm. 'Old Sarky', as we called him, beckoned to me.

'Studying hard, Mr Cushing?' he purred. 'I hear you're leaving us soon. Made up your mind about what you're going to do in the hard world outside? No? Then let me make a suggestion, Mr Cushing. Judging by your scholastic attainments I suggest you get yourself a job as a trick rider in a circus!'

I should have liked to have seen his face two years later when I was racing up and down the stage of the Connaught Theatre, Worthing in a period play – perched on a penny farthing!

But the years between nine and 18 were not entirely wasted academically. For I studied art in the evenings under Mr Percy

Rendell of the Croydon School of Art. I have had reason to be grateful for that art training. During one period in my career, apart from an occasional week or so at a small theatre, I was unable to get work on the stage for 18 months. Married, in debt and desperate, I turned to commercial art and earned a living as a silk scarf designer. And I have found that art enables me to relax when I am not acting. Apart from landscapes and drawing, I sculpt miniature figures and make model houses from paper and glue.

When I left school I did what my father wanted me to do. I joined the Coulsdon and Purley Urban District Council as a surveyor's assistant. In reality, I was a glorified office boy.

During the two years I was with the council, I continued to take part in my old school's plays. I was more successful as an amateur actor than as a professional surveyor's assistant. The plans I drew up were architects' nightmares. One had a garage in front of the house leading onto the kerb. Another, highly decorative chimneys placed in impossible positions. Yet another showed a semi-detached house with a bathroom extending into the adjoining house. It was said of my plans that any resemblance to a real building was purely coincidental. Yet I was still taking art lessons and apparently making progress. I can only assume that my urge to create was stronger than my regard for facts.

My heart, of course, was still in acting. So I applied to the Guildhall School of Music and Drama for a scholarship. Veteran actor Allan Aynesworth interviewed me.

'And what can I do for you, laddie?' he inquired benignly.

I still spoke badly. 'I wanna go on the stage,' I announced.

Aynesworth glared. 'This isn't an audition,' he snapped. 'Speak in your normal voice.'

I protested: 'This *is* me normal voice. I wanna go on the stage!'

The old actor exploded. 'No, no! Go away! And change that awful voice before you come to see me again!'

I then called on James Cairns-James, of the original D'Oyly

Carte Opera Company, for advice. He gave me a list of approved phrases on which to practise.

Now I have always been fond of fresh air. Even today, whenever possible, I learn my lines in the open. To improve my diction and practise voice projection I used to go for long walks over the nearby downs, bawling such lines as: 'How now, brown cow? The moon in June is full of beauty.' I became known as 'the Madman of Purley'.

My chief at the office was not impressed with my surveying. One day he told me so. He had caught me playing darts with the sharp-pointed surveyor's instruments. 'Young man,' he said, 'as a surveyor you give one of the worst performances I've seen. I'm sure you could do better on the stage. My advice to you is – go out and survey the theatre. And the best of luck to you.'

So there I was at 20 with stage ambitions but no recognised training or professional experience. By then I had improved my diction but had decided not to re-apply for a drama school scholarship. That left the hardest – and, in my opinion, the best – training ground. Repertory. The nearest repertory company was at Worthing, Sussex, at the Connaught Theatre.

This period in my life taught me the value of persistence. Bill Fraser was then running the company. Each week I wrote to him for a job. After my 21st letter I received a reply. It was short but it looked hopeful. It said: 'Please, Mr Cushing, come and see me.'

When I walked into Bill Fraser's office he barked: 'Who are you?'

'I'm Peter Cushing,' I revealed, and waited expectantly.

'Look, Mr Cushing,' said Fraser wearily. 'I only wanted to see you in order to tell you this: please, please, stop writing to me for jobs.'

I must have paled from the shock of this anti-climax because, in a kinder tone, he went on: 'I'm sorry, son, but look at it from my end. What experience have you had? What possible use to us could you be?'

I started to tell him – and I think my enthusiasm must have hypnotised him. For he gave me a part in JB Priestley's *Cornelius*.

It was only a walking-on, role, but at last I was an actor – a professional actor.

THREE

My first professional stage appearance with the Worthing Repertory Company taught me an important rule.

I was playing one of the gum-chewing, teddy-bear-coated creditors in JB Priestley's *Cornelius*. Suddenly I got what I thought was a brainwave. I would impress on the audience the coarseness of the character I was playing. Ostentatiously, I spat the gum into the palm of my hand, then stuck it under my heel. Result: I distracted everyone – the cast, the audience, the stage manager. I learned then that every significant action should be worked out previously – and that unless an actor has been instructed to move, he must remain still.

My official title at Worthing was assistant stage manager – the grandiose expression for odd-job man. Apart from stage appearances, it was my duty to look after three lots of props at the same time. I had to return last week's props, handle those for the current play, and get the props for next week's play. To distinguish them, they were marked green, red and blue.

I was paid 15s a week, was at the theatre from 8.00 am to midnight, and loved every minute of it.

My digs – bed and breakfast – cost me 15s a week. Which left me nothing. I was – and still am – a non-smoker and teetotaller. But even so, you must be wondering how I managed about food.

My breakfast was always a huge one. My other meals I got at the theatre. For the food on the stage was real food, supplied by various companies in return for mentions in the programme. I made a point of scanning advance scripts for eating scenes. North Country plays were popular with me: they often featured a high tea.

Whatever its dramatic merits, I did not care for St John Ervine's *Anthony and Anna*. The chief character, an American invalid suffering from indigestion, had to be fed on charcoal biscuits. No other food was supplied for this play. By the end of the week I felt I could portray the invalid with more conviction than the leading actor!

I think those early experiences left their mark. I can still go through most of the day without food. At home, unless my wife is there to remind me, I simply forget to eat and just drink numerous cups of tea.

Talking of drinking reminds me of a party in those Worthing days. I was put in charge of the drinks – probably because I was teetotal. Drinks were a mystery to me. I mistook a decanter of gin for a flask of water. As the whisky began to run low, I added a liberal quantity of what I thought was water to each nip of Scotch. I kept to ginger beer. Soon everyone – except me – was drunk. But in the morning I did not feel so good, either. I had practically carried the producer a mile to his digs.

I played many kinds of parts at the theatre. As I have already mentioned, I even rode a penny farthing round the stage.

After I had been with the Worthing Rep for some months, Peter Coleman – who now runs the Palmers Green Intimate Theatre in North London – came from Southampton as guest producer and leading player. When he returned to Southampton's Grand Theatre, he took me with him as assistant stage manager and small-part player.

I learned a lot more in the next nine months. I found that acting is like painting: it is not what you put in that matters, but what you leave out. I put too much into the small but important part of John Fairweather in *Lean Harvest*. The script described the character as 'slightly merry'. I staggered onto the stage with balloons tied to the ends of my tie, bottles of gin sticking out of my pocket. So much 'a drunk' was I that no one understood a word I said.

When we put on the pantomime *Dick Whittington*, I was King Rat. To liven things up we worked in an acrobatic routine. And I nearly killed the actor playing the Cat. I hope that was not why he gave up acting! He now owns a pub called The Cat and the Fiddle.

I was soon playing juvenile leads at Southampton – and getting £3-10s a week, which was then generous pay for repertory actors. I left Peter Coleman to join the William Brookfield Players at the Theatre Royal Rochdale – for the then princely salary of £5 a week.

At that time the goal of all repertory actors was Harry Hanson's Court Players. I joined them at the Theatre Royal Nottingham. There I met my boyhood hero, Tom Mix, and his horse Tony. Tom, who could neither read nor write, asked me to look over his contract for him.

In the same company was Peter Gray, an excellent actor with whom I have been friends ever since. At Nottingham I played practically everything from character juveniles and dashing juvenile leads to old butlers. My debut as an ancient family retainer prompted Peter to quip: 'You look so old you can't possibly be alive.'

During one of those inevitable 'resting' periods I was in a bus at Croydon, Surrey, reading through the vacancies in a stage journal when I spotted a personal advertisement. It read: 'Will Peter Cushing please get in touch with Dominic Roche.' I did – and Roche gave me a three-week engagement at Burnley.

I drove there in a car I bought for £5. Surprisingly, it held together for that journey, and for others – to Scarborough Opera House, to Lowestoft, and then back to Harry Hanson's Court Players, who had moved to Peterborough – where, incidentally, they are still.

I was then 23 – and ambitious. I knew that I could never achieve fame in a repertory company. So where to now but Hollywood?

I had saved £50. My father helped me with more money. In September 1938, I bought a one-way ticket to New York.

FOUR

The first thing I did when I arrived in New York was to buy a one-way ticket to Los Angeles. Then I checked in at a YMCA, where I paid for 20 days in advance. Next I wrote letters to the New York offices of every major American film company, telling them I was 'going to the coast'.

After that I felt I could act the part of a tourist with a clear conscience. I hailed a brightly painted taxi, and it was then that I got my first experience of the proverbial American generosity.

Every New York taxi driver is compelled to display his photograph, name, age and address inside his vehicle. This one, Michael Phelan, was four years older than I, but from his photograph he could have passed as Peter Cushing. Our real-life likeness was less striking. However, when I told him how much his picture resembled me, he studied my face, then the photograph, and said solemnly: 'Bud, we must be long-lost relatives. Which part of the old country you from?'

I had heard that not all Irish-Americans like the British, so I was not happy about telling him I came from London. But Phelan just said: 'Zat so, brother? Well, I guess your folks must have come from Ireland way back.'

All day he showed me round the city, refusing payment. 'It's for free, Pete,' he would explain when I tried to press money on him. 'You're one of the family, ain't yuh?'

For some inexplicable reason he seemed proud of his newly found 'relative'. So I stopped arguing. I just could not bring myself to spoil his happiness. Whenever he saw an acquaintance – which was often – he stopped and introduced me as his cousin from County Cork. By the time I got away from Mike I was beginning to believe it. I had even begun to speak with just the slightest hint of a brogue!

In New York I saw Hollywood film stars in the flesh for the first time, acting in Broadway theatres. Two who impressed me with their command of stage technique were Franchot Tone and Sylvia Sidney, who were co-starring in *The Gentle People*.

On the train to Los Angeles a musical trio of college boys were making the journey pay for itself. I joined them as treasurer. My job, as you will have guessed, was to pass the hat round. Their repertoire comprised two songs – 'Franklin D Roosevelt Jones' and 'My Melancholy Baby'. After three days of it the music got monotonous, so I retired from busking. But today, whenever I hear those tunes I feel nostalgic.

California! 'California the Golden' they call it. The description did not apply when I arrived at Los Angeles. It was pouring with rain. Still, like everything else in California, the rain was something special. It brought out the wonderful scent from the orange groves.

After the stuffiness of a New York late summer and days cooped up in the train, the crisp Californian air went to my head. I began to feel like a film star before I had even seen the inside of a studio. I hardly noticed the rain as I walked the four miles to Hollywood, where I checked in at the YMCA. (Before returning to Britain, I was to see the inside of many more YMCAs in the States and Canada.)

'I'm staying ten days,' I informed the reception clerk. 'By which time I shall be in films.'

His only comment was a terse 'Oh, yeah?'

I had just enough money to pay for two days and offered the cash in advance.

The clerk gave me a level look. 'That's OK, bud,' he said. 'Pay me when you leave.'

Within ten days I got into films. When I paid the clerk, I said: 'What made you trust me – when you knew I was practically broke?'

His answer I treasure. 'Well, you're British aren't you?' he said. 'That's why I trusted you.'

For 25 cents I bought a map of the film stars' homes. The man who sold it to me said he had been selling maps in Hollywood for five years – but had never himself seen a star. No wonder he looked cynical!

It was bluff that got me into films. Director James Whale was looking for an expert fencer to play opposite Louis Hayward in a film of the Alexandre Dumas classic *The Man in the Iron Mask*. I had never handled a foil in my life. But the job meant four months' work at 75 dollars a week. So I told Whale I had fenced since I was a boy and was now a British champion.

I got the job. But the film's technical adviser on duelling, a Frenchman named Cavens, was the best swordsman in Hollywood. How could I hope to fool him!

I acted on a hunch. 'M'sieur Cavens,' I said, 'I know nothing about fencing, but I badly need to keep the job.'

What followed was another of those individual acts of kindness that have helped me throughout my career. Cavens grinned and said: 'I know. I knew it as soon as you picked up the sword. But because you have respect for my intelligence, I will teach you all there is to know about fencing.' And he did. So it was to gallant M'sieur Cavens that I owed the authentic-looking sword-play in the TV comedy *Tovarich*.

I met Joan Bennett and the late Alan Hale, who were in the film. And I was soon able to buy a car for $200. Things were looking up.

FIVE

Without the experience I gained in repertory I should not have been able to tackle my second Hollywood part – the most important role I played in the film city.

George Stevens, who was later to direct such films as *A Place in the Sun* and *Shane*, was then about to start a hospital drama, *Vigil in the Night*, from the AJ Cronin novel. The dialogue director, Robert Coote, was looking for an actor who could speak a modified Lancashire dialect that would be understood by American audiences.

I played second lead to co-stars Carole Lombard and Brian Aherne. The critics were kind to me. Some likened my acting to that of Spencer Tracy. This was gratifying because I had always admired his work. But I shall best remember *Vigil in the Night* because it gave me the opportunity to play opposite the sparkling Carole Lombard, who was to die in an air crash three years later.

Carole had excelled in crazy comedies and this was her first dramatic role. The one-time Mack Sennett bathing belle from

Indiana who became Clark Gable's third wife followed this with other dramatic successes.

I think Carole had a premonition about that last journey in 1942. She tossed a coin to see whether she should go by train instead. The plane won. She waved gaily as it took off. It was a gesture typical of the impulsive Carole. Her sudden death shocked and saddened those of us who had known her.

But to return to my story. Hollywood headlines have to be seen to be disbelieved. When I read that Britain had declared war on Germany, my first reaction was to wait for the next edition denials. But this 'sensation' was the real thing.

At my medical examination I was graded 4C. My rugger injuries had deteriorated over the years. I was told to remain in California and await further instructions. The studio I was with, RKO, feared I might be sent away at short notice. So, understandably, they gave me only small parts. If you are an afternoon viewer you have probably seen me – without knowing it – in one of those parts. Next time the Laurel and Hardy film, *Chumps at Oxford**, is shown, study the faces of those moustachioed dons. I am the one who looks like stage wide-boy Arthur English, trying to cash in on culture.

Repeatedly I tried to join up. The answer, always the same, got monotonous. 'Stand by,' I was told. 'Just stand by.'

I seemed to be of little use to anyone. For the first time since I started acting, I was really depressed. A film part restored my confidence.

I was playing Clive of India in a short – *The Hidden Master*. The highlight of the film was that famous episode in the young Clive's life when he puts a loaded gun to his head, pulls the trigger – and nothing happens. A friend then takes the gun, aims at the wall – and fires.

Something happened to me in that scene. I felt then that I would one day achieve success as an actor. And I realised that

* Working title of *A Chump at Oxford*.

every experience, pleasant or unpleasant, would help me to put conviction into my work.

Louis Hayward, with whom I played in my first Hollywood film, *The Man in the Iron Mask*, was then married to London-born Ida Lupino. I was a frequent guest at their home. So frequent, in fact, that one day Ida, a practical joker, started a story about her 'adopted son' staying with them. A puzzled columnist followed up the story. He wrote: 'Ida Lupino is always speaking about her adopted son. He lives with them. People are always surprised when they meet him because he is 6ft 2in Peter Cushing*, the RKO actor.' Ida, then 21, carried the joke further. She gave me a signed photograph. It reads: 'To my son. Love always. Mother.'

I have no complaints against Hollywood. Before I went there I had heard and read stories about the 'ignorance' of American film-makers. I did not find it so. I found the people of Hollywood always generous and often extremely talented. A trained artist myself, I discovered that many directors could talk knowledgably about paintings. I met producers who, apart from their executive ability, had a remarkable acting talent. Some, when telling you the story of their latest film, would bring to life every character in the script.

With the bombing of London, graphically reported by the American press, I decided to fly to New York to see if I could hasten my return. But on the plane I realised that my right leg had become septic. I had neglected a burst blister and picked up an infection, probably in a swimming pool.

At Bellevue, the city hospital, the specialist said casually: 'We'll have to amputate.' I thought he was joking. But he went on: 'You left it too late. A week ago we might have been able to save it.'

I said: 'But I'm an actor. My career will be finished. Can't you try to do something?'

He mentioned a film star who had gained fame after he had lost a leg. But I felt no happier.

* Cushing (or the columnist quoted) was exaggerating his height here. He was six feet.

They managed to save my leg after all; but the expensive treatment used up nearly all my savings. I was stranded in New York.

SIX

Because of my health the services did not appear to want me. And even if it had been possible to get a berth on a home-bound ship, I was without money. I could not afford to stay even at the YMCA. I moved into a 'flophouse' on the corner of 42nd Street and Broadway. Flophouses are apartment houses where a 'deadbeat' can get a bed for 25 cents.

I then started the round of theatrical agents. After a few weeks of vague promises I realised I would have to work at anything – or starve. I became a car park attendant on Coney Island.

British cars have bumpers. American cars have fenders. These are aptly named. Their function, apparently, is to push other cars out of the way so that you can secure a place for your vehicle. Battered fenders are often a sign of enterprise in parking cars.

I did not know this. With great care, I managed to park one car, a Cadillac, on my first day. It was also my last day.

After he fired me, my boss, an excitable Italian, gave me a demonstration. It was like watching an aggressive drunk driving a dodgem car in the nearby fun fair. I think he was hoping I would join his rival.

I had had enough of car parks. I became a 'soda jerk'.

The drug store slang intrigued me. One phrase convinced me that most Americans are optimists. Whenever anyone ordered hash, I had to shout this to the kitchen: 'Here's a guy who wants to take a chance!' I could never understand why no one cancelled his order.

After a few months I had saved enough to live on for a few weeks while I tried the agents again.

It was the same story. But I could not keep away from the atmosphere of the stage. In the afternoons I used to wander into the empty Broadway theatres and just stand around, occasionally rearranging the props. I made a point of noting where they came from. So when someone came in unexpectedly I had my answer ready. I had been sent to see whether the props were satisfactory.

I could not overcome the feeling that I had stood on those stages many times before in the distant past. There seemed to be a link between myself and my grandfather, Edward Cushing*. He had been a friend of Dame Ellen Terry and toured the United States with Sir Henry Irving nearly half a century before.

Soon I had pawned everything of worth – except a gold watch of sentimental value. When I finally decided that, too, had to go, I was too late. It was stolen from my wrist while I slept in the flophouse.

I had one dollar and 35 cents left. I decided to do without breakfast and wandered around Central Park Zoo. This was free. But it was feeding time there and I felt out of it. So I strolled over to the lake, the New York equivalent to the Serpentine in London's Hyde Park. There I had an inexplicable urge to take out a boat. I could not afford the 25 cents and was feeling far from energetic – but I yielded to the impulse.

I rowed listlessly – till I noticed on the bottom of the boat a dirty piece of paper that reminded me tantalisingly of money. I examined it. It *was* money – a ten dollar bill that must have lain there for weeks. It had footprints on both sides. I rowed back to the bank like an Olympic champion.

For three weeks I lived on that ten dollar bill. I budgeted myself at 50 cents a day (then about 2s 6d). The flophouse – 25 cents. Food – 20 cents. The five cents that were left I splashed around recklessly!

I was able to exist like this because I found a small Greek café, on the edge of Little Italy, where for ten cents you were served with a doughnut and as many cups of coffee as you could drink. I was a regular twice-a-day customer, if not a profitable one.

One day in May 1941, I had an enormous meal there – free. It was when Hitler invaded Crete, and the British Army were fighting

---

* Cushing calls his grandfather Henry William Cushing in *An Autobiography*.

side by side with the Greeks in an attempt to repulse the Germans. The grey-haired café owner, who knew I was British, asked me to sit down at a table. Then he disappeared. He returned without his apron, and wearing a tie and jacket.

'Today,' he said, 'I shall be honoured if you will join me as my guest.' And his wife served us a magnificent dinner with all the trimmings, including champagne.

After that I felt I could no longer take advantage of his free cups of coffee. But he used to wait till he saw my cup was empty, then, before I could leave, he would pounce on me and force me to have another.

I hope to visit New York again. If the old Greek is still there, I shall try to repay his kindness.

SEVEN

After weeks in New York on a near-starvation diet of coffee and doughnuts, I began to wonder whether I should have more chance of getting work as an artist than as an actor. I had practised regularly since those evenings at the Croydon School of Art and had always liked painting, drawing and designing. So I decided to explore Greenwich Village, the artists' quarter, to find out the prospects.

Within 24 hours I had three pleasant surprises – none of them connected with art.

The first came when I was sitting in a café that was trying hard to give the impression of having been transported bodily from the Latin Quarter of Paris. There were three 'madly Bohemian' types at my table: a girl with long matted hair, a man with long matted hair – and Peter Cushing, 'the artist'. Suddenly we saw a dark-haired hefty six-footer in the doorway, pointing at me. He was convulsed with laughter. My companions ignored him and went on talking about abstract art in an abstract manner. They were apparently used to such interruptions.

When the man stopped laughing I recognised him as a Hollywood actor friend, John Ireland (who is now married to the film star Joanne Dru). 'On location, Peter?' he queried, and again burst into uncontrollable mirth. I grinned sheepishly, quickly pushed my hair back from my eyes, whipped off my canary yellow scarf and hid my stockingless sandalled feet under the table.

My second surprise was mixed with irony. John told me I was entitled to $18 a week under an unemployment benefit scheme to which I had contributed in Hollywood. Wryly I recalled the past six lean months when I could have drawn that weekly allowance and lived in comparative luxury!

There was irony, too, in my third surprise. Next morning, on my way to collect the week's benefit money, I checked in with an agent. He offered me an immediate five-month contract, playing in a summer camp at Warrensburg in New York State, about 200 miles from New York itself. There was no salary – but he promised good food, accommodation and sunshine. And, of course, I should be acting again. In such revivals as *The Petrified Forest*, *Macbeth* (in modern dress) and Noël Coward's *Fumed Oak*. I accepted.

We played to exceptionally appreciative audiences. Life in the camp was pleasant. But I felt that my place was in the services, or at least back in Britain, so I wrote to Toronto to Air Marshal Bishop, wartime director of the Royal Canadian Air Force. I asked to be taken into the RCAF in any capacity. Air Marshal Bishop pointed out my low medical category – 4C. He regretted there was little he could do, but advised me to cross the border and try to get a home-bound ship from Canada. I had no money to do this, but a theatrical producer who saw me act at Warrensburg signed me for one of the leads in a new Broadway play that was going into rehearsal in the autumn. It looked like the answer to my money problems.

I made my Broadway debut at the Mansfield Theatre in *The Seventh Trumpet*, a mystical war play. It mystified the audience, the critics – and the cast. The production survived for a fortnight. And by then I had saved $100 towards my passage home.

Next stop: Montreal, and when I arrived there I worked day and night. At night, as a reception clerk in the YMCA. For this I received breakfast, supper and a room. During the day, in the art department of a film studio. I slept in snatches between jobs.

When I had enough money for my passage home, I went north to Halifax. But no berths were available. While waiting, I worked as a cinema attendant. In the days when I played opposite the glamorous Carole Lombard in Hollywood I had dreamed of making a 'personal appearance' in a cinema. But not this kind!

At last, towards the end of January 1942, I was bound for home in the 5,500-ton SS Tilpala. In mid-winter on the Atlantic I had become a merchant seaman (temporary) on a banana boat built for the tropics. For the first time since the outbreak of war our convoy used a peace-time route. We were chased by the German battleship Tirpitz – but it was driven off by our escort.

One afternoon they put me on crow's nest duty. I sat in a barrel high up on the mast, my feet in several inches of rain water. I was up there for six hours. By the end of the watch my legs had frozen and I could not get down. Two men were sent to rescue me. The captain then ordered me to bed for the rest of the voyage.

In the middle of February we reached Liverpool. It was nearly four years since I had seen the shores of Britain. I was appalled at the jutting masts of the numerous sunken ships. My parents were then staying at my elder brother's poultry farm at Norwood Hill. No one expected me. When I walked in, my mother fainted.

Three days later, after being turned down for the services, I called at the ENSA offices in London's Drury Lane Theatre. Actor Henry Oscar was then chief of the Drama Department. He gave me a job immediately. Months later he told me: 'When you came into my office, I was astonished. I had been searching everywhere for a presentable young man with talent. But they were all in the services – or playing leads in the West End. You were exempt. You had played a leading role on Broadway; leads in Hollywood. Yet you insisted on working for ENSA. And when I asked whether you could learn the part in three days, you said – "Yes, of course." For just a few moments, I thought you were an escaped lunatic.'

I played opposite Sonia Dresdel in *Private Lives*. We toured the military camps, and I was able to see again the English countryside I had missed during those years in America. Three months later something happened that was to change my *own* private life and have an important effect on my career.

EIGHT

When Sonia Dresdel – my wife in *Private Lives* – left the cast, she was replaced by Helen Beck, a blue-eyed blonde with classical features. After nearly a year of fighting on the stage, we decided to try it at home! We were married on 10 April 1943 at Marylebone Register Office.

Helen was born in St Petersburg (now Leningrad), where her parents lived in luxury – till the 1917 Revolution when, almost penniless, they escaped to Britain with Helen, then a baby. Helen's father, Ernest Beck, was a Lancashire industrialist with cotton mills in Russia. They had been handed down for generations by his family, who, though British, had helped to pioneer the textile industry there. In Russia, Ernest married a Nordic beauty of Swedish-Polish parentage – Helen's mother.

Helen, an ex-musical comedy actress and dancer, played in Hollywood films in her early teens. She had been selected from 500 girls for a part in a Cochran revue staged in America. While in Hollywood she appeared with TV producer Eric Fawcett – who was then an actor – in the Victor McLaglen film *What Price Glory?* Later she switched to the legitimate stage and toured the United States.

If I am a success today, I owe it to the encouragement, strength and knowledge given me by my wife.

Helen and I had only £50 when we married. We had both been happy with ENSA, but health trouble forced me to leave. We rented a pleasant ground-floor studio flat at Kensington, London, which has been our home ever since. The full-length French windows of the lounge, overlooking an acre of lawn, make it ideal for painting or designing – my chief hobbies. Surprisingly, when a bomb burst 40 yards away, not a pane was cracked.

In May 1943, a few weeks after leaving ENSA, I was given two roles in the stage adaptation of Tolstoy's *War and Peace* – Alexander I, Emperor of Russia, and Captain Ramballe of Napoleon's army. It was a mammoth 32-scene production that lasted nearly four hours. We opened at the Grand Theatre Blackpool in June; at the Palace Theatre Manchester in July; and in September at London's Phoenix Theatre.

From my role as Captain Ramballe, many people seemed to get the impression that I was a real Frenchman. Five weeks later I was given the part of Frenchy in a war play, *Happy Few*, at London's Cambridge Theatre. At the Cambridge, 'the French actor' was seen by Elsie Beyer of HM Tennent Ltd. Result: when Eugene Deckers became ill, I took over as the Free French officer in Terence Rattigan's *While the Sun Shines* at the Globe. I acted with Michael Wilding, Hugh McDermott and Brenda Bruce (now a TV celebrity through her appearance on the panel of *The Name's the Same*).

Ronald Squire joined the cast and we went on tour. Edith Evans was then casting for Sheridan's *The Rivals*. She was co-director as well as Mrs Malaprop. She came to see Ronald Squire.

'Ronnie,' she said, 'have you any suggestions for *The Rivals*?'

Replied Ronnie: 'Yes – Peter Cushing as Faulkland.'

And Faulkland I became. We opened at London's Criterion Theatre in September 1945, after it was vacated by the BBC, who had moved in during the war.

When the run of *The Rivals* ended, my hardest period began. Soon I was heavily in debt. For 18 months I could find only an occasional week's work at the 'Q' Theatre, Kew Bridge, on the outskirts of London.

I used to look through my cuttings books, trying to reassure myself that I had talent. I had been acting for 11 years. In my early days I had soon reached the goal of repertory actors – Harry Hanson's Court Players. At 24 I had played second lead to Carole

Lombard in Hollywood. Two years later I had a leading role on Broadway. Then, important parts in London's West End. The critics had been generous to me. Even when the play was bad they had singled me out for praise.

Now I was puzzled. What was wrong?

Today I think I know the answer. Nothing was wrong. Earlier in my story I said that I felt I was destined to become an actor. I believe those 18 months of disillusionment, depression and frustration were put into my life to widen my emotions and to strengthen my character.

Because of those experiences I became a better actor.

But I do not think I could have got through that period without the encouragement given me by my wife. 'One day, Peter,' she said again and again, 'you will gain recognition from the public.'

Her prediction came true. In 1953 the public – the viewers – voted me the most popular TV actor. And because of the public's support I was able to play the kind of role – in the political thriller *Nineteen Eighty-Four* – that won me the Best Actor award from the TV producers and directors.

NINE

We had no money for Christmas 1945. I wanted to give Helen a present. I found a large piece of silk – she had been cutting up her grandmother's ball dress for dusters – squared it up, placed it over a pastry board and painted Dickensian characters on it.

It was my first attempt at designing scarves. I put it in a box I had painted. It was on Helen's pillow when she woke on Christmas morning. She was delighted, but wanted to know how I had got the money to buy it.

Some weeks later an actress friend of ours, Roberta Huby, asked Helen to lend her the scarf for a party. At the party was a North Country textile manufacturer. The next day he called and took me back to Macclesfield for a week, where he explained what he wanted. Then he sent me home with a contract as a silk scarf designer. Later I designed scarves for the Festival of Britain and the Coronation.

If I did not earn much on the stage during the next 18 months, I did have some interesting one-week engagements at the 'Q' Theatre. Then in 1947 Anthony Bushell interviewed me. He was casting for the American play *Born Yesterday*, which Laurence Olivier produced in London's West End.

'Do you speak American?' he asked.

I replied: 'No. I spent four years in the States, but I think only Americans can speak American.'

Three months later Bushell telephoned me: 'How would you like to play in the film *Hamlet*?'

I quipped: 'Has the part of Hamlet been filled yet?'

He laughed: 'Laurence Olivier is doing that. But I'll tell you what – as a sort of consolation prize you can play the court dandy, Osric.'

He then told me why he had got in touch with me. 'You made an impression on us when you refused to attempt that American accent,' he said. 'Especially after nearly every young actor in London mistakenly thought there was nothing to it. Soon after, I went to see a friend play at the 'Q'. I was struck by the acting of the Frenchman in *While the Sun Shines*. I looked at my programme – and the Frenchman's name was Peter Cushing. I made inquiries – and found you couldn't even speak French. I said to Larry – that's an actor. That's the man to play Osric. And Olivier said – "Test him".'

They tested me – and I passed. It was a small part – but an important one.

Olivier made no comment at the end of my first day's work as the foppish courtier, Osric, in *Hamlet*. But at six next morning I was in the make-up room, sitting under a hairdryer, when I felt a tap on my shoulder. It was Olivier. He said: 'I am taking the Old Vic Theatre Company on a tour of Australia and New Zealand. Would you care to come with us?'

It was the biggest acting opportunity of my career. I forgot about the hairdryer and nearly dislocated my collar bone as I thanked him.

Both Olivier and I dislike wearing wigs. He had dyed his hair dark blond for the part of Hamlet. I had let mine grow very long. He remarked: 'It's funny, but you and I are the only ones who look as if we have wigs on.'

One day, lost in thought on the set, I walked into a plaster pillar. I split my lip and broke a front tooth. My mouth was numb, and I thought my voice sounded odd. I was due in the recording theatre in two minutes' time and I told Olivier I did not feel I could do justice to the dialogue.

'Nonsense, Peter,' he said. 'It's just your imagination. Forget your tooth and lip. Pretend we're both acting before an audience. That'll do the trick.'

He was right. But one thing went wrong during the first take. The rest of my broken tooth shot out and hit Olivier on the nose.

My wife, Helen Beck, who was then an actress, also joined the Old Vic Company for the tour. She later gave up her career in order to help me with mine.

Before we left Britain in 1948, I designed the 'Hamlet scarf'. It was based on the film's costumes and characters – including myself. It sold well in Britain and America. The Queen Mother (then the Queen) graciously accepted one of the scarves at the *Hamlet* première, which was held while we were in Australia.

Life was hectic for the next year on that Australasian tour. We put on nine shows a week. I played the hypocritical Joseph Surface in Sheridan's *The School for Scandal*, the weak, frightened Duke of Clarence, brother of the king, in *Richard III*, and, in contrast, acted with Helen in an ultra-modern play, Thornton Wilder's *The Skin of Our Teeth*.

For sponsored radio in Australia I took the lead in *Beau Brummell*. This version of the romantic dandy's life was different from that in Anatole de Grunwald's recent TV play. But I found the recording, with which I was presented, useful while rehearsing the television role.

When we returned, we opened at London's New Theatre, adding Chekhov's *The Proposal*, a 20-minute sketch, to our repertoire. I played Lomov, a droll character.

As a boy with stage ambitions I had studied the technique of those master clowns, Chaplin and Buster Keaton. Now came the pay-off. The ovation was the most moving stage experience I have had. Even the normally cynical gallery audience – the real theatregoers – cheered wildly. On the opening night I had to take eight encores. After the fourth, emotion got the better of me. Laurence Olivier had to push me onto the stage.

TEN

While rehearsing for a new play in London's West End, Bridget Boland's *Damascus Blade* with John Mills, I was taken ill. I shall never forget Laurence Olivier's kindness to me then. For some time he had been considering putting me under contract. And he did – the day after I was ordered to bed. Yet he knew I would be unable to work for at least six months. Throughout my illness he paid me a weekly retainer.

I had not fully recovered when I took one of the leads in a play at the Opera House Manchester in November 1950. It was adapted from Molière's comedy *Le Malade imaginaire*. Its title: *The Gay Invalid*. Which was exactly how I felt! I played opposite a fair-haired girl whom I was later to partner on TV in the serial *Pride and Prejudice* and *Beau Brummell*. Her name, of course, is Daphne Slater.

During the Festival of Britain I was with Sir Laurence Olivier at the St James's Theatre, London, playing in Shakespeare's *Antony and Cleopatra* and Shaw's *Caesar and Cleopatra*. In September 1951 Olivier and the company left for America. I preferred to stay behind as I had already spent four years in Hollywood and New York.

One day TV producer Harold Clayton sent for me. Evidently my stage disguises had been effective. For he said: 'I've seen you act for the past nine years. I sent for you because I wanted to know what Peter Cushing looked like.'

I hope the impression he got had nothing to do with his next action. He cast me as a drunken actor in JB Priestley's *Eden End*.

To clear up any suspicions, I repeat that I am teetotal.

But my TV debut nearly drove me to drink. After the response of theatre audiences, the silence at the end of the television play seemed almost an accusation. I felt I had given the worst performance of my career. My clothes were sticking to me after the strain of this exacting new medium. I left the studio at once and went home to bed.

Helen had been watching the play at a friend's house. When she returned she praised my performance. She had always been my most candid critic – but this time I thought she was telling a white lie. I spent a gloomy, sleepless night. Next morning I was pecking at an early breakfast when the telephone rang.

'It's the BBC,' said Helen.

'I bet they're cancelling the repeat,' I muttered.

But it was that distinguished producer, the late Fred O'Donovan. 'A great performance,' he shouted. 'Look, laddie, on Christmas Day I'm putting on a Priestley comedy, *When We Are Married*. I say that you're just the boy for the juvenile lead.'

I did not argue. That telephone call was the forerunner of many that were to show me how TV renews old friendships.

From the time I played Mr Darcy in the serial *Pride and Prejudice* till my portrayal of the spiv in the comedy-thriller *Portrait by Peko* 18 months later, I suffered from TV nerves. The symptoms, in my case, were acute pains across the eyes, forcing me to close them for a few seconds every now and then. Despite treatment by a specialist, head pains troubled me when I played Lebel in *Asmodée*, Vadassy in the serial *Epitaph for a Spy*, and Petrovsky in *Anastasia*.

My favourite TV part was in *Tovarich* with film star Ann Todd. When the BBC asked her whether she would play in *Tovarich*, she replied: 'Yes – but only opposite Peter Cushing.' I was flattered, because till we started rehearsals we had never met. She had seen me only on TV.

Among my other TV plays, Peter Ustinov's *The Moment of Truth*, Terence Rattigan's *The Browning Version* and the recent *Richard of Bordeaux* afforded me interesting roles. I also enjoyed *Beau Brummell*. But the controversial *Nineteen Eighty-Four* provided me with my most memorable part. The role was physically exhausting – but it was worth doing because of the play's important message.

The variety of parts I have been fortunate enough to play on television won for me some contrasting film parts. The one I enjoyed most was in Graham Greene's *The End of the Affair*, with Deborah Kerr and Van Johnson; it was directed by the brilliant Edward Dmytryk.

Incidentally, it was the only recent film I have been able to make in Britain. The others were made in Spain – *The Black Knight*, with Alan Ladd as the hero, myself as the bearded, double-dyed villain; and *Alexander the Great*, with a fine cast headed by Richard Burton, Fredric March and Claire Bloom. I play the Persian General Memnon. The film is to be shown soon.

And now – what of the future?

A TV play, I have heard it said, is like a newspaper. Once seen, it is discarded and forgotten. There are not even records of television performances. Because of union rules, a play cannot be filmed for the mid-week repeat. To these observations I reply: more people see a TV play in one night than see a film in a month, a stage play in a year.

I shall not deny that TV is the most difficult medium of all. It combines the film's technical restrictions with the concentration needed for a sustained stage performance. But I shall always be eager to appear on television. For if it had not been for viewers' appreciation of my work, I should have had no story to write.

STAGE, SCREEN AND RADIO

Note: The following chronology has been made as complete as possible, but PC's numerous guest appearances as 'himself' on radio and television have been omitted.

For the record, he was the subject of BBC Radio's *Desert Island Discs* in 1959 and *Be My Guest* in 1971, together with the TV documentaries *Peter Cushing: A One-Way Ticket to Hollywood* (1989) and *The Human Factor: For the Love of Helen* (1990). Among his narrator credits were the Australian TV documentary *A Land Looking West* (1977) and the two-part *Flesh and Blood: The Hammer Heritage of Horror* (1994), the second instalment of which was broadcast posthumously.

Under 'Stage', the theatre in which PC performed is given for each engagement. 'Radio', 'Television' and 'Film' note the chief production companies in each case. The chief country (or countries) of origin are also provided in the last of these categories, while the years attached to films are those of production (not necessarily release).

STAGE

1936
Connaught Theatre Worthing:
Cornelius, It Pays to Advertise, Bees on the Boatdeck, The Man at Six, Potash and Perlmutter, Aloma of the South Seas, The Midshipmaid, The Middle Watch, Anthony and Anna

1937
Grand Theatre Southampton:
Lady Precious Stream, Winter Sunshine, Lean Harvest, Dick Whittington
William Brookfield Players, Theatre Royal Rochdale: *Marigold*

1938
engagements at Burnley, Scarborough, Lowestoft, Peterborough
Harry Hanson's Court Players:
Blondie White, The Greeks Had a Word for It, Fresh Fields (Penge Empire), *This Money Business, Love from a Stranger, The Island, Sunshine Sisters, The Phantom Light, Black Limelight, Count Your Chickens, Sweet Aloes, Springtide, Whistling in the Dark, Hay Fever* and 15 other plays (Theatre Royal Nottingham)

1939

Summer Stock, USA: *Love from a Stranger* (Palm Springs)

1941

Summer Stock, USA: *Biography, The Petrified Forest, Pound on Demand / Fumed Oak* (double-bill), *Night Must Fall, The Ghost Train, Macbeth* (Warrensburg, New York)
Broadway: *The Seventh Trumpet* (Mansfield Theatre)

1942-43

UK tour for ENSA: *Private Lives*

1943

Grand Theatre Blackpool, Palace Theatre Manchester then Phoenix Theatre, West End: *War and Peace*
'Q' Theatre, Kew: *The Morning Star*

1944

'Q' Theatre, Kew: *The Dark Potential, The Fifth Column, The Crime of Margaret Foley, Watch on the Rhine, Private Lives*
Cambridge Theatre, West End: *Happy Few*
Globe Theatre, West End: *While the Sun Shines*

1945

Globe (continued) plus UK tour: *While the Sun Shines*
Criterion Theatre, West End: *The Rivals*

1946

Criterion (continued): *The Rivals*
'Q' Theatre, Kew: *They Came to a City, The Seagull, While the Sun Shines, Tonight at 8.30, The Curious Dr Robson*
Theatre Royal Windsor: *The Rivals*

1948

Old Vic tour of Australasia: *Richard III, The School for Scandal, The Skin of Our Teeth*

1949

New Theatre, West End (Old Vic season): *Richard III, The School for Scandal, The Proposal*

1950

Manchester Opera House: *The Gay Invalid*

1951

Festival Theatre Malvern then Garrick Theatre, West End: *The Gay Invalid*
St James's Theatre, West End (Laurence Olivier's Festival Season): *Caesar and Cleopatra, Antony and Cleopatra*

1952

Manchester Opera House then tour: *The Wedding Ring*

1954

UK tour: *The Soldier and the Lady*

1956

Duchess Theatre, West End: *The Silver Whistle*

1959

Aldwych Theatre, West End: *The Sound of Murder*

1965

Yvonne Arnaud Theatre Guildford then Garrick Theatre, West End: *Thark*

1975

Horseshoe Theatre Basingstoke: *The Heiress*

FILM

1939

Edward Small Productions-UA (USA): *The Man in the Iron Mask*
Hal Roach Studios (USA): *A Chump at Oxford*
RKO Radio (USA): *Vigil in the Night*
RKO Radio (USA): *Laddie*

1940

Republic (USA): *Women in War*
Columbia (USA): *The Howards of Virginia*
MGM (USA): *John Nesbitt's Passing Parade – The Hidden Master* [short]
MGM (USA): *John Nesbitt's Passing Parade – Dreams* [short]
MGM (USA): *John Nesbitt's Passing Parade – The Woman in the House* [short] *
MGM (USA): *John Nesbitt's Passing Parade – Return from Nowhere* [short] *
[* PC's scenes recycled from *Dreams*]

1941

Columbia (USA): *They Dare Not Love*

1942

Canadian Ministry Films (Canada): *We All Help* [short]

1946

Crown Film Unit (GB): *It Might Be You* [short]
Crown Film Unit (GB): *The New Teacher* short]

1947

Two Cities (GB): *Hamlet*

1952

Romulus (GB): *Moulin Rouge*

1953

Warwick (GB-USA): *The Black Knight*

1954

Coronado (GB): *The End of the Affair*
Republic (USA): *Magic Fire*

1955

Rossen Films-UA (USA): *Alexander the Great*

1956

Harlequin (GB): *Time Without Pity*
Hammer (GB): *The Curse of Frankenstein*

'Mine's a MINOR' says PETER CUSHING APPEARING IN THE FILM 'MAGIC FIRE'

2/9 for 20

PLAIN OR CORK TIPPED ALSO IN SMALLER PACK

ISSUED BY GODFREY PHILLIPS LIMITED

1957
Hammer (GB): *The Abominable Snowman*
Rank (GB): *Violent Playground*
Hammer (GB): *Dracula*

1958
Hammer (GB): *The Revenge of Frankenstein*
Warner Bros (USA): *John Paul Jones*
Hammer (GB): *The Hound of the Baskervilles*

1959
Hammer (GB): *The Mummy*
Triad (GB): *The Flesh and the Fiends*
Charter (GB): *Suspect*

1960
Hammer (GB): *The Brides of Dracula*
Aubrey Baring Productions (GB): *Cone of Silence*
Hammer (GB): *Sword of Sherwood Forest*
Mijo (GB): *Fury at Smugglers' Bay*
New World (GB): *The Hellfire Club*
Pennebaker-Baroda (GB): *The Naked Edge*

1961
Hammer (GB): *Cash On Demand*
Hammer (GB): *Captain Clegg*
Constantin-Criterion (Germany-Ireland): *Im Namen des Teufels* [The Devil's Agent] *
[* PC's scenes deleted]

1962
White Cross (GB): *The Man Who Finally Died*

1963
Hammer (GB): *The Evil of Frankenstein*
Hammer (GB): *The Gorgon*

1964
Amicus (GB): *Dr Terror's House of Horrors*
Hammer (GB): *She*

1965
Amicus (GB): *The Skull*
Aaru [Amicus] (GB): *Dr Who and the Daleks*
Planet (GB): *Island of Terror*

1966
Aaru [Amicus] (GB): *Daleks' Invasion Earth 2150 A.D.*
Hammer (GB): *Frankenstein Created Woman*
Amicus (GB): *Torture Garden*

1967
Foundation (GB): *Some May Live*
Planet (GB): *Night of the Big Heat*
Titan (GB): *Corruption*
Tigon (GB): *The Blood Beast Terror*

1969
Hammer (GB): *Frankenstein Must Be Destroyed*
Titan-Lucinda (GB): *Incense for the Damned*
AIP-Amicus (GB): *Scream and Scream Again*
Chrislaw-Trace Mark (GB): *One More Time*

1970
Hammer-AIP (GB): *The Vampire Lovers*
Amicus (GB): *The House That Dripped Blood*
Amicus-British Lion (GB): *I, Monster*

1971
Hammer (GB): *Twins of Evil*

Amicus-Metromedia (GB): *Tales from the Crypt*
Hammer (GB): *Dracula A.D. 1972*
Hammer (GB): *Fear in the Night*
AIP (GB): *Dr Phibes Rises Again*
Granada-Benmar (Spain-GB): *Pánico en el Transiberiano* [Horror Express]

1972
World Film Services-LMG (GB): *The Creeping Flesh*
Amicus-Harbor (GB): *Asylum*
Charlemagne (GB): *Nothing But the Night*
Amicus-Harbor (GB): ~ ~ *And Now the Screaming Starts!*
Hammer (GB): *Frankenstein and the Monster from Hell*
Hammer (GB): *The Satanic Rites of Dracula*

1973
AIP-Amicus (GB): *Madhouse*
Amicus (GB): *From Beyond the Grave*
Amicus (GB): *The Beast Must Die*
Hammer-Shaw Brothers (GB-Hong Kong): *The Legend of the 7 Golden Vampires*

1974
Hammer-Shaw Brothers (GB-Hong Kong): *Shatter*
Films Christian Fechner (France): *La grande trouille* [Tender Dracula]
Tyburn (GB): *The Ghoul*
Tyburn (GB): *Legend of the Werewolf*

1975
Lawrence Friedricks Enterprises (USA): *Shock Waves* [Death Corps]
Combat (GB): *Trial by Combat*
Poseidon-Getty (GB-USA): *The Devil's Men*

1976
Amicus (GB): *At the Earth's Core*
Lucasfilm-Twentieth Century-Fox (USA): *Star Wars*
Ottokar Runze-Orfeo (Germany-Spain): *Die Standarte* [Battleflag]
Cinévidéo-Tor (Canada-GB): *The Uncanny*

1977
Naxos-Film (Germany-USA): *Hitlers Sohn* [Hitler's Son]

1978
Barkarow-Melsom (GB): *The Detour* [short; PC as narrator]
Elsinore (GB-Zambia): *A Touch of the Sun*
Badger (GB): *Arabian Adventure*

1980
Almena-Fort (Spain-USA): *Misterio en la isla de los monstruos* [Mystery on Monster Island]

1981
MB Diffusion (Spain-USA): *Asalto al casino* [Black Jack]

1982
Paramount-Kingsmere (USA-GB): *Top Secret!*
London Cannon (GB): *House of the Long Shadows*
London Cannon (GB): *Sword of the Valiant – The Legend of Gawain and the Green Knight*

1985
Compact Yellowbill-Tambarle (GB): *Biggles*

RADIO

1941
NBC (USA): *Outward Bound, The Grandpa Family, Bitter Sweet*

1943
BBC: *Mendelssohn, Destination Unknown*
BBC: *The Lay of Horatius*

1946
BBC: *Wednesday Matinée – A Fourth for Bridge*
BBC: *Orley Farm* [serial]

1947
BBC: *Saturday Matinée – The Face of Teresa, Radio Theatre – It Speaks for Itself*

1948
ABC (Australia): *Beau Brummell*

1949
BBC: *Saturday-Night Theatre – Alien Corn*

1951
BBC: *PC 49 – The Case of the Tenth Green*

1954
BBC: *A Book at Bedtime – Natural Causes*

BBC: *Morning Story – The Bride in the Bath*
BBC: *The Gay Lord Quex*

1955
BBC: *Wife for Sale*

1964
BBC: *Loyal Servant*

1966
Stanmark: *Doctor Who* [not broadcast]
BBC: *The Strong Are Lonely*

1967
BBC: *The Burnt Flowerbed*

1973
BBC: *The Price of Fear – The Man Who Hated Scenes*

1977
BBC: *Aliens in the Mind* [six-part serial]

1990
BBC: *Human Conflict*

TELEVISION

1951
BBC: *Eden End*
BBC: *When We Are Married*

1952
BBC: *Pride and Prejudice* [six-part serial]
BBC: *Bird in Hand*

BBC: *If This Be Error*
BBC: *Asmodée*
BBC: *For the Children – The Silver Swan*

1953
BBC: *Number Three*
BBC: *Asmodée* [repeat performance of

1952 production]
BBC: *Epitaph for a Spy* [six-part serial]
BBC: *Wednesday Theatre Presents – A Social Success*
BBC: *Rookery Nook*
BBC: *The Road*
BBC: *Anastasia*
BBC: *The Noble Spaniard*
BBC: *Portrait by Peko*

1954
BBC: *Tovarich*
BBC: *Beau Brummell*
BBC: *The Face of Love*
BBC: *Nineteen Eighty-Four*

1955
BBC: *The Creature*
BBC: *The Moment of Truth*
BBC: *The Browning Version*
BBC: *Richard of Bordeaux*

1956
BBC: *Home at Seven*

1957
BBC: *Sunday-Night Theatre – Gaslight*

1958
BBC: *The Winslow Boy*
BBC: *Uncle Harry*

1962
ABC: *Drama 62 – Peace with Terror*

1963
BBC: *The Spread of the Eagle*
[episodes four to six – *Julius Caesar*]
BBC: *Comedy Playhouse – The Plan*

1964
BBC: *Star Story – The Yellow Cat* [not transmitted]

BBC: *Story Parade – The Caves of Steel*

1965
BBC: *Cribbins*
BBC: *Thirty-Minute Theatre – Monica*

1967
ABC: *The Avengers – Return of the Cybernauts*

1968
BBC: *Sir Arthur Conan Doyle's Sherlock Holmes* [16-part series]

1969
BBC: *The Morecambe and Wise Show* [two episodes]

1970
BBC: *The Morecambe and Wise Christmas Show*

1973

BBC: *The Morecambe and Wise Show*
ITC: *The Zoo Gang – The Counterfeit Trap*
Anglia: *Orson Welles Great Mysteries –*
La Grande Breteche

1974

ITC-Rai: *Space: 1999 – The Missing Link*

1976

Avengers Film & TV: *The New Avengers*
– The Eagle's Nest
ABC Circle (USA): *The Great Houdini*
[TV movie]

1978

Thames: *The Morecambe and Wise Show*

1980

ITC-Cinema Arts: *Hammer House of*
Horror – The Silent Scream
Hallmark (USA): *A Tale of Two Cities*
[TV movie]
Thames: *The Morecambe and Wise*
Christmas Show

1983

Anglia: *Tales of the Unexpected – The*
Vorpal Blade
20th Century Fox (USA): *Helen Keller*
The Miracle Continues [TV movie]

1984

Tyburn: *The Masks of Death* [TV movie]

AWARDS

1953-54

National Television Award – *Daily Mail*
– for Outstanding Actor of the Year

1955

Guild of Television Producers and
Directors Best Performance Award
(Winston Smith in *Nineteen*
Eighty-Four)

1956

Television Top Ten Award – *News*
Chronicle – for Best Actor (Viewers'
Gallup Polls)

1973

Licorne d'Or Award – Convention
Française du Cinéma Fantastique,
Paris – for Best Actor (Mr Grimsdyke
in *Tales from the Crypt*)

1976

Best Actor Award – Festival
Internacional de Cinema Fantàstic
i de Terror, Sitges (Dr Lawrence in
The Ghoul)

1983

Best Actor Award – Festival
Internacional de Cinema Fantàstic
i de Terror, Sitges (Sebastian
Grisbane in *House of the Long*
Shadows) – shared with Vincent
Price, Christopher Lee and John
Carradine for the same film

INDEX

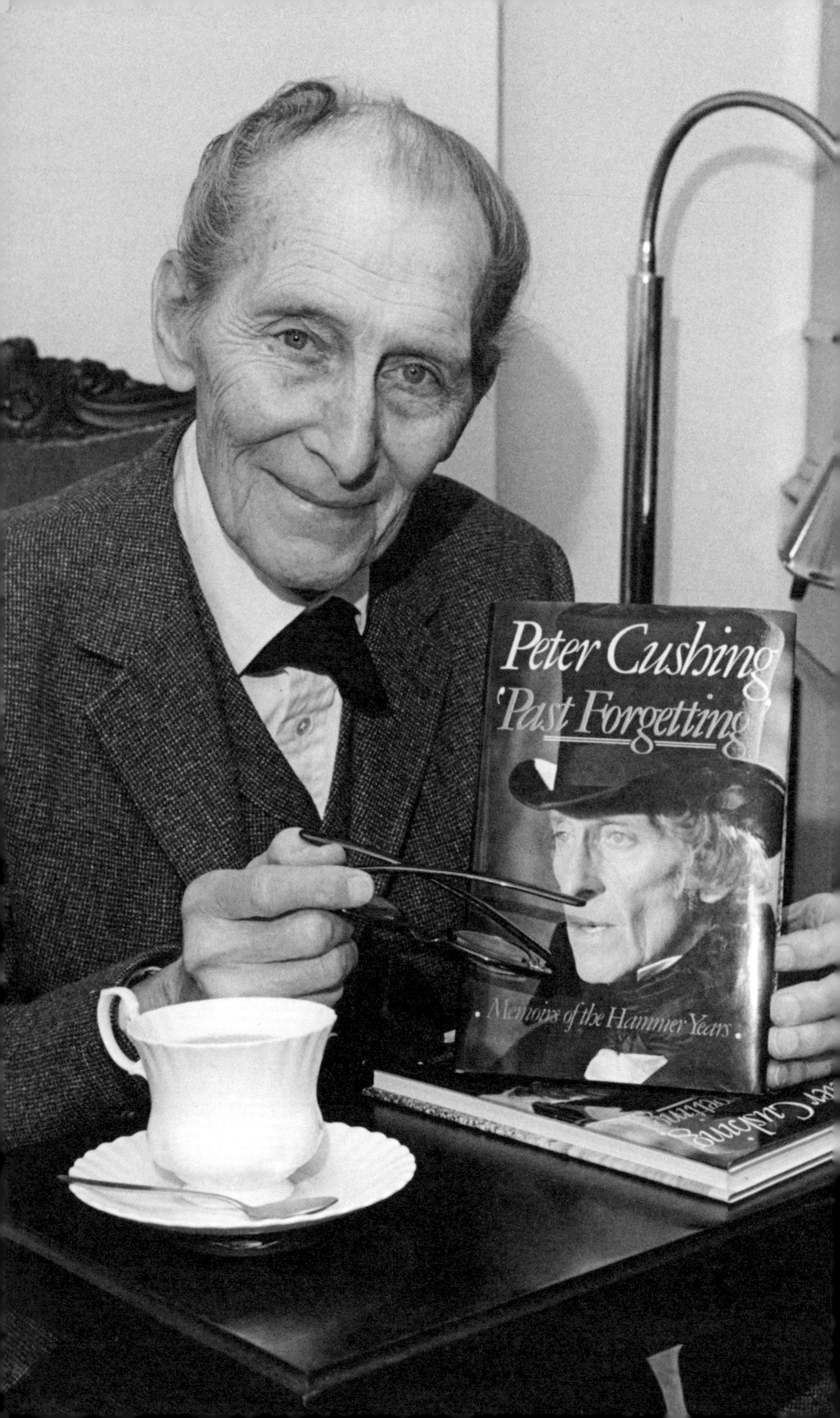
Peter Cushing
'Past Forgetting'
Memoirs of the Hammer Years

ACKNOWLEDGEMENTS

The publishers and the estate of Peter Cushing gratefully acknowledge Tom Johnson for his help in making this book possible.

The publishers also wish to thank Jo Ware for her assistance in preparing the manuscript, Colin Bourner, the British Film Institute, Bernard Broughton, Joyce Broughton, Rosemary Burrows, Karen Daniels, Derek Handley, David Miller, Jonathan Rigby, Adrian Rigelsford and Paul Taylor.

All pictures are courtesy the estate of Peter Cushing and the following copyright holders. Any errors or omissions will be corrected in future editions.

Frontispiece: On the beach at Whitstable, 1960s.
Page 26: With Helen at Airlie Gardens, 1956. Photo by Shaw Wildman.
Page 184: *The Revenge of Frankenstein* © Hammer Film Productions/Columbia Pictures.
Page 284: Tango-ing days in Oxford bags, 1936.
Page 286: *Alexander the Great* © CB Films/Rossen Films/United Artists.
Page 314: *The Hound of the Baskervilles* © Hammer Film Productions/United Artists.
Page 317: Advertising Minors cigarettes, 1956.
Page 321: With Barbara Kelly in a *Woman's Own* promotion, 1957.
Page 324: *At the Earth's Core* © Amicus Productions/American International Pictures.
Page 325: *Cash On Demand* © Hammer Film Productions/Columbia Pictures.
Page 326: *Dr Terror's House of Horrors* © Amicus Productions/Regal Films International.
Page 327: *The Gorgon* © Hammer Film Productions/Columbia Pictures.
Page 328: *The Hellfire Club* © New World Productions/Regal Films International.
Page 330: *The Mummy* © Hammer Film Productions.
Page 331: *The Satanic Rites of Dracula* © Hammer Film Productions/Warner Bros.
Page 332: *Tender Dracula* © Les Films Christian Fechner/AMLF.
Page 333: *Twins of Evil* © Hammer Film Productions/The Rank Organisation.
Page 335: Publicising *'Past Forgetting'*, 1988 © Colin Bourner.

Picture section one
Page 4 (top): *A Chump at Oxford* © Hal Roach Studios/United Artists.
Page 4 (middle): *Vigil in the Night* © RKO Radio Pictures.
Page 4 (bottom): *The Hidden Master* © Metro-Goldwyn-Mayer, *Women in War* © Republic Pictures.
Page 8 *Hamlet* © The Rank Organisation/ITV Studios International.

Picture section two
Page 2 (top): *Tovarich* © BBC Television, *The End of the Affair* © Coronado Productions/Columbia Pictures.

Page 2 (middle): *Beau Brummell* © BBC Television.
Page 2 (bottom): *The Black Knight* © Warwick Film Productions/Columbia Pictures, *Nineteen Eighty-Four* © BBC Television.
Page 3 (top): *Richard of Bordeaux* © BBC Television, *Alexander the Great* © CB Films/Rossen Films/United Artists.
Page 3 (bottom): *Home at Seven* © BBC Television, *The Creature* © BBC Television.
Page 4 (bottom): *The Curse of Frankenstein* © Hammer Film Productions, *Gaslight* © BBC Television.
Page 5 (top): *Violent Playground* © The Rank Organisation/ITV Studios International, *Uncle Harry* © BBC Television.
Page 5 (bottom): *Dracula* © Hammer Film Productions.
Page 6 (top): *Suspect* © Charter Film Productions/British Lion Film Corporation.
Page 6 (middle): *Sword of Sherwood Forest* © Hammer Film Productions/Columbia Pictures.
Page 6 (bottom): *The Brides of Dracula* © Hammer Film Productions/Universal Pictures.
Page 7 (top): *The Naked Edge* © Pennebaker-Baroda Productions/United Artists, *The Plan* © BBC Television.
Page 8 (top): *Daleks' Invasion Earth 2150 A.D.* © Aaru Productions/Studiocanal, *Sherlock Holmes* © BBC Television.

Picture section three
Page 1 (bottom): *Frankenstein Must Be Destroyed* © Hammer Film Productions/Warner Bros, *The Vampire Lovers* © Hammer Film Productions/American International Pictures/MGM.
Page 2 (top): *The House That Dripped Blood* © Amicus Productions/Cinerama.
Page 2 (bottom): *Horror Express* © Benmar Productions/Granada Films/Scotia International, *Tales from the Crypt* © Amicus Productions/Metromedia Producers Corporation/Twentieth Century-Fox.
Page 3 (top): *Nothing but the Night* © Charlemagne Productions/The Rank Organisation/ITV Studios International.
Page 3 (bottom): *Frankenstein and the Monster From Hell* © Hammer Film Productions/Avco Embassy.
Page 4 (top): *And Now the Screaming Starts!* © Amicus Productions/Cinerama Releasing Corporation.
Page 4 (bottom): *The Legend of the 7 Golden Vampires* © Hammer Film Productions/Shaw Brothers/Warner Bros.
Page 5 (top): *Star Wars* © Lucasfilm/Twentieth Century-Fox, *Hammer House of Horror* © Chips Productions/Cinema Arts International/ITC/ITV Studios International.
Page 6 (top): *A Tale of Two Cities* © Hallmark Hall of Fame Productions/Marble Arch Productions/Norman Rosemont Productions.
Page 7 (top left): Peter Cushing © Joyce Broughton.
Page 7 (top right): Peter Cushing and Joyce Broughton © Colin Bourner.
Page 7 (middle): *This is Your Life* © Thames Television/Fremantle.
Page 7 (bottom): Peter Cushing © Colin Bourner.
Page 8 and back cover: Peter Cushing © Carlo Pangrazio.